MW00710222

THE NURTURING OF TALENT, SKILLS AND ABILITIES

EDUCATION IN A COMPETITIVE AND GLOBALIZING WORLD

Additional books in this series can be found on Nova's website under the Series tab.

Additional e-books in this series can be found on Nova's website under the e-book tab.

FINE ARTS, MUSIC AND LITERATURE

Additional books in this series can be found on Nova's website under the Series tab.

Additional e-books in this series can be found on Nova's website under the e-book tab.

THE NURTURING OF TALENT, SKILLS AND ABILITIES

MICHAEL F. SHAUGHNESSY
EDITOR

nova publishers

New York

Copyright © 2013 by Nova Science Publishers, Inc.

All rights reserved. No part of this book may be reproduced, stored in a retrieval system or transmitted in any form or by any means: electronic, electrostatic, magnetic, tape, mechanical photocopying, recording or otherwise without the written permission of the Publisher.

For permission to use material from this book please contact us:
Telephone 631-231-7269; Fax 631-231-8175
Web Site: http://www.novapublishers.com

NOTICE TO THE READER

The Publisher has taken reasonable care in the preparation of this book, but makes no expressed or implied warranty of any kind and assumes no responsibility for any errors or omissions. No liability is assumed for incidental or consequential damages in connection with or arising out of information contained in this book. The Publisher shall not be liable for any special, consequential, or exemplary damages resulting, in whole or in part, from the readers' use of, or reliance upon, this material. Any parts of this book based on government reports are so indicated and copyright is claimed for those parts to the extent applicable to compilations of such works.

Independent verification should be sought for any data, advice or recommendations contained in this book. In addition, no responsibility is assumed by the publisher for any injury and/or damage to persons or property arising from any methods, products, instructions, ideas or otherwise contained in this publication.

This publication is designed to provide accurate and authoritative information with regard to the subject matter covered herein. It is sold with the clear understanding that the Publisher is not engaged in rendering legal or any other professional services. If legal or any other expert assistance is required, the services of a competent person should be sought. FROM A DECLARATION OF PARTICIPANTS JOINTLY ADOPTED BY A COMMITTEE OF THE AMERICAN BAR ASSOCIATION AND A COMMITTEE OF PUBLISHERS.

Additional color graphics may be available in the e-book version of this book.

Library of Congress Cataloging-in-Publication Data

ISBN: 978-1-62618-521-0

Published by Nova Science Publishers, Inc. † New York

CONTENTS

PREFACE

Across the life span, from birth to death, many are involved in the on-going pursuit of greatness, and enhancing their own skills, talents and abilities. Some individuals have direct responsibility for their pupils and protégés, others, like parents attempt to enhance the potential of their children as best they can.

This text examines the development, nurturing and enhancement of skills, talents and abilities in a number of different areas. Some of these areas are academic in nature, some interpersonal, some musical and artistic. Some are ephemeral in nature, some direct and observable.

In this text, a number of leading scholars in their own areas will discuss the identification of talents, skills and abilities, and others will demonstrate and delve into the lengthy process by which " experts " are made and fostered. Different procedural endeavors will be examined and explored. In some realms, direct instruction is imperative as we propose to develop a certain type of thinking and in other realms we are attempting to enhance talents, and arrive at a "magic synthesis" if you will, of in-born talents combined with years of direct and indirect instruction.

In the first chapter, Enid Zimmerman explores the realm of art, artistic talent and provides some examples of aesthetics and the development of the skills and talents of the "artist". Jason Paulk and Jason Vest and Kayla Paulk follow with an exploration into the development of the most human inborn talent- the talent of the human voice- both alone, or when combined with choir or backed with a musical instrument, orchestra or accompaniment. Mark Dal Porto and Tracy Carr round out this section with an exploration of the realm of musical composition and it's place in the realm of music.

In the domain of thinking, Colin Hannaford examines the realm of mathematical thinking, and the problems associated with the development of this thinking skill. Dr. Linda Brody follows with her years of experience in terms of working with mathematically precocious children.

She is followed by the historian par excellence, Dr. Donald Elder, who discusses the domain of historical thinking, examining, and exploring the past. Dr. Jerry Everhart provides an overview of the field of science, examines the past history of scientific instruction, and takes us "back to the future" where we could have a truly qualitatively superior science education and program.

Gerard Casey of Trinity College, Dublin, Ireland, tackles the philosophical issues of thinking like a philosopher, examining philosophical issues, and the development of a spirit of philosophy in today's technological, computerized, electronic world.

Lisa Rivero and Roya Klingner focus their energies on a group of children and adolescents that have a good deal of intellectual energy- those children labeled as " gifted " ; or highly able or those with potential.

John Baer and Ken Kierwa, along with Greg Schraw provide an examination of three distinct, disparate realms-John Baer, well known for his work in creativity, insists that "In the Development of Creative Thinking, Metaphors Matter". As is well known by most in education, the past few years have seen a rise in standardized, one size fits all curriculum packages, and the domain of creativity has been somewhat neglected. John Baer attempts to re-energize that realm, and provides some metaphorical thinking to assist in this development.

Greg Schraw examines a number of domains that result in the formation of a scholar – researcher as he examines the role of deliberate practice in the development of graduate researchers. It is at the graduate level that scholars are formed, investigative thinking encouraged, statistical competence fostered and realms of needed research examined.

Ken Kierwa revisits a domain that over the years always seems to be explored- the realm of the chess master- and the realm of the " expert " and " novice " and the difference between the two. In his chapter, he delves into some of his work in examining the role of the parent in the development of chess skills.

In the inter-personal realm, psychiatrist Adam Blatner shares his years of expertise in the realm of counseling. In this increasingly intricate, complex world, we all seem to need assistance, nurturance, support, and emotional sustenance as we try to cope with the stressors of the world, while trying to reflect on our talents, skills and abilities and nurture them as time permits.

Skills, talents, abilities- we all have them, some of us nurture them, some of us encourage them and all of us should treasure them. It is hoped that this book will assist those who mentor individuals with talent, coach individuals with skills and abilities and nurture the education of those who possess extraordinary talents and potential.

Michael F. Shaughnessy

In: The Nurturing of Talent, Skills and Abilities
Editor: Michael F. Shaughnessy

ISBN: 978-1-62618-521-0
© 2013 Nova Science Publishers, Inc.

Chapter 1

DEVELOPMENT OF SKILLS, TALENTS, AND CREATIVE ABILITIES IN VISUAL ARTS EDUCATION

*Enid Zimmerman**

Professor Emerita of Art Education and Gifted and Talented
Education, Indiana University, Bloomington, IN, US

INTRODUCTION

Artistically talented visual arts students in schools often face unfair challenges due to practices that do not support their abilities and interests. There are prevalent beliefs held by parents, community members, art teachers, and these are frequently reinforced by administrative practices at local, state, and national levels, that predicate against best educational practices for development of art skills, talent, and creative abilities. In this chapter, research about development of artistically talented students' and their teachers' skills, talents, and creative abilities are discussed and suggestions are offered for supporting best practices.

DEFINITIONS AND ISSUES RELATED TO GIFTEDNESS AND TALENT

There are no agreed upon definitions of the terms *gifted*, *talented*, or *creative.* The term *gifted* often refers to those people who have superior academic abilities and the term *talented* to those with superior abilities in the visual and performing arts. In educational settings, outstanding students often are identified as gifted in academics or talented in the arts. Recently, however, talent has come to be defined as possessing superior abilities in a single school subject, such as mathematics, language arts, science, or the fine arts. The term *gifted*

---

* Corresponding author: Enid Zimmerman. E-mail: zimmerm@indiana.edu.

and talented, in many educational contexts, has been replaced by *talent development*, a term that emphasizes processes of nurturing talents, rather than working with predetermined gifts (Feldhusen, 1992). Talented students require instruction and their instruction needs to be qualitatively different from that offered to students who do not have the same degree of abilities. There are many views about interrelationships between abilities of highly able students in academics and arts areas. One is to ignore art talent development as a component of programming for academically talented students. Another is to view students' academic achievements as separate from their abilities in the visual arts. A third is to claim lack of evidence that students with talent in the arts also are talented in academic areas. Dichotomizing arts and academic abilities often results in programs where the arts are not valued in the education of high ability academic students. The arts, however, can offer much to support achievements of both artistically talented students and those who are talented in academic areas as well.

Arbitrary separation of intellectual and artistic performance has been questioned for many years although some researchers have asserted positive relationships between intelligence and abilities in art (Clark and Zimmerman, 2004; Eisner, 1994; Tiebout and Meier, 1936) and that high ability academic students also may be talented in the arts (Schubert, 1973; Vernon, Adamson, and Vernon, 1977). Gardner (1983) and Arnheim (1969) both firmly established a claim for artistry as resulting from intelligent behavior and not just simply as a visual expression of emotion. Eisner (1994) claimed that affect and cognition are processes that cannot be separated. Cognition can be expanded through different kinds of intelligences as people confront and solve problems. Decisions to use language arts, science, social studies, mathematical, or visual and performing arts skills and understandings to confront meanings are rewarded differently in different cultures. If a culture places less value on arts than academic education, high ability students may have little exposure to the arts and few opportunities to express their abilities in visual form. It is important to educate students to use their imaginations and spatial abilities as they attempt to solve problem without relying solely on their mathematical or verbal skills. On the other hand, artists working in fields such as graphic design need to use their mathematics and language arts skills effectively in addition to their visual thinking skills. Unfortunately, American education often has embraced a view that the arts do not require the same intellectual and cognitive talents associated with high academic abilities. Such a view has promoted intellectual talent and abilities only in predominantly academic areas, especially those being tested with standardized measures, and has made the arts peripheral to this enterprise. Students can possess multiple gifts and talents in several domains (such as mathematics and the visual arts), within several arts areas (such as painting and modern dance), and/or specializations within one area (such as watercolor painting or digital drawing). If art talent development is considered an important part in the education of all students, those who are talented in the arts should be viewed as intellectually endowed as those with high academic abilities.

ISSUES RELATED TO CREATIVITY

Relationships among giftedness, talent development, and creativity are important and challenging areas of research and practice. Over these years, support for creativity in art education has waivered from a high point in the 1960s and 1970s, to its decrease during the

1980s, and until recently when it has garnered popularity again. Creativity and its role in art education needs to be reconsidered with emphases not only on students' creative self-expression, cultural identity, technology use, and realities of the global economic sector, but also on students' creatively as evidenced through their own artwork and in the strategies that their art teachers use in their pedagogical practices.

Many contemporary psychologists and educators agree that *creativity* is a complex process that can be viewed as an interactive system in which relationships among person, process, products, and social and cultural contexts are of paramount importance (Csikszentmihalyi, 1996, Feldman, 1999; Gruber, 1989; Sternberg, 1999) All creative work, according to Sternberg (1999), happens in one or more domains, people are not creative in a general sense; they are creative in particular domains such as science or the visual arts. Creativity from this point of view is an individual characteristic as a person reacts with one or more systems within a particular social context.

Talented individuals fit well in certain domains of knowledge within their own cultures and may be recognized as highly competent by members in their fields of expertise (Csikszentmihalyi, 1996; Feldman, 1982; Gardner, 1999; Winner and Martino, 1993). Creative persons, however, often do not fit easily within a domain of knowledge and it is only after much time and effort that they may be able to establish a body of work that comes to be valued.

DISPOSITIONAL FACTORS: TALENT AND CREATIVITY

Talent and creativity are not fixed traits; they can be nurtured and developed as art students and art teachers meet challenges daily in their personal and professional lives. Research has demonstrated that there is no common set of creative traits for all individuals. Many dispositional factors influence talented art students as they create their own artwork and art teachers as they instruct their students in creative educational environments. Attributes often associated with talented art students and teachers include being curious, open-minded, energetic, and having a keen sense of humor (Clark and Zimmerman, 2004).

Although visual arts identification programs often emphasize a superior final product or performance, attention also should be paid to arts processes that may ultimately lead to products or performances. Students' methods of discovery and delving deeper into problems sometimes can be more indicative of arts understandings than their actual solutions.

It is clear that there are many ways to describe and categorize artistically talented students and not all of these are by observation of their artworks. Art talent development should not be understood only as a single-minded quest for depicting the world realistically. Although examining art products for evidence of talent is common, however, students also can be identified according to behavioral characteristics such as well-developed drawing skills, high cognitive abilities, interest, task commitment, and motivation (Clark and Zimmerman, 2004: Hurwitz and Day, 2001).

Talented students' artworks should be considered in terms of perceptual qualities, expression and skills with media, and conceptual qualities including themes, puns, paradoxes, and metaphors. Other characteristics include intensity of application and early mastery of cultural forms, production of a large volume of work over a sustained period of time, nurturance from family and teachers, and thematically specialized work (Pariser and Zimmerman, 2004; Pariser, 1997).

Artistically talented students also create imaginative worlds, are intensely involved in a specific domain, experiment with spatial and naturalistic renderings, and see the world differently than their peers (Milbrath, 1998; Winner, 1996). Milbrath (1998) found that the most telling difference between the artwork of talented and less talented children were matters of quality and kind.

Talented art students come from widely diverse backgrounds, including differences in gender, racial, cultural, and socioeconomic attributes that are found in all communities. In a study of teen-age girls and boys who attended a summer program for talented art students, comparing girls with boys, cultural stereotyping was apparent in choices of girls' subject matter and media and their lack of practical planning for their future careers (Zimmerman, 1995a). Similarly, in a case study of a talented art student in the United States, from his early years through college, it was concluded that talent does not develop without an enormous amount of work, practice, and study, coupled with direct assistance, guidance, and encouragement (Clark and Zimmerman, 2004; Zimmerman, 1995b). An individual's talent involves interplay of many forces and artistic developments and is not an automatic consequence of maturation; it is a learned set of complex skills and abilities that to a large extent are greatly influenced by the culture and educational opportunities available within that culture.1

Figure 1. Artworks by talented first and second grade students in New York City.

---

[1] Note: I have group permissions for all these artworks, as I was teacher or director of programs where these artworks were created. I take full responsibility for their publication.

DIFFERENCES BETWEEN TALENTED
AND CREATIVE STUDENTS

Differences between talented people and creative ones are relevant for considering how art teachers develop their students' talents and their own talents and creative abilities. Talented people can be viewed as advancing societal norms and creative individuals as opposing societal norms and proposing new norms (Sternberg, 2001). From this point of view both talent and creative development are needed. Artistic creativity has been defined as a range of processes that include knowledge of art concepts and traditions in a culture, highly developed visual thinking skills, and intrinsic motivation (Amabile, 1983).

An ability to become emotionally involved and focus on finding a personal vision was identified by Dudek and Cote (1994) as relevant throughout a creative person's successful engagements with art making.

Figure 2. Self-portrait created by the talented art student in the Zimmerman study.

In his research, Feist (1999) determined that dispositional factors that distinguish creative artists and scientists tended to ones that were manifest in being open to new experiences, self-confident, self-accepting, driven, ambitious, impulsive, and less conventional and conscientious than others in the general population. Student creative dispositions that often challenge teachers include questioning rules, being disorganized, being absentminded, ignoring convention, tending to be overly emotional, and being fascinated with childhood experiences (Dudek and Cote, 1994; Feist, 1999). Creative traits often are dichotomous such as displaying a great amount of physical energy and a need for quiet times; being playful and disciplined, being extroverted and introverted, being humble and proud, being traditional and rebellious, and being passionate yet at the same time objective about their own work (Csikzentmihalyi, 1996; Davis, 1992; Gardner, 1999).

It is clear that there are many ways to describe and categorize characteristics of students with talents and creative abilities in the visual arts, and no single set of characteristics will ever comprehensively describe all covert or overt manifestations of such abilities. Use of multiple criteria systems is recommended in all identification programs for supporting art talent development.

When multiple criteria systems are used they should include a number of different kinds of identification instruments and procedures and diverse measures of various aspects of students' abilities, backgrounds, behaviors, interests, skills, achievements, and values. In addition, multiple criteria can include measures such as self, parent, teacher, and peer nomination forms; work samples; student process portfolios; student attitude questionnaires; grades in art classes; and standardized tests.

TEACHING CHARACTERISTICS FOR DEVELOPING TALENT AND CREATIVITY

Talent and creative abilities can be developed by adapting teaching strategies that balance a student's generation of new ideas, critical thinking abilities, and abilities to translate theory into practice (Sternberg and Williams, 1996). Art teachers who model creative behaviors and construct their own art products often are successful in development of student creative behaviors evidenced in their art classrooms. All art teachers, like their students, possess talent and creative abilities and similar to intellectual abilities in other areas, some have a lot, some an average amount, and some a small amount (Clark in Clark and Zimmerman, 2004).

Most people view creativity as either associated with a few eminent individuals or as everyday creativity. Kaufman and Beghetto's (2009) *Four C Model of Creativity* provides a useful framework for understanding how art teacher and student creativity can be acknowledged and encouraged beyond concepts of everyday creative acts to those of eminent creativity (Gregory, in press; Lu, in press). In the Four C model, creativity extends from mini-c, to little-c, to Pro-c, to Big-C.

Mini-c Creativity: Transformative Learning is evident in those who do not have a large amount of domain knowledge but want to satisfy personal goals. It is an important concept for creative teaching and learning through which personal knowledge and understandings can be constructed through meaningful insights as learning focuses on new subject matter, how to use tools and materials, engage in art making, and produce tangible results. In *little-c:*

Everyday Creativity, emphasis is on mastering tools and media, attention to detail, internal motivation, and becoming skillful in a craft. *Pro-c Creativity: Professional Expertise* includes individuals who are professional creators and who have required knowledge, skills, and motivation to engage in creative work in a chosen profession, but have not reached domain changing status. With acquired expertise and advanced schooling, talented art students and art teachers often progress from *little-c* to *Pro-c* status, but they do not often attain *Big-C: Eminent Creativity* status that includes remarkable and lasting contributions made by those considered recognized 'experts' in a particular domain. Although these conceptions of the *Four C Model of Creativity* are represented as distinct, they can be viewed on a continuum that is similar to stages of structured learning experiences in the visual arts (Clark and Zimmerman, 2004).

In their students' artwork, art teachers, as a result of their art teaching, generally see evidence of *mini-c* and *little —c* levels and those, who teach students at higher levels of education, sometimes see their students achieve *Pro-c* levels. Successful teachers of artistically talented and creative students are knowledgeable about their subject matter and able to communicate instructions effectively. They select important learning experiences that challenge their students to attain advanced levels of achievement (Pariser and Zimmerman, 2004).

Feldman and Goldsmith (1986), who studied children who were prodigies in many different areas, were persuaded that progress in all areas, including the visual arts, is the result of intensive and prolonged instruction that results in generation of high level students' skills and abilities. The impact of educational opportunities, educational settings, and the role of art teachers on development of artistically talented students are all important for developing art skills, talent, and creativity. In a case study of an art teacher of talented middle art students who fostered both talent and creativity in his students; it was found that he helped his students develop self-expression through transformational experiences (Zimmerman, 1990, 1992a). This teacher, who possessed a wealth of knowledge about art history and the contemporary art world, emphasized cognitive and affective skills in his teaching, helped his students reach their potential when boredom or frustration prevented them from learning; attended to preparation, organization, and anticipated students' problems; and possessed many art-making skills. He also was able to relate this knowledge to his students; critically reflected about his role as a teacher; presented his students with learning experiences that emphasized feelings of competence, encouraged risk taking; provided feelings of belonging; took time to understand each student's sensibilities and competences; and was knowledgeable about best pedagogical practices.

EDUCATIONAL INTERVENTIONS THAT FOSTER DEVELOPMENT OF ART SKILLS, TALENT, AND CREATIVITY

A misconception about art teachers and art classes is that visual art classes present a time in the school day for students to be to be 'creative.' Art teachers often are regarded as purveyors of an undemanding time in school where creativity in art class means coloring pre-formed handouts, mixing paint colors, and making lots of pretty pictures. From this viewpoint, all an art teacher needs to do is provide materials and students will be creative and experience a break from engaging with important school subjects that dominate the majority of time they spend each day in educational institutions.

Art teachers however can be powerful influences in developing all students' creative art abilities by being knowledgeable about subject matter, communicating effectively, using directive teaching methods, making classes interesting and challenging, and helping students become aware of contexts in which art is created. This means that art teachers go beyond teaching skills and encourage independent thought, spontaneity, and originality in all their students, especially those who are talented and creative.

Differentiated instruction is an important concept in curriculum planning for developing art skills, talents, and creative abilities that focus on students learning strategies that are more qualitative than quantitative. Adding more of the same content is not equivalent to learning experiences that are qualitatively different than those generally offered to most students. Differentiated learning experiences in art education should include a variety of approaches to content, process, product, and assessments that are promoted though both individual and whole class instruction (Clark and Zimmerman, 2004; Kaplan, 1979).

Through differentiated instruction, talented art students can engage with real and tangible work and use critical thinking and arts-based problem finding, shaping, and solving skills, thus replacing discrete, predetermined curricula with focus on meeting their needs through flexible, open-ended, and differentiated curricula. Such an integrated, differentiated approach to curriculum for artistically talented students supports teaching and learning focused on experiences that lead to increased and accessible understandings in art as well as connections to other disciplines.

Figure 3. Visual narratives created by two middle school students in the IU Summer Arts Institute, a program for talented visual art students at Indiana University in Bloomington, Indiana.

Developing each artistically talented student's self-identity and ability to make meaning through art processes and products that resemble the work of professionals should be an integral component of differentiated curriculum for talented art students (Clark and Zimmerman, 2004)

Educators have suggested a number of strategies for developing curricula that support art talent development in different subjects including art. Some of these suggestions include having students: (1) practice problem finding as well as problem shaping and solving techniques; (2) use unfamiliar materials that elicit more novel thinking and lead to new ideas, (3) rely on both visual and verbal materials; (5) be exposed to curricula with open-ended outcomes that allow for unforeseen results; (6) follow their own interests and work in groups as well as independently; (7) choose environments that support their talents; and (8) encounter a wide range of tasks intended to encourage, reinforce, and enhance emerging talents (Clark and Zimmerman, 2001; Costantino, Kellam, Cramond, and Crowder, 2010; Mumford, Reiter-Palmom, and Redmond, 1994; Sternberg and Williams, 1996; Zimmerman, 2005).

In respect to art education for artistically talented students specifically, curricula should: (1) emphasize study of the methods of art inquiry including art history, art criticism, art making, aesthetics, and popular art and visual culture, (2) focus on both convergent (structured) and divergent (unstructured) tasks needed for art skill building and self-expression; and (3) assure that original products, based on local and global art concerns and addressing real audiences, are evaluated and displayed in public arenas (Clark and Zimmerman, 2004).

Without support of such teaching and instructional strategies, students will have limited opportunities to develop their talent in any subject. In art class as in any other school subject, there is not one method of teaching to ensure a positive impact on a developing student's skills, talents, and creativity. Teachers need to select methods that make sense to them, for their students, and in the context where teaching is taking place.

Creativity itself should not be viewed only as an outcome-based experience; rather, its transformational aspects should be emphasized. Creativity often is observed to be valuable mostly for its *extrinsic* outcomes such as for the production of new products, technology, economic entrepreneurship (Florida, 2002; Freedman, 2007), and to offset routine work and standardized assessments (Partnership for 21st Century Skills, 2010). From this standpoint, creativity is needed to ensure that students have access to methods of reading ideological content of visual images (Duncum, 2007) and to promote social justice with art as a vehicle of social transformation (Bastos, 2010; Freire, 2006). Creativity also can be viewed as an in-process, *intrinsic*, transformational experience in which each individual has access to experiences that embody self-expression and creating a body of work based on his or her own abilities and concerns (Zimmerman, 2010). In order to express individual themes and concerns, understandings about skills and materials are needed to express personal ideas and to experience creative acts because these are good and worthwhile in and of themselves.

In all phases of teaching for creativity, from ideation through art making, the focus always should be on the student. Some general art teaching strategies for promoting creativity development include transforming students from learners to active investigators who hunt for information, make connections, and then construct their own knowledge (Marshall, 2010); focusing on process as well as products; and helping students create a body of their own work so they can develop personal themes in-depth (Zimmerman, 2009).

Figure 4. Artwork created by middle school students in the IU Summer Arts Institute, Bloomington, Indiana.

Generating a supportive educational environment in which creativity development can take place should focus on student meaning-making through a prolonged engagement with a problem or problems by concentrating on being playful without constraints when working with materials thereby freeing students' minds to function creatively (Salen and Zimmerman, 2004); encouraging risk taking by experimenting with materials and ideas without fear of sanctions against incorrect solutions, errors, or mistakes; and promoting deep involvement, passion, and imagination (Graham, 2003). Such a supportive educational environment can introduce security, openness, and expressive freedom; enable self-directed work with choice options; emphasize trusting students' capacities and encourage them to generate surprising conclusions (Gude, 2010); and maintain a climate that is individualized and co-operative rather than competitive. Art students, however, cannot achieve successful outcomes in their individual or collaborative bodies of work without support of teacher or mentor intervention. Thomas' (2009) study about art students' creative autonomy concludes that total independence is a fiction as art students who take risks are dependent on their teachers for reassurance and help. Such collaboration between students and teachers includes trust, good faith, and even tough love at times.

COMMUNITY-BASED PROGRAMS AND ASSESSMENT OF STUDENTS' TALENTS, SKILLS, AND CREATIVE ABILITIES

Adaptation of local community values is important for developing equitable, differentiated community-based curricula for talented art students linked to daily living and not confined to school walls. Such activities involve building connections between communities and schools where community members, teachers, and students participate.

In these communities, communication and collaboration can be increased among a variety of groups of people in rural, urban, suburban settings, and in contemporary times, in communities that are virtual and exist in a world wide web of social connections (Clark, Manifold, and Zimmerman, 2007).

Although there are generic frameworks developed for educating artistically talented students, developing programs for these students, with active involvement of local community members, can establish a positive contribution to their education. As examples, two programs for talented art students will be briefly described, including one for seven rural, underserved, economically challenged elementary schools in United States and another for two elementary and three secondary schools in neighborhoods with different socio-economic backgrounds in Hong Kong.

In the program in the United States, goals were to develop programs to enable students from different racial and ethnic backgrounds to retain their cultural heritages and at the same time to adapt practices considered necessary to function locally and globally. Art and classroom teachers designed and implemented differentiated identification procedures, curricula, and evaluation programs that focused on meeting the needs of culturally diverse, artistically talented students from communities in southern Indiana, northern New Mexico, and southeastern South Carolina (Clark and Zimmerman, 1997; 2004).

Curricula were planned based on the input of a number of local constituencies and schools decided on goals and themes for their programs. Several procedures were found helpful in success in the education of these rural and underserved talented students, including meeting with an official from each community to solicit and guarantee prolonged support; holding a series of meetings with school principals, local teachers, and parents of highly able students to ensure understanding of the program's goals and activities; and involving local people who understood community needs and values.

In evaluating this program, locally designed assessment measures were used because they were sensitive to pluralistic issues and reinforced achievements of the students in each diverse community.

Different measures were used to determine students' and teachers' progress and achievements. Sources for assessment of students' developing understandings, skills, and techniques about the visual arts included: (1) portfolios of unfinished work; (2) peer critiques, self-evaluations, contracts, diary notes, and student journals; (3) journal notes produced by the teacher, (4) video interviews, (5) work produced by students, (6) teacher, student, and parent assessments, and (7) group presentations and public art exhibitions. It was one of the goals of this program to have students present their artwork publicly in local contexts to community members and other interested audiences. Also taken into consideration were feedback from parents and community members who were involved in assessment programs in the local schools and communities in which students lived.

Community-based approaches to art education also formed the basis of a program for teaching talented art students in Hong Kong (Clark, Zimmerman, Goodie, Wso, and Ho, 2003). Goals for this program were to develop and use a range of tools for identifying primary and secondary students in selected schools who were talented in the visual arts. Then, along with consultants, parents, artists, and teachers a differentiated curriculum for students talented in the visual arts was developed that focused on local cultures.

Figure 5. A contemporary Native American shield created by a 4th grade student in Project ARTS.

In Hong Kong, each participating school was located in a neighborhood with a different history and population. Research about local art and cultural backgrounds was highlighted in the curricula at each school, with a focus on cultural pluralism and social equity for all students and with respect for a variety of life styles. Different groups of local people involved in this Hong Kong program included local consultants, parents, teachers, and students, who developed community-based identification instruments, curricula, and assessment programs.

At the conclusion of the art talent program, students, parents, and teachers were interviewed about their impressions and reactions to various aspects of the art talent program. Respect for local cultural life and use of community resources and for involving parents and community members were discussed very positively because they did not rely only on art standards issued from the Hong Kong government. Participants became aware of the need to use local resources, both people and places, as integral parts of a program planning for talented art students.

NEW TECHNOLOGIES THAT SUPPORT DEVELOPMENT OF SKILLS, TALENTS, AND CREATIVITY ABILITIES

New technologies offer pathways for art teachers to teach toward creativity and develop their students' skills and talents by reinterpreting traditional forms, breaking boundaries, and using social communication that encourages studying about artists who use digital media. Digital technologies provide new tools, media, and environments for communicating with others around the world and offer opportunities to be creative in ways that have not before been possible. Teachers and students can share content in innovative ways and respond to one another's concerns through social media such as blogs, Facebook, Twitter, etc. The current Net-generation represents a culture of participation in an international community that uses cyberspace for discourse (Hagel and Seely Brown, 2010) in which every day computer users can serve as peer gatekeepers and mentors.

Manifold (2009a, 2009b) studied creative adolescents and young adults, who are fans of popular culture narratives and make art inspired by these themes through on-line communication. She found that recognition and support within a community of like-minded others was important for talent and creativity development and suggested teaching strategies that could contribute to meaningful art education curricula for secondary level students to produce positive changes in developing talented students' skills and creative abilities.

Concomitant with the use of new technologies is a social view of learning in art education associated with talent and creativity development that supports knowledge and skill acquisition as socially constructed through interactions when students learn collaboratively with each other (Congdon, in press; Hausman, Hostert, and Brown, in press; Shin, 2010; Tillander, 2010). This emphasis on collaborative and cooperative learning is referred to in a number of research reports as 'distributed cognition' (Freedman, 2003). An example is Stanford University's d.school (Design School) whose mission is to "foment personal transformation" (Antonucci, 2011, p. 48) through teaching methods that encourage creativity and innovation. Groups of students who represent a diverse number of interests come together to investigate and propose solutions to social and institutional problems at local and local and global levels.

Figure 6. A painting, about Hong Kong becoming an official part of Mainland China; created by a high school student in a program for talented art students in Hong Kong.

They develop "creative confidence … and problem solving approaches that augment the knowledge and skills they acquire in their degree programs at Stanford's seven schools" (p. 53). The physical space at the d.school was redesigned to avoid a hierarchical situation where an instructor stands before a class of students; rather, spaces are designed with furniture and walls that can be rearranged and diverse materials can be used for solving practical problems. There is an initiative now to bring d.school design thinking to K-12 classrooms in the United States and abroad.

Although it has been assumed, especially by those researchers and practitioners who view creativity mainly for its extrinsic outcomes, that human creativity has increasingly become a group process, although some current research demonstrates that the if "you want people to work together effectively … [there is a need] to create architectures that support frequent, physical, spontaneous interactions" (Kohane cited in Lehrer, 2012, p. 25). Architectural configurations at Disney and Pixar Animation and MIT are used as examples of how people from different backgrounds and points of view can be enabled to come together in unpredictable ways to encourage group dynamics that unfold and creativity can abound. Art classrooms, as compared to most other physical spaces in K-12 public school settings, have potential to offer architectural configurations where creative teaching and learning can occur through both teachers' pedagogical practices and students' meaningful art making experiences and achievements.

CULTURAL VARIABILITY AND EXPRESSIONS OF SKILLS, TALENTS, AND CREATIVITY

Teachers and students can only be recognized as talented and creative in areas that are valued within their own cultures (Sternberg and Lubart, 1999). For example, Wang Yani at a very young age demonstrated a talent for mastering a highly conventionalized, non-naturalistic, representational system used in traditional Chinese brush painting (Pariser and Zimmerman, 2004). What is considered a valued ability in one culture, such as being able to copy art works with precision, may not be valued in another. In contemporary post-industrial cultures, change is encouraged with emphasis on producing a product that is both novel and appropriate within a particular culture.

In addition to these criteria of novelty or originality, some scholars have added criteria of appropriateness or usefulness in respect the cultural context in which these contributions occur (Csikszenmihalyi, 1996; Florida, 2002; Runco, 2007). While some aspects of creativity appear to be universally valued, diverse cultures also can nurture creativity in specific domains, which consequently help shape a particular way of life (Misra, Srivastava, and Misra, 2006). In this view of creativity, less emphasis is placed on final products than on the creative process itself. In many traditional cultures conformity and adhering to traditions may be valued more than novel solutions to problems. Creativity depends on previous knowledge, and, therefore, to some extent on reproduction (Freedman, 2010).

In production of new ideas, objects, and images, creativity builds upon former concepts and in this way honors and reinforces tradition. Renewing and revitalizing something that already exists, such as Navajo weaving, African masks, or American folk art sculpture, also can be considered creative, dynamic, and changing with focus not on novelty but on self-expression within a traditional environment.

Figure 7. A *mashup* of a gargoyle from Notre Dame and reference to the Leave No Child Behind Act of 2001, created by Enid Zimmerman.

Creative acts then may be understood as acts of transformation that arise out of respect for a particular art form. Peat (2000) suggested that renewing and revitalizing something that already exists should also be viewed as creative. For example, students can create *mashups* that use web applications in which existing visuals are combined to create new images or videos. The old can become new and be renovated and reinterpreted by extending the energy of what has been created in the past (Congdon, in press).

CONCLUSION

In times of economic challenges and emphasis on standardized testing in the US and aboard, talented and creative art students need to receive differentiated education programs best suited to their own, their community's, and their country's needs. Art talent and creative abilities should be conceived of as multidimensional, with emphasis on development of technical skills, cognitive capacity and affective intensity, and interest and motivation in the arts. Art talent development should focus on students' backgrounds, local and global cultural contexts, personalities, skill development, processes and final products, and cognitive and affective abilities. Such development should be viewed as a learned set of complex abilities, and not an automatic consequence of maturation, in which carefully constructed educational interventions are essential. It therefore is appropriate for art talent development and aspects of creativity to be defined and put into practice in terms of educational interventions and how they are responsive to the educational needs of artistically talented and creative students. Programs for talented art students in any school and at any level should require participation of communities of interested parents, local crafts people, historians, and other community members. It is apparent that all students need to be prepared for a new information age. Those artistically talented students, who will later become practicing artists, should be prepared to think creatively and develop skills and abilities appropriate in a rapidly changing world. Educational interventions in art education that foster skill, talent, and creative development are needed to help these students generate solutions to real life problems. From local, national, and global perspectives, therefore, contemporary notions about creativity need to be reconsidered to acknowledge a more inclusive paradigm in which teachers and students from different backgrounds all can be included in an environment of changing notions about skill, talent, and creative development.

In any societal context, art teachers and their artistically talented students, can develop personal and professional creativity. These teachers can participate in the contemporary information age through developing educational interventions in art education that foster creative thinking, imagination, and innovation in which interconnection with others globally should be a goal. Visual art education has a major role to play in an increasingly visually oriented world by encouraging and supporting all students' and art teachers' talents, creative abilities, and imaginations. A conception of development of skill, talent, and creativity in the visual arts should foster art learning in which talented and creative students and their teachers are encouraged and rewarded to find and solve problems in unique ways that take into account their skills, talents, and creative abilities.

REFERENCES

Amabile, T. (1983). *The social psychology of creativity*. New York, NY: Springer-Verlag.

Antonucci, M. (2011, March/April). *Sparks fly*. Stanford, 46-53.

Arnheim, R. (1969). *Visual thinking* (Vol. 3). Berkley and Los Angles: University of California Press.

Bastos, F. (Ed.). (2010). Art education and social justice [Special double issue]. *Art Education, 63 (5)*.

Clark, G., Manifold, M. C. and Zimmerman, E. (2007). Meeting the needs of artistically talented students who reside in real and virtual, rural communities in the United States. *International Journal of the Gifted, 23(3), 319-329.*

Clark, G. and Zimmerman, E. (1997). *Project ARTS: Programs for ethnically diverse, economically disadvantaged, high ability, visual arts students in rural communities*. Washington, DC: US Department of Education. Research for this report was supported under the Javits Act Program (Grant NO. R206A30220).

Clark, G. and Zimmerman, E. (2000). Greater understanding of local community: A community-based art education program for rural schools. *Art Education, 53 (2), 33-39.*

Clark, G. and Zimmerman, E. (2001). Art talent development, creativity, and enrichment programs for artistically talented students in grades K-8. In: M. L. Lynch and C. R. Harris (Eds.), *Teaching the creative child K-8* (pp. 211-226). Needham Heights, MA: Allyn and Bacon.

Clark, G. and Zimmerman, E. (2004). *Teaching talented art students: Principles and practice*. New York, NY: Teachers College Press.

Clark, G., Zimmerman, E., Goodie, E., Wso, E., and Ho, A. (2003). *Report for a pilot project on the redevelopment of gifted and talented Students in the visual arts*. Arts Education Section of the Education Department, Hong Kong.

Congdon, K. (in press). Creativity and folk art: Making connections through Innovation and grounding in cultural contexts. In: F. Bastos and E. Zimmerman (Eds.), *Creativity research and practice in art education*. Reston, VA: National Art Education Association.

Costantino. T., Kellman, N., Cramond, B., and Crowder, I. (2010). An interdisciplinary design studio: How can art and engineering collaborate to Increase students' creativity?' *Art Education, 63*(2), 49-53.

Csikszentmihalyi, M. (1996). *Creativity: Flow and the psychology of discovery and invention*. New York, NY: HarperCollins.

Davis, G. A. (1992). *Creativity is forever*. Dubuque, IA: Kendall/Hunt.

Dudek, S. Z. and Cote, R. (1994). Problem finding revisited. In: M. A. Runco (Ed.), *Problem-finding, problem solving, and creativity* (pp. 130-150). Norwood, NJ: Ablex.

Duncum, P. (2007). Nine reasons for continuing use of an aesthetic discourse in art education. *Art Education, 60*(2), 46-51.

Feldhusen, J. F. (1992). *Talent identification and development in education (TIDE)*. Sarasota, FL: Center for Creative Learning.

Eisner, E. W. (1994*). Cognition and curriculum reconsidered*. New York, NY: Teachers College Press.

Feist, J. (1999). The influence of personality on artistic and scientific creativity. In: R. J. Sternberg (Ed.), *Handbook of creativity* (pp. 273-296). New York, NY: Cambridge University Press.

Feldman, D. H. (1982). *Developmental approaches to giftedness and creativity*. San Francisco: Jossey-Bass.

Feldman, D. H. (1999). The development of creativity. In: R. J. Sternberg (Ed.), *Handbook of creativity* (pp. 169-186New York, NY: Cambridge University Press.

Feldman, D. H. and Goldsmith, L. T. (1986). *Nature's gambit: Child prodigies and the development of great potential*. New York, NY: Basic Books.

Florida, R. (2002). *The rise of the creative class*: *And how it's transforming work, leisure, community, and everyday life*. New York, NY: Basic Books.

Freedman, K. (2003). *Teaching visual culture: Curriculum, aesthetics and the social life of art*. New York, NY: Teachers College Press and Reston, VA: National Art Education Association.

Freedman, K. (2007). Artmaking/troubling: Creativity, policy, and leadership in art education. *Studies in Art Education, 48*(20), 204-217.

Freedman, K. (2010). Rethinking creativity: Contemporary principles and practices. *Art Education, 63* (2), 9-15.

Freire, P. (2006). *Pedagogy of the oppressed* [30th anniversary issue ed.]. New York, NY: Continuum.

Gardner, H. (1999). *Intelligences reframed: Multiple intelligences for the 21st century*. New York, NY: Basic Books.

Graham, M. (2003). 'Responding to the demise of artistic development.' *Studies in Art Education* 44(2), 162-177.

Gregory, D. (in press). Creativity: Unmasking the process and product of art educators as professional pro-c artists. In: F. Bastos and E. Zimmerman (Eds.), *Creativity research and practice in art education*. Reston, VA: National Art Education Association.

Gruber, H. E. (1989). The evolving systems approach to creative work. In: D. B. Wallace and H. Gruber (Eds.), *Creative people at work: Twelve cognitive case studies* (pp. 3-24). New York, NY: Oxford University Press.

Gude, O. (2010). Playing, creativity, possibility. *Art Education,* 63(2), 31-37.

Hagel, J. and Seely Brown, J. (2010). *The power of pull: How small moves, smartly made, can set big things in motion*. New York, NY: Basic Books.

Hausman, J., Hostert, N. and Brown, W. K. (in press). Pedagogy toward a creative condition. In: F. Bastos and E. Zimmerman (Eds.), *Creativity research and practice in art education*. Reston, VA: National Art Education Association.

Hurwitz, A. and Day, M. (2001*). Children and their art: Methods for the elementary school* (7th ed.). San Diego, CA: Harcourt College Publishers.

Kaplan, S. N. (1979*). Inservice training manual: Activities for developing curriculum for the gifted*. Ventura, CA: Ventura County Superintendent of Schools Office.

Kaufman, J. C. and Beghetto, R. A. (2009). Beyond big and little: The four c model of creativity. *Review of General Psychology,* 13, 1-12.

Manifold, M. (2009a). Fanart as craft and the creation of culture. *The International Journal of Education through Art,* 5(1), 7-21.

Manifold, M. (2009b). What art educators can learn from the fan-based artmaking of adolescents and young adults. *Studies in Art Education,* 50 (3), 257-271.

Marshall, J. (2010). Thinking outside, and on the box: Creativity and inquiry in art practice. *Art Education,* 63(2), 16-23.

Milbrath, C. (1998*). Patterns of artistic development: Comparative studies of talent*. New York, NY: Cambridge University Press.

Misra, Girishwar, Ashok K. Srivastaveda and Indiwar Misra (2006), Culture and facets of creativity: The Indian experience. In: J. C. Kaufman and R. J. Sternberg (Eds), The international handbook of creativity, (pp. 421-455). New York, NY:Cambridge University Press

Mumford, M. D., Reiter-Palmon, R. and Redmond, M. R. (1994). Problem construction and cognition: Applying problem representations in ill-defined domains. In: M. A. Runco (Ed.), *Problem finding, problem solving, and creativity* (pp. 3-39). Norwood, NJ: Ablex.

Pariser, D. (1997). Conceptions of children's artistic giftedness from modern and postmodern perspectives. *Journal of Aesthetic Education,* 31(4), 35-47.

Pariser, D. and Zimmerman, E. (2004). Learning in the visual arts: Characteristic of gifted and talented individuals. In: M. Day and E. Eisner (Eds.), *Handbook for research and policy in art education* (pp. 379-405). New York, NY: Lawrence Erlbaum.

Partnership: 21st century skills (2010). Educator preparation: A vision for the 21st century. Draft 02.15.10. http://www.p21.org/

Peat, F. D. (2000). *The black winged night: Creativity in nature and mind*. Cambridge, MA: Perseus.

Runco, M. A. (2007). *Creativity-Theories and themes: Research development and practices.* Burlington, MA: Elsevier Academic Press.

Salen, K. and Zimmerman, E. H. (2004). *Rules of play: Game design fundamentals.* Cambridge, MA: MIT Press.

Shin, R. (2010). Taking digital creativity to the art classroom: Mystery swap box. *Art Education, 63*(2), 38-42.

Schubert, D. S. P. (1973). Intelligence as necessary but not sufficient for creativity. *Journal of Genetic Psychology, 122,* 45-47.

Sternberg, R. J. (Ed.). (1999). *Handbook of creativity.* New York, NY: Cambridge University Press.

Sternberg, R. J. (2001). What is the common thread of creativity? *American Psychologist, 56* (4), 360-362.

Sternberg, R. J. and Lubart, T. I. (1999). Concept of creativity: Prospects and paradigms. In: R. J. Sternberg (Ed.), *Handbook of creativity* (pp. 3-15). New York, NY: Cambridge University Press.

Sternberg, R. J. and Williams, W. M. (1996). *How to develop student creativity.* Alexandria, VA: Association for Supervision and Curriculum Development.

Thomas, K. (2009). Creativity in artmaking as a function of misrecognition in teacher-student relations in the final year of schooling. *Studies in Art Education*, 51(1), 64-76.

Tiebout, C. and Meier, N. C. (1936). Artistic ability and general intelligence. *Psychological Monographs,* 48(213), 95-125.

Tillander, M. (2011). Creativity, technology, art, and pedagogical practices. *Art Education*, 64 (1), 40-46.

Vernon, P. E., Adamson, G. and Vernon, D. (1977). *The psychology and education of gifted children.* Boulder, CO: Viewpoint.

Winner E. and Martino G. (1993). Giftedness in the visual arts and music. In: K. A. Heller, E. J. Monks and A. H. Passow (Eds.), *International handbook of research and development of giftedness and talent* (pp. 253-281). New York, NY: Pergamon Press.

Winner, E. (1996). *Gifted children: Myths and realities.* New York, NY: Basic Books.

Zimmerman, E. (1992a). A comparative study of two painting teachers of talented adolescents. *Studies in Art Education, 33* (3), 174-185.

Zimmerman, E. (1992b). Factors influencing the graphic development of a talented young artist. *Creativity Research Journal, 53,* 295-311.

Zimmerman, E. (1995a). Factors influencing the art education of artistically talented girls. *The Journal of Secondary Gifted Education, 6*(2), 103-112.

Zimmerman, E.(1995b). It was an incredible experience: A case study of the impact of educational opportunities on a talented student's art development. In: C. Golomb (Ed.), *The development of gifted child artists: Selected case studies* (pp. 135-170). Hillsdale, NJ: Lawrence Erlbaum.

Zimmerman, E. (2005). Should creativity be a visual arts orphan? In: J. C. Kaufman and J. Baer (Eds.), *Creativity across the domains: Faces of the muse* (pp. 59-79). Mahwah, NJ: Lawrence Erlbaum.

Zimmerman, E. (2009). Reconceptualizing the role of creativity in art education theory and practice. 50th Anniversary issue, *Studies in Art Education, 50* (4), 382-399.

Zimmerman, E. (2010). Creativity and art education: A personal journey in four acts (2010- Lowenfeld Lecture), *Art Education, 63* (5), 84- 92.

In: The Nurturing of Talent, Skills and Abilities
Editor: Michael F. Shaughnessy

ISBN: 978-1-62618-521-0
© 2013 Nova Science Publishers, Inc.

Chapter 2

NURTURING VOCAL TALENT

Jason Paulk, Kayla Paulk† and Jason Vest‡*

Eastern New Mexico University, Portales, New Mexico, US

INTRODUCTION

Singing—the first art—has existed for many thousands of years and continues to gratify the audiences that enjoy great performances and the individuals who provide them. The authors of this chapter agree that every human being has the potential to use their voice in an artistic and expressive way to create meaningful music; therefore, everyone has the potential to develop their vocal talent. The main limitation in the development of vocal talent is self-imposed, a result of commitment deficiencies rather than innate abilities.

This chapter includes three sections, detailing three specific areas of nurturing singers' talents: Jason Vest discusses working with solo voices; Kayla Paulk illustrates the work of solo singers in collaboration with a vocal coach; and finally, Jason Paulk illuminates an approach to developing voices in the choral rehearsal process.

DEVELOPING SOLO VOICES

Singing is a very personal action to us as humans. It feels so natural precisely because it is an outgrowth of one's self, a prolonging of the comparative brevity of expression found in our speech. And yet, singing is not used to communicate the banal details consigned to speech. More often, humans utilize song to convey or conjure emotions and heightened experience, whether positive or negative. One cannot say when song began because it feels as if it has always been with us. J.R.R. Tolkien puts forth in his story, *The Silmarillion*, that the earth and surrounding universe were all created through song. The great religions of the earth

---

* Jason Paulk. E-mail: Jason.Paulk@enmu.edu.
† Kayla Paulk. E-mail: Kayla.Paulk@enmu.edu.
‡ Jason Vest. E-mail: Jason.Vest@enmu.edu.

share singing as a central practice in their worship and praise. Even so, people often lament, "I wish I had learned how to sing" or "I wish I weren't tone deaf."

If song is so common to our childhood experience, from our mother's lullabies (where we cared little about her readiness for the performing stage) to schoolyard nursery rhymes, why is it often uncommon to adult experience? Almost everyone has a favorite song they loved to sing as a small child, where we first began to use our voices to trill out lilting melodies. It should be the case that, if we learn to sing at a young age, even preliminarily, our vocal talent should then increase in a linear or even a logarithmic manner as our intellect and physical abilities also augment. It seems, however, that only a chosen few mature with gifted voices. Is this natural selection of talent happening within our society? What creates the difference between those who are truly vocally talented and those who are not? The reasons may be varied, but usually can be reduced to aural experience, musical education, physical makeup, desire, and most importantly, work ethic.

How much singing occurred in your house during your childhood? Did your family sing together on a regular basis? Were you an active participant in school music classes? The chances are that the answers to these questions influenced your current vocal ability. Our brains are innately built to process music and it has lately been shown that there is little difference in the way the musically trained and untrained hear and understand music, meaning that everyone is at least somewhat musically adept. Lyle Davidson, in his chapter of the 1994 book *Musical Perceptions*, points out that adults with no formal training can solve musical problems as well or better than the average undergraduate music major. However, assembling knowledge of tonality into a framework from which one may sing and reproduce musical notation accurately with the voice requires a much deeper development of knowledge and skills (Davidson, 1994). Potential students of singing with little aural experience or practice using their voice accurately will find themselves at a disadvantage.

Marty Heresniak, writing in the *Journal of Singing*, called those inexperienced at matching pitch "bluebirds." He points out that the reasons for their vocal deficiencies can be many, including organic, cognitive, and functional causes (Heresniak, 2004). When these bluebirds enter the studio, they are most often not voice majors and do not have the goal of singing professionally. Even so, the occasional incoming freshman voice major enters as a "bluebird." Because they have not gathered vocal models and years of appropriate imitation, their progress is initially very slow. Within the confines of an undergraduate degree, there is not usually enough time for them to develop the integration of skills necessary to be successful and they change majors or leave the program. The needed skills include not only vocal frames of reference but also at least a basic knowledge of music theory, aural skills, and piano.

Singing, in concept, is actually simple. It is exactly because of that simplicity that the skill is so difficult to master. Much of the work of a voice teacher is focused on encouraging good behaviors and eliminating unnecessary tension, making the voice "simple" again. "Tension probably is the greatest enemy of the public performer," wrote James McKinney in *The Diagnosis and Correction of Vocal Faults* (McKinney, 1994, p. 35). Singing is an extension of the speaking voice and as such, should be freely produced. This assumes, however, that the speaking voice is produced in a healthy way, which it often is not. In addition, students often struggle with tension caused by collapsed posture. Many others find progress difficult because of health challenges that do not allow them to accomplish important points of technique, including pain with deep inspiration, temporomandibular joint disorder, asthma, allergies, and a myriad of other problems that can afflict the aspiring singer. Much like medical disorders are often treated with physical therapy, the relief of physical tension in the voice requires a similar approach. A systematic approach must be prescribed by the voice teacher and closely followed by the student if these hindrances are to be overcome. It is usually at this point, when the "fun" of singing is joined by the work of singing, that a student's desire is truly tested.

Many years ago a television show aired featuring an award-winning karate dojo. The owner of the organization was asked about the secret of his success in competition and he offered the following, "Flash is trash without basics." Mathilde Marchesi, a singer and voice teacher who studied with the famous Manuel Garcia and taught some of the most famous voices of the early twentieth century, proclaimed similarly, "Every art consists of a technical-mechanical part and an aesthetical part. A singer who cannot overcome the difficulties of the first part can never attain perfection in the second, not even a genius" (Marchesi, 1970, p. xviii).

There are many singers with whom we associate frequently that could be called talented. They sing in their offices, at the karaoke bar, in their cars with the radio, or even for an American Idol audition! If they have not benefited from voice lessons, they have most likely sung in a choir or have benefited from good models during childhood. A singer with "raw talent," though, has no guarantee of success if they continue to serious voice study. A colleague once told me, and it has proven to be true, that potential will break your heart. Many enter a course of study in voice with excellent groundwork laid (we might call them "very talented") and so their potential for success is enormous. They begin their study and initially succeed, but when they are suddenly in deep water, facing concepts, literature, and techniques for which they have to spend hours and hours practicing, they prefer to get out of the pool rather than learn to swim. Fortunately, many more choose to take the plunge and commit their time to learning the skill of singing. While the groundwork of which we spoke above puts someone ahead of the game, it is true that with time and work anyone can learn to sing well. Using the voice in a beautiful manner should not just be the province of the talented nor are we born as singers and non-singers. All humans are born with lungs, larynx, and resonating spaces, and thus all truly have equal opportunity when it comes to vocal talent. While not all may become professional opera singers, all humans can use their voices to communicate in the peculiar way only singing affords.

As with all talents, a foundation should be laid upon which all other aspects of the singing rest. The first of the basics that must be learned in solo singing is that of breathing. Before moving further with breathing, one should consider the structure in which breathing occurs, namely within the rib cage. It helps to think of the entire skeletal system as the steel frame of a building and consider that the frame must be correct to support the energy of breathing and phonation. Therefore, before inspiration even occurs, the singer's posture must be such that ideal breathing can occur. Marchesi states at the beginning of her singing method, "The attitude of the pupil, in singing, should be as natural and easy as possible. The body should be kept upright, the head erect, the shoulders well thrown back, without effort, and the chest free. In order to give perfect freedom to the vocal organs whilst singing, all the muscles surrounding those parts should be completely relaxed" (Marchesi, 1970, p. xi). Richard Miller, perhaps the most famous classical singing teacher and writer of the late twentieth century, agreed with Marchesi and described the posture for singing as "axial" and "noble" (Miller, 2004, pp. 35, 39).

Maintaining an open and elevated posture with the ribs allows the lower ribs to pull on the outer edges of the diaphragm, thus when inspiration begins the diaphragm descends into the thorax. This is perhaps one of the most difficult sensations for students of singing to grasp because it is opposite to habitual breathing patterns of everyday experience. Most subconscious breathing done throughout our lives is clavicular and intercostal, much higher than the low engagement needed in classical singing to produce a strong, supported tone.

Furthermore, few students understand at first the amount of energy and engagement in the entire body that is required to sing correctly. However, a teacher cannot just tell a student to use more energy and sing louder, as this will also produce undesirable effects in the voice. Instead, while singing, the sensation of continuing to inhale is sustained as long as possible through the phrase. This is often called *appoggio* or *la lotta vocale*, both terms implying a contest where the muscles of inhalation do not give in to the muscles of exhalation (Miller, 2004, pp. 1-17). This feeling of opening and expanding while singing allows the ribs to stay open, the diaphragm to not immediately release, and takes pressure off of the throat, which then remains free to phonate. As Giovanni Battista Lamperti succinctly stated, "To sing well you must continually feel 'hollow-headed,' 'full-throated,' 'broad-chested' and 'tight-waisted'" (Lamperti, 1957, p. 29). From this *appoggio* style of support the voice should arise naturally and without localized effort, as a balanced tone containing the strength of the low vocal register and ease of the high register.

Finally, an ideal resonating space must be created to amplify the harmonics of the voice in a desirable manner. Resonating strategies will be different for differing styles of music, but the lining up of vowel formants with harmonics is the best solution for all styles. In other words, the singer adjusts the space in the throat and mouth to amplify frequencies in just the right way depending on the pitch and vowel being sung. Many defects can impede the singer's ability to do this, including tongue and jaw tension, habitual rising of the larynx, weak muscles of the soft palate, and a general misconception of how one should sound when one sings. A common message given by the singing teacher is that the sound the student hears is not the sound their audience hears. Our ears truly do deceive us. Therefore, one must find the right sensations in practice and lessons and then replicate that feeling in performance.

When a singer gains a solid grasp of the basic functioning of their voice, they can then begin to communicate the text of the song in a meaningful way. The goal is that technique becomes second nature through repetition of correct habits and the performer can then focus completely on the acting or presentation of the song. This complete coordination takes a while to develop, sometimes many years of dedicated, daily practice before the student can synchronize the posture, breathing, resonation, and expression of an inspiring performance.

The teacher who wishes to help a student achieve fulfilling vocal execution must possess, in the words of James McKinney, "(1) comprehensive knowledge of the vocal mechanism and how it works, (2) ability to express yourself in terms the student can understand, and (3) some of the skills of a master psychologist." He goes on to state, "The teacher-student relationship must be based upon mutual respect and an awareness of the complex personal feelings that each person brings into the studio" (McKinney, 1994, pp. 13-14). As stated at the beginning of this section, singing is a very personal act, an outgrowth of our self in prolonged expression. While all have the privilege of developing a talent for singing, many are limited because of aural inexperience, physical challenges, lack of desire, and numerous other reasons.

These challenges can be overcome in time with the proper technique and requisite desire, and the most gifted singers, as well as the least gifted, can acquire the capacity to deliver a truly stirring performance.

DEVELOPING VOICES THROUGH VOCAL COACHING

The Value of Collaboration

As people who live and work in social communities, the ability to collaborate well with others is a necessary and valuable attribute. Collaborative groups pool their resources, varied experiences and knowledge, enabling them to be more comprehensive and successful than an individual with more limited resources. In a 2006 research study by Peter D. Hart Research Associates, Inc., conducted on behalf of The Association of American Colleges and Universities, teamwork skills and the ability to collaborate with others in diverse group settings ranked as the first and most important skill employers look for in new hires. This research demonstrates that those with strong collaborative skills are best equipped to work together with others toward a common goal. As anyone who has attended an office, town hall or other group meeting has witnessed, shared knowledge and experience within a group generally promotes learning and increased consensus.

Advanced singers in the world of vocal performance frequently seek the opportunity to collaborate with gifted vocal coaches, who specialize in the following roles: learning assistance for opera roles, language coaching, refining artistic nuances for the performance of art songs, and preparation for a collaborative voice and piano recital. Likewise, in the university setting, advanced students often have the opportunity to study with a vocal coach, who in supplement to their regular applied voice lesson, offers practical guidance in recital repertoire selection, provides accompaniment for recital performances, assists in teaching language fluency, phrasing, ensemble, communicating with an audience and the nurturing of vocal artistry.

Voice and Piano Collaboration

Collaboration is an inherent element in the art and discipline of music. Though solo music does exist, most musicians perform in collaboration with others. Even solo musicians rely on the collaboration of others to bring their art forms to life: the solo pianist joins the orchestra for a concerto, the maestro conductor elicits music from the people who comprise the orchestra, and the soprano is almost always accompanied by either a pianist or orchestra, sometimes joining forces with other singers.

No matter the medium, musicians who collaborate together become more facile and dynamic musicians in the process, being informed by and informing their collaborators simultaneously as they make music together. In vocal music, myriad collaborative opportunities exist. A singer may collaborate with other musicians in small ensembles (duets, trios, quartets, quintets, etc.) and large choral ensembles.

Perhaps no other collaborative experience in music is as varied as that of the collaborative pianist (accompanist), whose title alone carries the proverbial torch for collaboration in the musical arts. Singers will inevitably work with a collaborative pianist numerous times during their careers and learn many vital skills during the process.

The role of the collaborative pianist can be considerably diverse. On any given day, the pianist may accompany a voice lesson or recital, rehearse with a quartet, record the accompaniment of a saxophone solo to aid a student in practice, accompany numerous auditions, collaborate in a choral rehearsal or concert, perform a piano solo with an orchestra, accompany a musical theatre performance, join a jazz combo, play in a church setting, or serve as a vocal coach for singers.

Of all the roles available to an accompanist, it is the role of the vocal coach that best allows the pianist to directly nurture the talents, skills and abilities of the singer, as the vocal coach works in tandem with the voice teacher to offer the student a comprehensive and collaborative pedagogical experience.

The Collaborative Pianist As Vocal Coach

A vocal coach serves as a partner with and liaison between the singer and the private voice teacher. Where a private teacher's role is to aid the singer in developing good vocal technique through vocal modeling and instruction, healthy posture, efficient and effective breathing, artistry through song and many other attributes of vocal development, the role of the vocal coach, though not designed specifically for technically developing the voice, is to guide the singer in all other facets of vocal performance, including diction, note learning, artistry, historically informed performance practice, and myriad key concepts. Because the majority of vocal coaches are trained pianists rather than singers, their work is most successful when focused on all aspects of training the singer outside of vocal technique, as that responsibility should belong solely to the trained voice teacher.

Many components of the development of singers can successfully be taught by coaches, enabling the voice teacher to focus primarily on vocal development in lessons and lending the singer the vocal coach's additional perspective on concepts the teacher may not have time to fully develop.

Equipping the Singer for Success in Vocal Coaching

In order for a singer to gain maximum benefit from vocal coachings, identifying a coach with a solid foundation in diction (native and foreign language), song literature, a facile piano technique, excellent accompanying skills, and a basic understanding of healthy vocal technique are prerequisite. Additional skills in conducting, vocal pedagogy, foreign language fluency/immersion and education are also beneficial. A coach who possesses such a broad and comprehensive foundation of training will have the ability to develop the talents, skills and abilities of a singer in numerous ways.

The singer whose vocal coach is also an accompanist will have a teacher who can perform dual roles in the lesson: coach-teacher and coach-accompanist. Because many voice teachers are not pianists and often lack the skills to play the accompaniments of representative vocal repertoire, a coach-accompanist is able to provide accompaniment for the singers in coachings while offering instruction simultaneously. Not only does this aid the singer in learning how it feels and sounds to sing a song with accompanimental support, but it also provides the singer with an additional perspective on areas in which he may need guidance. If a singer sings with an inconsistent tempo, the coach-accompanist will feel and hear that, and can address that with the singer. If the singer has an unsteady sense of rhythm, the coach-accompanist will recognize the misalignment of rhythm between singer and pianist, and is better equipped to address rhythmic integrity. When a singer has an unbalanced or uneven sense of tempo rubato or graduated ritard, a good coach-accompanist can use the accompaniment to demonstrate for the singer many examples of balanced tempo rubato or a gradual ritard.

Additionally, by playing the accompaniment in coaching lessons, the coach-accompanist introduces the entire harmonic structure and overall affect of a song or aria to the singer. As many singers are unable to play accompaniments for themselves (notably orchestral reductions of operatic arias and complex song accompaniments), they far too often rely on recordings to help them understand the entire scope of a piece. As the coach-accompanist plays an accompaniment for a singer, the tempo is more pliant than a recording, it is possible to pause for collaborative study of various musical components, dynamic alterations can be explored and the singer gains a more complete synthesis of the song (or aria) in its entirety. With a coach-accompanist at the piano, a depth of musical exploration, analysis and synthesis is available, helping the singer develop musical analysis skills for future study of new repertoire.

For the coach-accompanist to best assist the singer, knowledge of the vast song and operatic repertoire is essential. How deeply a coach understands a song or aria will have a direct influence on the depth of understanding and, subsequently, level of performance the singer can achieve. Equipped with this knowledge, a coach can offer suggestions of quality editions of repertoire (including cadenza books and vocal exercises) and extant recordings of works the singer is studying.

Additionally, a coach will be able to assist the singer in creating era-specific ornamentations, including extended melismatic cadenzas, appoggiaturas, trills, etc. Because vocal coachings do not focus primarily on building and shaping the voice, there is time available for teaching guided self-discovery of numerous tools such as these, which provide the singer with important skills of independent musicianship. A significant benefit of the young singer working with a coach-accompanist is the set of foundational tools being learned for a lifetime of musical collaboration. When the singer graduates from the vocal studio to transition to graduate school, a young artist program, an opera apprenticeship or, ultimately, a career as a professional singer, there will be many people involved in their continued development: a voice teacher, vocal coach, agent, and a conductor may all be involved in the work of a young singer. When a singer learns to work with more than one musical influence in a single musical project, their education and experience are deeper and more comprehensive, as they are influenced by several supporters. When a young singer is able to receive instruction from and collaborate with varied musical influences, that singer will be able to interact and work with a wide variety of people and personalities. Whether introverted or extroverted, humble or egocentric, of a fixed or open mindset, musicians, like people, are individually unique. The singer with multiple pedagogical influences will adapt well to the life of a professional singer and all it entails.

Collaboration beyond the Vocal Studio

When considering collaborative opportunities for the singer in the vocal arts, perhaps the quintessential opportunity for collaboration among large groups of singers is the choral experience. In a choral setting, where a group of people sing together and work toward common musical goals, a musical environment is created which depicts the essence of collaboration. Whether in an opera, professional, community or collegiate choral experience, the choral experience can offer a wealth of developmental opportunities for the singer. Infused with both a healthy and pliant vocal technique learned in the studio and dynamic artistry, independent analysis skills and resourcefulness learned in the coaching studio, a singer can approach a choral experience as a well-prepared and significantly contributing leader of the ensemble, adding the choral art to his already extensive resume of vocal pedagogy.

DEVELOPING VOICES IN THE CHORAL SETTING

Participation in choral organizations is very high throughout the world. For example, in the United States, approximately 22.9% of households reports that a family member regularly sings in a chorus, meaning approximately 42.6 million Americans regularly attend choir rehearsals and perform choral concerts with approximately 250,000 choruses comprised of professional, community, educational, and religious organizations (Chorus Impact Study, 2009).

For the vast majority of singers who populate the world's choruses singing is avocational, and as such, they need considerable direction in their pursuit of vocal development. Most have never had private voice lessons, many do not possess music reading skills beyond a very basic level, and vocal ability levels vary dramatically between individuals in the ensemble, from rank beginners to accomplished performers. Herein lies the great challenge of developing vocal talent in the choral setting: balancing the needs of each individual singer with the overarching performance goals of the choral instrument.

The choral curriculum addresses three specific domains of development, including the psychological, the physical, and the musical. These domains will be discussed in brief detail below, providing approaches and pedagogies employed to develop awareness, fluency, and mastery in each specific area.

Psychological Development

Pablo Picasso is credited with saying, "Every child is an Artist; the problem is how to remain one once you grow up." Singers in ensembles often have to be reminded how to enjoy being "at play." Psychological issues that are at work in the choral setting include overcoming inhibitions, fear of judgment, risk taking, and developing intrinsic motivation, just to name a few.

The choral rehearsal environment, as any classroom environment, either supports and encourages or limits student achievement. This foundational concept cannot be overstated and research exists that proves the classroom environment that encourages intrinsic motivation through the combination of internal and external rewards causes the brain's dopaminergic hormones to facilitate neural synaptic transfer, providing for learning fluency. Conversely, stressful conditions and socio-emotional deprivation inhibit dopamine production and therefore limit transfer for learning (Braun and Bock, 2007).

What does a supportive environment look like? A supportive environment is a positive place that accepts individuals with varying abilities and nurtures ensemble members' pride in their work, reinforces the benefits of teamwork, encourages risk-taking, and helps students develop intrinsic motivation through setting high expectations and through teaching students how to take control of their own educational outcomes.

Furthermore, creating opportunities for students to become completely integrated and invested in the choral rehearsal process is an important hallmark of the supportive environment. The psychologist, Mihalyi Cziksentmihalyi, suggests that when students are working at a high level of concentration on an enjoyable task they can reach a mindset that is totally engrossing, dispensing of all worries and thoughts of other problems. This "flow" experience, as he describes it, becomes the reward for intense focus and dedication to the task (Elliott, 1995, p. 114). Understanding the importance of engagement and flow is important for keeping students focused during the learning process.

Assisting students in the discovery of musical elements and vocal techniques that can be improved in the rehearsal process—through a spiral curriculum (Bruner, 1960)— is very important. By revisiting common building blocks of healthy singing in each new piece of repertoire, common musical goals are realized by each singer. A singer's perception of their "ability" or "talent" is sometimes mistakenly thought of as their capacity to sing a piece "correctly." This is rarely a healthy perspective. Research by music psychologists point out that young singers "who think ability is a repertoire of *skills* that can be continuously expanded through instruction and experience are more likely to focus on the task at hand, display greater intrinsic involvement, and are less preoccupied with learning as a test of their worth" (Covington, p. 53).

By assisting singers in developing self-assessment tools—listening skills, physical and vocal awareness—conductors create a continually formative process in which individuals set their own goals in tandem with the goals of the ensemble. This focus on self improvement becomes a major contributor for engagement in the choral rehearsal process because each person understands what it takes to be personally involved and takes responsibility for the group's progress.

Why do people sing in choirs? The answers are as numerous and varied as the individuals who populate the choirs in which they sing.

No matter the reasons, it is incumbent upon teachers to find varied ways to engage, motivate, and inspire individual singers. Six specific constructs of musical meaning were discovered through research by Hylton (1981) in a survey of nearly 700 high school choral singers. These students responded that they found meaning in the following aspects of choral singing: the psychological, communicative, integrative, musical-artistic, spiritualistic, and achievement (Richmond, 1981, p. 797).

Developing talent for most singers, therefore, means finding ways to assist them in their quest for meaning in these various areas of ensemble singing.

Physical Development

Singers cannot expect to develop significant vocal achievement without an understanding and awareness of their bodies. Somatic awareness is achieved through multiple experiential methods in the choral rehearsal. Activities for developing kinesthetic awareness are included in the warm-up period of rehearsals in order to allow singers the opportunity to connect with their core muscles, release tension, and prepare for supportive and flexible inhalation and exhalation, which is exaggerated when singing as compared to normal daily communication.

Great success can be achieved by using examples from real life events in order to achieve a specific goal of bodily awareness and optimal physical function (Ehmann, 1982).

Important conceptual areas for physical development include: understanding of the main elements of alignment from head to toe; freeing tension that inhibit free phonation, good support, and energized tone production; understanding of major muscles involved in support and respiration (lower abdominal and intercostals muscles for increased capacity of and efficiency for airflow); learning to use the articulators (lips, tongue, teeth) for clear and effective communication.

Many of these elements can be addressed in creative physical exercises that are enjoyable for group process. For example: a conductor might ask the choir to stand at "attention," and then flop over like a "rag doll." Now the ensemble of rag dolls might pull themselves into a tall and regal position as if being controlled by a marionette.

This type of exercise not only connects each individual to their own specific postural needs, but it encourages creativity and imagination, clearly a need in all areas of development. Another helpful tool for the conductor is the use of exaggeration. Singers can be asked to exaggerate a collapsed posture, or a misaligned chin and head on top of the spine, followed immediately by an "inspired posture," and a "noble" head position.

Musical Development

The elements in this category are far beyond the scope of one chapter and so numerous that is difficult to parse the few that can be addressed here. Three categories will be discussed, including theoretical reasoning, vocal attributes, and issues related to ensemble cohesion.

Theoretical Reasoning

Singers in ensembles should have the opportunity to learn a system for reading a musical score, whether in the form of *solfeggio*, number system, or note names. Likewise, singers should develop a secure sense of rhythm, an understanding of meter, and an ability to count accurately in order to learn new music by sight-reading instead of having to rely on rote learning. Pitch and rhythm fluency is to music performance what phonemic fluency is to early elementary school reading development.

Once beyond the basic elements of the grammar of music, assisting in the understanding of harmony (how chords are constructed and tuned effectively) and form (phrase shapes and overall structure) are important elements of concern.

Vocal Attributes

Numerous warm-ups are employed in the choral rehearsal, usually in the opening minutes, in order to facilitate the successful accomplishment of vocal concepts. Some teachers call this the "skill building" portion of the rehearsal, and it is, perhaps, the most important time in rehearsal because the fundamental quality of voice production and technique is developed herein. A few of the specific concepts frequently addressed include developing a pleasing timbre, opening the vocal tract, resonance, *appoggio* (breath management), tuning, vowel modification, glottal onsets, and an evenness of voice production throughout the range. These fundamental vocal qualities will be consistently reinforced during rehearsal of the repertoire.

Voice building, a term coined by Frauke Haasemann, employs a non-threatening approach to group vocal techniques by employing many everyday activities, sounds, and experiences into the choral rehearsal. This approach is highly beneficial and encouraged for use with amateur choirs and singers with little experience. Using creative sounds to develop high registers such as police sirens and train whistles, "mooing" cows to develop resonance in the low voice, and "yawn-sighs" to blend registers (from top to bottom), students begin to learn vocal pedagogy without even realizing. Applying those sounds in the repertoire becomes second nature and builds an important foundation of vocal skill from which can be built an artistic singing voice. Other vocal skills that are often effectively developed through group voice building include: varied timbre, range extension, staccato, martellato, opening of the vocal tract, resonance, inhalation/exhalation, breath support, vowel modification, and many others.

While it is still beneficial to employ the same types of creative pedagogical techniques with advanced choirs, advanced singers need to begin to understand the semantics and science of singing by experiencing appropriate usage of terminology. Don Miller discusses the importance of the commonality of language and expectations for singers in the forward for his excellent book, *Resonance in Singing* (Miller, 2008). Being technically accurate with terminology—that is, employing terms that accurately describe a physiological function, such as lifting the soft palette, focusing the tone toward the hard palette, achieving "singer's ring," developing *appoggio*, *chiaroscuro*, etc.—will prepare singers to understand the commonly understood vocabulary employed amongst voice users in the field. Speaking too frequently in metaphors, aphorisms, and descriptive language can often unfortunately obscure the central message for singers. Besides, with great advances occurring in vocal pedagogy, technology, and the proliferation of numerous resources available to guide teachers, specific technical vocal terminology is becoming ubiquitous.

Ensemble Cohesion

Singing in a choir is a completely unique opportunity compared with singing as a soloist; that is to say, the "choral instrument" is much greater than the sum of its parts. The artistry and emotional impact of many voices singing together can be very compelling, evidenced by a thousand years of choral music composition. People have sung together for enjoyment, ceremonial purposes, and for worship of God for many centuries, and will continue to do so because of the unifying nature of the activity.

Becoming unified as a choir is often challenging for untrained voices due to the many various vocal attributes represented in the ensemble. Obviously, every voice has its own distinct make-up of harmonics that make it sound unique. In order to achieve cohesion and unity as a choir, singers must develop a sensitive ear and flexibility in their approach to singing, learning to balance their own unique timbres within a section of unique sounds, in order to become a unified section. Only then can a choir begin to sing in tune; individual sections must sing as unit before parts can tune to each other.

A few of the important artistic elements involved in this cohesion process includes: a strong sense of internal rhythm so vowel shapes and consonants can occur simultaneously; learning to sing a legato line with constant breath flow, as opposed to singing pitch to pitch in a pedantic manner; understanding articulation as it relates to small units of the musical measure and larger units of the musical phrase; tuning concepts related to chord structure; and a varied approach to vocalism depending upon the style of the music being performed (composer, period, compositional style, etc.).

CONCLUSION

Singers come in all shapes, sizes, and with varied experiences. Likewise, their vocal apparatuses and bodies (literally, their *instruments*) come in varied states of health and wellness. In part, due to the individual goals and differences in each person's voice, and in part due to the fact that voice teachers, vocal coaches, and conductors construct art with invisible instruments in an ephemeral genre, challenges abound in practical vocal pedagogy. It is the hope of the authors that the material presented in this chapter provides a pragmatic framework for approaching the nurturing and development of vocal talent in the areas of solo voice instruction, collaborative voice instruction, and in the choral singing process.

REFERENCES

Braun, A. and Bock, J. (2007). Born to Learn: Early Learning Optimizes Brain Function. In: W. Gruhn and F. H. Rauscher (Eds.), *Neurosciences in Music Pedagogy* (pp. 27-52). New York, NY: Nova Science Publishers.

Bruner, J. (1960). The Process of Education. Cambridge, MA: Harvard University Press.

Chorus America. (2009). The Chorus Impact Study: How Children, Adults, and Communities Benefit from Choruses. Retrieved from http://www. chorusamerica.org/advocacy-research/chorus-impact-study

Covington, M. (1983). Musical Chairs: Who Drops Out of Music Instruction and Why? In: K. Deans (Ed.), *Documentary Report of the Ann Arbor Symposium on the Applications of Phsychology to the Teaching and Learning of Music: Session III Motivation and Creativity* (pp. 49-54). Reston, VA: MENC.

Davidson, L. (1994). Songsinging by Young and Old: A Developmental Approach to Music. In: R. Aiello and J. Sloboda, *Musical Perceptions* (pp. 99-130). New York: Oxford University Press.

Ehmann, W. and Haasemann, F. (1982). *Voice Building for Choirs*. Chapel Hill, NC: Hinshaw Music, Inc.

Elliott, D. (1995). *Music Matters*. New York, NY: Oxford University Press.

Hart, Peter D. Research Associates, Inc. (2006). How Should Colleges Prepare Students to Succeed in Today's Global Economy? Retrieved August 12, 2012, from http://www.aacu.org/leap/documents/Re8097abcombined.pdf

Heresniak, M. (2004, September/October). The Care and Training of Adult Bluebirds: Teaching the Singing Impaired. *Journal of Singing,* 61(1), 9-25.

Katz, M. (2009). *The Complete Collaborator: The Pianist as Partner.* New York, NY: Oxford University Press.

Lamperti, G. B. (1957). *Vocal Wisdom.* New York: Taplinger Publishing Company.

Lindo, A. (1916). *The Art of Accompanying.* New York, NY: G. Schirmer.

Marchesi, M. (1970). *Bel Canto: A Theoretical and Practical Vocal Method.* New York: Dover Publications, Inc.

McKinney, J. C. (1994). *The Diagnonis and Correction of Vocal Faults.* Long Grove, Illinois: Waveland Press, Inc.

Miller, D. (2008). *Resonance in Singing—Voice Building through Acoustic Feedback.* Princeton, New Jersey: Inside View Press.

Miller, R. (2004). *Solutions for Singers.* New York: Oxford University Press.

Montgomery, A. (2006). *Opera Coaching: Professional Techniques and Considerations.* New York, NY: Routledge Taylor and Francis Group.

Moore, G. (1945). *The Unashamed Accompanist.* New York, NY: The Macmillan Company.

Richmond, J. (2012). The Sociology and Policy of Ensembles. In: McPherson, G. E. and Welch, G. F. (Eds.), *The Oxford Handbook of Music Education.* New York, NY: Oxford University Press.

Spillman, R. (1985). *The Art of Accompanying: Master Lessons from the Repertoire.* New York, NY: Schirmer Books.

In: The Nurturing of Talent, Skills and Abilities
Editor: Michael F. Shaughnessy

ISBN: 978-1-62618-521-0
© 2013 Nova Science Publishers, Inc.

Chapter 3

USING THE STUDY OF LANGUAGE TO HELP DEVELOP MUSICAL SENSITIVITY

Mark Dal Porto and *Tracy Carr*

Eastern New Mexico University, Portales,
Roosevelt County, New Mexico, US

INTRODUCTION

Language is an extremely powerful tool for human communication and expression. Words alone have the ability to express a wide variety of emotions. A true orator is well aware of the power and expression of the spoken word.

Music too, has the power to create and evoke powerful emotions. The ancient Greeks believed in the Doctrine of Ethos – a philosophy that the type of music one listens to, or more specifically, the scales or modes of a piece as well as the specific type of musical instruments used, can strongly affect the listener's logos (rational behavior) and pathos (emotional behavior). Similarly, in 1752, J. J. Quantz wrote in On Playing the Flute: "For that which does not come from the heart does not easily reach the heart."

Hence, the connection between these two modes of communication, music and language, as well as the ability to express emotion in both disciplines is further explored here.

By associating the universal principles of language with music, it can help one better understand, as well as become more sensitive to, the aesthetic details found in music.

If this integration of art forms (language, poetry, and music) can be used to acquire greater sensitivity in music, then it would seem logical that it could also be used as a springboard to promote greater musical talent as well as a higher emotional intelligence quotient (often abbreviated as EI for Emotional Intelligence or EQ for Emotional Quotient).

Language, of course, is universal and has its own internal system. Its structure is composed of the following elements: grammar, phonology, morphology, syntax, and semantics.

All of these facets of language have analogies that can be made to music's internal language structure as listed below:

---

* Corresponding author: Mark Dal Porto. E-mail: Mark.DalPorto@enmu.edu.

1   Grammar – how words combine to form sentences (how musical components are arranged, chord progression)
2   Phonology – speech sounds and pronunciation (musical articulation, the harmonic series)
3   Morphology – form and structure of words (harmony in music)
4   Syntax – phrase and sentence structure (musical phrases, cadences, chord progression)
5   Semantics – meanings of speech forms, word meanings (transmission of meaning and emotion in music)

The association of the principles of language with the study of music is a largely untapped region of study. Therefore, we have been attempting to relate the structure, function, and classification of these language principles to music and have found them both to share some similarities. Illustrating these various linguistic functions can help one to better understand more abstract musical concepts through the more natural process of language which we naturally tend to acquire in infancy.

Thus, we have found that having a greater understanding of how language relates to music can enhance one's ability, perception, understanding, and emotional sensitivity for music. By especially increasing one's emotional sensitivity to music, this enhanced "EQ" can only make one better equipped to develop and nurture musical talent.

We can now consider in more detail each of the aforementioned qualities of language and their corresponding musical elements.

MUSICAL GRAMMAR

Listen to and compare the following two chord progressions of Example 1 (See the end of this article for where you may hear all of the examples from this paper online.):

Example 1a. Chord progression #1.

Example 1b. Chord progression #2.

The first progression (1a) follows a normal grammatical arrangement of tonal harmony (drives convincingly toward a final resolution of the main tonal center or key) whereas the second progression (1b) seems to wander and lack a sense of purpose or direction in seeking a final key resolution.

Even so, both of these progressions may be usable to the composer depending on what the composer's intent is. If the composer is looking to create fulfilled expectations, then the first progression would seem more appropriate.

However, if the composer is seeking to create a more yearning, unresolved emotional affect, then the second progression would seem to be the better one. In either case, the point is that traditional music has an internal set of tonal and harmonic materials that tend to create a sense of logical flow culminating in a drive towards a tonal center. When this goal is delayed or denied, then a different emotional affect (usually a sense of heightened tension) is created.

The study of the consistency by which these materials have been used in the past and the codifying of such procedures are referred to as music theory. These theoretical principles might also be referred to as basic harmonic grammar.

We will return to these two progressions after first considering other principles of comparison, specifically those involving musical phonology, morphology, and syntax.

MUSICAL PHONOLOGY

Phonology deals with speech sounds and pronunciation which may be likened to articulation in music. Musical articulation deals with the way notes are attacked (staccato, legato, portamento, etc.) and serves to enhance the emotional character of the musical material. Additionally, timbre is an aspect of sound. Musical timbre is a by-product of the harmonic (or overtone) series. These are the presence of higher pitches in the sound spectrum when a sound is produced. Generally speaking, more harmonics will occur the louder a note is played. For musical pitches, they follow a precise mathematical pattern. For example, when a C2 is played on the piano, the following "harmonics" (Example 2) will tend to occur:

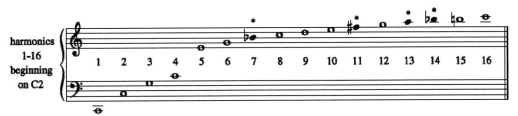

*dark noteheads indicate pitches that deviate markedly from our equal-tempered tuning system.

Example 2.

Example 2 illustrates the first 16 harmonics of the note C2 (the first being the fundamental pitch C2, the "perceived" tone). These upper pitches are present in varying degrees in the spectrum even though one is not usually aware of them because they are almost always softer in volume than the fundamental pitch. The fundamental is the primary tone that is heard, but the specific "power" of each of these additional harmonics gives whatever instrument is playing this fundamental pitch its characteristic and recognizable "timbre."

The exact amount of volume each harmonic possesses determines the tone's unique "phonological" timbre distinguishing one instrument's "color" or timbre from another.

MUSICAL MORPHOLOGY

Morphology deals with the form and structure of words. Its musical equivalent is notes and harmony. For instance, a musical note might be compared to a phoneme.

A phoneme is the smallest basic unit of sound. An example might be the letters /l/ and /t/ to distinguish between the words lip and tip. Next, a musical motive might be compared with a morpheme. A morpheme is the smallest unit of meaning (such as the word run or an –s, which is a plural marker for nouns). However, a word can contain more than one morpheme or unit of meaning (such as the word redo meaning again to do) or a word can contain several phonemes (basic units of sound) but only one morpheme or meaning (such as the word ma-hog-on-y).

A motive on the other hand, is the smallest basic idea in music. It is a germinal, embryonic motif often used as a building block for further development. As an example, one of the most famous musical motives in all music is the beginning of the following work (Example 3):

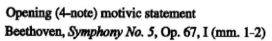

Example 3.

Finally, a musical chord might be likened to a word. A chord is a harmonic element that combines three or more notes simultaneously (often used to harmonize melodies) and can produce a wide variety of emotional effects depending on the composer's choice of chord and the way it is spread out or "voiced."

MUSICAL SYNTAX

Syntax deals with phrase and sentence structure. Sentence punctuation has its analogy in music in what are called cadences; these are sometimes brief points of rest or repose, a caesura of motion, or more often, simply a harmonic or melodic goal. Cadences are defined by the harmonic progression that concludes a phrase of music (a phrase can be defined as a musical idea longer than a motive, usually a few measures in length, and terminated by a cadence). There are four traditional cadences recognized in music. These are:

1   Authentic Cadence (V-I or vii°-I), This is considered the strongest of the four cadences in establishing a sense of finality. Of the authentic variety, there are two types: perfect and imperfect. A perfect authentic cadence ends the phrase with a V-I chord progression with both chords in "root position" and scale degree one in the top voice for the I chord (analogous to a period or exclamation point at the end of a sentence). An imperfect authentic cadence is a V-I chord progression with: (a) one or both chords not in "root" position, (b) with some other chord tone other than scale degree 1 on top when the I chord is reached, or (c) is a vii°-I chord progression.

2   Plagal Cadence (IV-I). Also conclusive sounding (analogous to a period or exclamation point at the end of a sentence). A plagal cadence is also sometimes called an "amen" cadence as it's frequently used as the final ending cadence found in hymns.

3   Half Cadence (any chord progressing to a V). Incomplete sounding (analogous to a comma in a sentence).

4   Deceptive Cadence (V to some chord other than I). Incomplete sounding (analogous to a question mark at the end of a sentence).

Other types of cadences are possible and are usually classified as derivatives of these.

A phrase in music has been likened to being similar to a sentence in language. Hence, using this definition, a phrase could then be said to equal a "musical sentence."

However, most phrases in music do not seem to give a sense of "completion" (as in an actual sentence) and therefore this terminology is misleading.

In spite of this, examples can be found where a phrase appears to sound like a complete musical sentence as in the following (Example 4):

Example 4.

Each phrase (or line) of the above example ends with a perfect authentic cadence giving the strongest sense of completion. Consequently, here we have two independent musical phrases that each provides a sense of being a complete "sentence."

The next two examples (5a and 5b) each consist of two phrases (again one phrase per line), the first phrase punctuated with a half cadence and the second with a perfect authentic. Thus, only the second phrase of each example gives a sense of completion.

Therefore, the entire two phrases together give a total sense of only one "sentence" (containing in effect two "clauses") with the midway point punctuated with a "comma" and the final phrase concluding the "sentence" with a "period."

Example 5a.

Example 5b.

Musically speaking, examples 5a and 5b also illustrate what is known as a musical period in its overall construction. This terminology is different as compared to when one speaks of a literal period ending a sentence. A musical period consists of at least two phrases which go together to form an antecedent/consequent relationship between one another. This is achieved here by the first cadence being weaker or incomplete-sounding (at the end of the first phrase) and the second cadence being stronger (at the end of the second phrase) giving a sense of completion. Thus, the two phrases together create a sense of unity linking two dependent clauses into a complete "musical sentence."

Both 5a and 5b may also be referred to as a parallel period since phrase one is similar to phrase two within each example. The term contrasting period is used for a period that contains dissimilar phrases.

The next musical excerpt for solo piano (Example 6) illustrates two phrases, the first punctuated with a deceptive cadence and the second with a half cadence. Both give a sense of incompletion. The first cadence can be likened to a question mark and the second to a comma.

Example 6.

In looking at the previous examples (4, 5, and 6), we can see that a phrase in music can occasionally be likened to a "sentence." However, most musical phrases do not give a sense of being a complete sentence and therefore seem to function more in the manner of a partial sentence or "clause." However a composer handles their integration of musical phrases within the course of a composition ultimately depends on the emotional affect intended for the listener.

In modern poetry, syntactic distortion is common. An example of this is the work of E. E. Cummings in which the following poem illustrates this technique (the original punctuation and spacing have been preserved):

My sweet old etcetera- E. E. Cummings (1894-1962)

Original:

my sweet old etcetera
aunt lucy during the recent

war could and what
is more did tell you just
what everybody was fighting

for,
my sister

isabel created hundreds
(and
hundreds) of socks not to
mention shirts fleaproof earwarmers

Rewritten:

Aunt: What is more, Aunt Lucy
could tell you what everybody was
fighting for during the recent war.

Sister: Sister Isabel created
hundreds (and hundreds) of socks,
not to mention shirts, fleaproof
earwarmers, wristers, etc.

etcetera wristers etcetera, my
mother hoped that

Mother: My mother hoped that I
would die bravely.

i would die etcetera
bravely of course my father used
to become hoarse talking about how it was
a privilege and if only he
could meanwhile my

Father: And only if he could of
course, my father used to become
hoarse talking about how it was a
privilege (to die bravely).

self etcetera lay quietly
in the deep mud et

Himself: Meanwhile, I lay quietly in
the deep mud (dreaming of your
smile, eyes, knees, and of your . . .
etc.)

cetera
(dreaming,
et cetera, of
Your smile
eyes knees and of your Etcetera)

"my sweet old etcetera". Copyright 1926, 1954, © 1991 by the Trustees for the E. E. Cummings Trust. Copyright © 1985 by George James Firmage, from COMPLETE POEMS: 1904-1962 by E. E. Cummings, edited by George J. Firmage. Used by permission of Liveright Publishing Corporation.

By rewriting the poem (as done in the right hand column), we can create five more "syntactically correct" sentences. The rewritten and original versions can be compared to the following two chord progressions which began our discourse (Example 8):

Example 8a. Chord progression #1.

Example 8b. Chord progression #2.

The second progression (8b) is like the Cummings poem in that the chords used do not follow the normal grammatical arrangement of syntax logic. Notice when hearing this example how the harmonies seem to wander and lack a sense of purpose or direction which may be heard by most listeners as creating an emotional affect of unanswered longing.

However, the first chord progression (8a) exhibits a stronger sense of normal harmonic syntax (comparable to my rewritten version of the Cummings poem). Why? This is because 8a exhibits a stronger sense of direction primarily in its drive toward the ultimate resolution of the central key of C major. All of the chords in the first example pull gradually toward this center of gravity ending with a perfect authentic cadence.

The second progression, although perhaps fresher-sounding in its approach, is not what would be considered normal harmonic movement in music.

This does not mean that the second progression is inferior musically or not useful. It simply depends on the emotional affect the composer intended to create. These two progressions are shown as an example of the affect created by intentionally distorting the harmonic syntax (as in the Cummings poem and example 8b) or by creating a more traditional harmonic progression (or syntactically correct arrangement as illustrated in our rewritten sentences of the Cummings poem and in example 8a).

As already mentioned, a musical phrase has its analogy in most cases to a clause and only occasionally as a complete sentence. A section in music can also be likened to a paragraph where a certain thought, idea, or subject prevails (as compared to music where a certain musical idea or melody might be featured).

A movement in music can be related to a short literary work or to an individual "chapter" in a larger work. Finally, a complete multi-movement musical work (containing several movements) can be equated to a book, play, novel, or any other literary work containing separate divisions, acts, or chapters.

MUSICAL SEMANTICS

Musical semantics is probably a more philosophic area to touch upon as it deals with musical meaning (as opposed to word meanings). Unless the music itself contains words or is instrumental music that contains a written "program" provided by the composer (defined as "program music"), much of it is simply open to the opinion of the listener. Listen to the following two excerpts (Example 9a and 9b) that occur from the same work:

The first (9a) occurs near the beginning of the work (in the first movement) and the second (9b) occurs near the end (of the fourth and final movement). The first might be likened to some listeners as a depiction of "nature at sleep" while the second could be said to symbolize "triumphant victory over life." However, these are just two possible interpretations out of a myriad of possible responses.

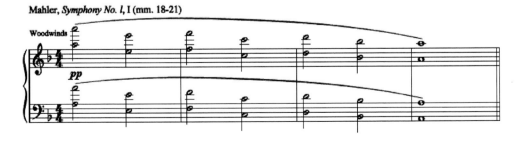

Example 9a.

Example 9b.

The two examples are clearly related melodically, but the character of each is entirely different. The first is played slowly and very quietly by woodwinds against a quiet string background. The second is much faster and played extremely loud by French horns accompanied by a full orchestral background. What could be said of this transformation in character that occurs during the course of the work? The storm clouds that metaphorically appear in the first movement reappear again in the last but ultimately resolve at the end in a blaze of glory. The listener probably cannot help but to sense that there is an "internal program" suggested by the music, but what exactly is it? Thus, we see that music cannot express fundamental meanings as can language, but often relies on its emotive power to convey only a hint of definitive meaning. Perhaps its true "meaning" can only be determined by how it makes one "feel".

Music has aptly been called "the art of the emotions" and often depends on its emotional qualities to try and communicate its "message" beyond the power of word meanings. Music, like poetry, is often purposely ambiguous in its meaning to allow the listener or reader the experience of determining its meaning through something that is already "known" to them. When that "known" element becomes clear to the listener, then that work's ultimate "meaning" will also become clearer and can then lead to a more sensitive and powerful musical experience.

CONCLUSION

We have considered but just a few examples of some basic structural similarities between music and language and how they express emotion. By comparing some of the universal principles and structure of language with music, a greater understanding and appreciation of music can emerge. It can also demonstrate the sometimes "hidden" logic of musical expression to be one that is backed by universal principles of language, communication expression, and emotion. Finally, by having a greater understanding of how language relates to music, this knowledge can help to increase one's emotional sensitivity to music.

REFERENCES

Bernstein, L. (1976) *The Unanswered Question*. Harvard University Press, 1976.
Quantz, J. J. (1975) *On Playing the Flute*. English translation from German, Macmillan, 1975.
To hear any of the examples in this article, go to: http://tinyurl.com/95z7s7b

In: The Nurturing of Talent, Skills and Abilities
Editor: Michael F. Shaughnessy

ISBN: 978-1-62618-521-0
© 2013 Nova Science Publishers, Inc.

Chapter 4

THE SOCRATIC METHODOLOGY, THE DEVELOPMENT OF MATHEMATICAL THINKING SKILLS, AND THE SPIRITUAL REVIVAL OF THE WEST

Colin Hannaford[*]
Oxford, England

INTRODUCTION

It was only after he discovered that his parents' murder was the result of the wholesale corruption and criminality of Gotham City that mild-mannered reclusive billionaire Bruce Wayne decided to make it his duty to cleanse Gotham of its criminals and fraudsters, and of all the political chicanery and injustice that kept them free.

Today, it is hard to imagine an ordinary person not affected by the collapse of common spiritual values and common morality that Western societies have recently experienced.

This is no longer the stuff of comic-book heroes. It is here and now.

The moral values which once everyone accepted as natural, the values which made our countries prosperous and safe, the moral values which encouraged young people to believe in their society, and in their ability to succeed through honesty and hard work, these moral values are now scorned by the new mega-rich as strictly for the ninety-nine percent: not for them.

It is also hard to imagine a more unlikely savior of these values, of honesty, humility, resourcefulness, and self-reliance, than the average mild-mannered mathematics teacher.

I am sure most of you are seen in this way by your colleagues and your pupils, even by yourselves. Waiting within you, however, is a hero or heroine, fully equal to Bruce Wayne and Barbara Gordon (even as played by Ms Michelle Pfeifer in black latex).

---

[*] Corresponding author: Colin Hannaford. E-mail: democracy@maths90.freeserve.co.uk.

SOME BASICS OF MATHEMATICAL THINKING

Let me explain what makes mathematics teachers uniquely able to save their pupils from losing confidence in these simple values and sliding down the slippery slope into self-disgust and moral degradation.

The first reason that makes this possible is that mathematics is culturally neutral. Every major civilization throughout history has played some part in its development; so that every modern nation feels proud of sharing in its present development.

The second is that mathematics is the only truly universal subject. It is taught in all countries, in all schools, in all languages, with the same practical intention of enabling proficient students to continue to work with others anywhere.

The third is that it is itself essentially a language of argument. It should not be taught to youngsters as a plethora of mysterious rules to be applied without question and without understanding, but to encourage them to develop their skills in critical, informed and receptive argument. This is essential in understanding mathematics properly. It will prepare them for study in all other sciences. The same skills are vital for democracy's health and success.

The fourth reason is that the teaching of mathematics has never been imagined as having any moral consequence. As a science, of course, mathematics has none. But, as we shall see, its teaching can have very great and inescapable moral consequences. The choice is only whether they will be bad or good. My purpose in this chapter is to argue that teaching mathematics as if it has no moral, social, or ethical consequences has been indispensable in wrecking our democracy, in giving power to the fraction of our societies interested only in increasing their own privileges and wealth, in making a cheap joke of the notion of government 'of, by, and for the people'.

The fifth reason is that mathematics lessons have never before been used deliberately in this way. It is, in a most important sense, invisible. It is the equivalent of Batman's cloak.

Given all these positive conditions, it will be obvious that mathematics teachers, knowing at firsthand the moral and ethical demands their training made on them, and wrapped, at least for the first few crucial years, in their cloak of invisibility, are most able to restore the spiritual and democratic values of any country. And if the people of any nation under God want this to happen, He must surely arrange for its mathematics teachers to be instructed in the best way to succeed!

The first step is to become acquainted with the Socratic Methodology which I developed whilst a Head of Mathematics in the British European School, United Kingdom, together with Dr Hartmut Koehler, Director of Studies, Stuttgart LEU, Germany, with support from Professor Eva Vasarhelyi, Director of the Department of Mathematical Didactics, Eötvös Lorand, University, Hungary, and Professor Dr Hani Khoury, Chair of Mathematics, Mercer University, Georgia, US.

It is strange now to remember when I first became dissatisfied with the way I was teaching mathematics.

This was over thirty years ago. I had been appointed a head of mathematics of the British European School outside Oxford, one of twelve international schools created by the European Union and teaching multi-national, multi-lingual, mixed-ability pupils for the European Baccalaureate, preparing them for university entry anywhere in Europe and the US.

This was not only a highly prestigious position; it also provided me with almost complete pedagogical freedom and official encouragement to find a way to teach mathematics better.

It soon became apparent to me that I was held to be a highly successful teacher - hence my appointment, aged 36 - because I was actually so highly successful in teaching the majority of my pupils to be obedient: whether or not they understood what they were doing. The more obvious this became, the more disgusted I was with myself. Surely I should achieve more than this!

Still more serious was my increasing realization that I was also responsible for my pupils' moral degradation. They had all come to me as eager young innocents: incapable of meanness, incapable of sustained deception. Within a few years, this would change: permanently, disastrously.

Given the freedom I enjoyed, I was able to stand back and reflect on the results of my teaching. I had been trained to teach at the School of Education of Cambridge University, one of the most highly-regarded in the world.

How could there be anything wrong with the methods it had taught me to use? My pupils did well in their exams. This must surely mean that they understood what they were doing!

The hardest obstacle to my own understanding was to accept that it was I who was failing. I was finally obliged to face the truth.

The truth was that only a very few actually did understand.

The even nastier truth was that I was obliging the majority of my pupils to learn to conceal that they did not understand. I was forcing them to be systematically dishonest. Most were just copying, more or less accurately, my instruction. Copying, for them, was 'understanding'.

A much smaller fraction always could understand my instruction as I intended. They were being obliged to believe that the others were stupid or lazy. As a result of this, they were not only learning to be contemptuous of anyone less able than themselves, but also to be selfish and unwilling to share their achievements.

And finally - as even I had to admit - there was always a bewildered remainder simply being left behind. Because of the relentless pressure, which all teachers will know, to 'finish the syllabus', once they fell too far behind I had no time to help them. At first only confused and disappointed, they would become increasingly angry with me and contemptuous of the system.

It became irresistibly and painfully obvious that I was creating in my classroom exactly the same three mutual distrustful, mutually contemptuous divisions visible in the breakdown of civil responsibility and individual moral confidence in our societies.

These divisions have been created in children before they leave school. They enter societies already divided by previous generations. How easy then for unscrupulous politicians to tell them, as they have repeatedly told their parents, that all the faults of their society, all the obstacles they face in their individual lives, are caused by the dereliction or delinquency of one or other of the other divisions, or both. Societies become ever more polarised as political rhetoric becomes ever more poisonous. Decent debate become impossible: becomes, in fact, unwanted. Democracy dies.

I decided either to quit a job that I had begun to detest; or learn to do it better.

This turned out to be spectacularly easy and astonishingly enjoyable, both for me and my classes at all ages from 11 to 18.

My senior pupils had always passed their exams. Although none had chosen to be math specialists, for the next fifteen years they continued to achieve amongst the highest average Baccalaureate grades of all thirteen European Schools.

More to the point, when they left my final class they knew how to continue to study and learn unsupported.

Unsurprisingly, my orthodox colleagues were horrified by my temerity: even more by my success. Their noses being kept firmly pressed to the orthodox grindstone by their national inspectors. Mine were more tolerant. They were obliged to continue as before.

Every year I would begin by explaining to my youngest pupils how best to help their brain to learn intelligently and critically. This would be their first lesson of less than an hour.

Within another month they would be proving its truth for themselves:

"I want you all to hold out your two fists, pressed together in front of you. This is almost exactly the size and shape of your brain. You see that it's divided into two almost equal halves. Almost equal in size: but with very different powers. Approximately – remember that I say 'approximately' – the right side learns by remembering what it has seen or felt as patterns, of what it has done as routines; meanwhile the left side knows how to hear, how to speak, and how to ask questions. We may say that the right side remembers what has happened; the left side is capable of understanding why it happens. Most of the time the right side's memory is very accurate: this is how you learn to ride your bike: but, if you make a mistake, it will remember this mistake very accurately too, as part of a routine. How many of you have found, if you have once spelled a word wrongly, you seem to spell it wrongly again, and again. This is when we say a routine has become, what? – thank you! – that it has become 'corrupted'. We can only get it 'uncorrupted' by asking the left side to find the mistake. The right side cannot do this!"

This explanation is readily understood by even the youngest children not only because it corresponds completely with their own past experience; but also because it enabled me to further explain what would happen in the near future.

"Until now," I would continue, "you have learnt almost all your arithmetic, and reading and writing and spelling as routines. Many of you could go on learning mathematics with me like this. You might all be entirely successful - for another two or three years - and then, and I absolutely guarantee this, most of you will start to fail. Why do you think this would happen? Thank you, again! Because you would have been using less than half your intelligence; trying to pack everything you need to remember into your right brain as routines, without any understanding of why they work; and when, eventually, they begin to fail, as they will, you will have not the least idea of why they fail, or how to make them work. You will find that many grown-ups remember this. You may hear them say: 'Oh, I was never any good at mathematics at school. I soon found it was too difficult for me!' What do you imagine happened to them? Let's suppose that every one of you has an IQ 0f 110. What is one half of 110? Thank you: 55. Do you know what people with an IQ of 55 can do for themselves? Not a lot! Thank you. Even with the best training someone with an IQ of 55 will remain permanently aged about 8. Do you remember what you could do aged 8? This is what will happen to many of you if you don't start to learn that mathematics is not just a lot of patterns, a lot of rules, a lot of boring routines. It is a great adventure, very nearly the greatest adventure that human minds have ever begun; and to take part in this adventure you must learn to use all your mind: which means you must learn to question, to argue, to criticise, to love to be criticised – for this is learning too – above all to doubt that anything is true until, as if you are pinned on an ice-face with nothing but a hand-spike to save you, you must put your faith in it in order to move at all.

This is the adventure of mathematics. In order to learn mathematics properly, you must learn to use the left side of your brain: this side. This is where your brain keeps its ability to listen, to talk, to discuss, to argue, to disagree, and to think seriously about disagreement, because sometimes the other will see what you do not see. Then you need to be honest enough to be thankful for being told you are wrong."

"Sometimes," the White Queen famously told Alice in Wonderland: *"I think of six impossible things before breakfast!"*

When I first announced that I planned to teach my pupils to learn mathematics by arguing its explanations and statements within each class, my own British colleagues were immediately, and loftily, dismissive. *"How can they possibly learn anything by arguing about mathematics. They don't know any mathematics. They will just end up fighting!"*

But what seemed impossible to them turned out to be easiest of all!

I turned for help to the National Literacy Trust in London, which provided me with the following statistics.

They represent the approximate ability of the average child to retain knowledge after different kinds of class activity:

1	Listening	5%
2	Reading	10%
3	Audio-visual	20%
4	Demonstrations	30%
5	Discussion	50%
6	Practice by doing	75%
7	Explaining to others	90%

Many people - above all, many parents - continue to insist that 'proper' teaching must emphasise mainly the first three activities. Whole classes, of any size, should learn by listening or reading (silently), or by watching their teacher writing or drawing diagrams on a board and (also silently) copying this down. The teacher is totally in control. The class is totally occupied. There is no fooling about. There is no talking. Everyone seems to be busy.

Of course such lessons always appear impressive. But how many are learning anything? The hard fact is that the first three activities can be twenty times less effective than the last three.

Their exclusive use by any teacher will only spell disaster for children.

Modern classes of youngsters will always contain a few who find it difficult to understand the meaning of even a single sentence. Most, of course, can read, silently or aloud. They recognize the words. They can also pronounce them. The crucial fact is, however, that many just *do not comprehend what the words actually mean.* By the end of a paragraph they may be completely lost.

We blame such children for being inattentive, for being bored, disruptive, and even destructive. And they often are. Do you remember how often you were bored?

In truth, their situation is really terrifying. They sit through lesson after lesson in a daze. They may act as if they understand. They may have learnt to do what is praised, very often without the slightest idea of why it is praised. They have come into school with almost no experience of reasonable conversation, of the use of language to communicate, of the need for tolerance of mistakes, for patience in constructing comprehension and achieving agreement. This is not their fault. Almost certainly they did not choose to be like this. Nor do they want to fail. But unless they are taught to understand, they will fail. It is inevitable and terrible to watch. It is also entirely possible to prevent it from happening.

The most effective lessons will be those in which you ask selected children to read a text aloud, to show their comprehension by explaining in their own words what it means, to demonstrate their understanding by discussing their ideas with others, and then by using their ideas.

The reason for this is not difficult. Knowledge is created through associations. The brain best remembers whatever has caused it to combine the most functions, whatever has caused it to notice or create the most associations.

Sitting silently whilst listening and watching a teacher - however talented the teacher - does not do this. Reading and listening, reading aloud, discussing the meaning, searching for a better explanation, giving examples, explaining to others: these use far more energy; they involve many more functions of the brain, create many more associations. How many more? We can give a rough approximation. Up to twenty times more energy, functions, and associations: which is why reading aloud (and then explaining) makes it far more certain that your pupils will learn!

Whatever their age, they should also hear much of the explanation you have just read. It has convinced you. You should be able to convince them. Incidentally, the first time I dared to begin Reading Aloud with a senior class, I did not do this. Within minutes, there was an explosion of rage. One girl slammed down her book. *"We're not supposed to be able to read this rubbish, and understand it."* she shouted angrily. *"It's your job to teach it to us!"*

"Listen," I replied, as calmly as I could manage. It was obvious that the rest of the class agreed with her. *"Within a year you will be sitting alone in a study bedroom in some university, and in the room with you will be a pile of books."*

I paused whilst the rest of class contemplated this possibility, real for them all.

"There will be no-one else in the room. Unless by then you can open books and read them, with understanding, you might as well be dead. Now, pick up the book - and read."

The lesson continued successfully. But I should have tried to explain this first.

This I now recommend.

It is not strictly necessary, however, for everyone to have their own text-book. They can share. It is a good idea to keep a list of who has read already, and to try to ensure that everyone has a turn. You will soon discover that some read fluently; some excruciatingly badly or slowly; others too fast. Praise clear, steady, lively reading. It *must* attract emotion as well as thought.

You can demonstrate this by reading a really boring text or some mystery thriller as if you are King Lear or Joan of Arc. The point is to alert and excite the emotions, to make any text more memorable. It must be fun to read. Make it so.

No pupil's reading should be too long. Sometimes a few words may require an explanation, although often to you they may be most obvious. Be sensitive to text that is irrelevant, or poorly written, or just plain boring - and, when it is, say so. You are not there to defend a text, only to help your class understand what it may mean. If a text is really bad, correct it; but ask the class for suggestions as to how they would correct it. They must learn that writers also are fallible.

I cannot emphasize enough how important it is not to show any surprise when the first person or the next or the next whom you ask: *"What does it mean?"* helplessly answers: *"I don't know."* This is entirely natural. Say so, before asking the reader: *"Please read it again."*

Obviously you will not show amusement, ridicule, frustration, impatience, disbelief, or anger. The whole tone must be of relaxed and interested exploration of the ability of the class to learn. If someone is disruptive, ask that person to read or explain.

Your example throughout is vital. Everyone is learning from you as well as from the text. That *you*, the authority over *them*, listen peacefully, and interject helpfully, whilst they help each other to reach an agreed conclusion - even if this is only temporary - gives them a tremendously powerful social model to remember. They see and experience the sheer difficulty of achieving agreement. They will later be more cautious about dogmatism.

Nor is it always the cleverest in the class who will make the most useful contribution. Occasionally, it may be some shy soul who has really never before got anything right. When they are able to make the contribution that everyone agrees is useful or right, you will have helped to change those persons' view of themselves for the rest of their life.

Finally, once any necessary examples of practical work have also been read and explained, let them decide which exercises they will do, both in class and at home, and let them get on with it, where necessary helping one another. The noise level may be high, but most of it will be useful noise.

Of course, there will be the occasional lesson failure. This is normal too, and when they happen, you can always revert to the time-honoured activities numbered one to three in our list. As we have seen, they are not very effective, but all classes are used to them, and therefore well understand the discipline that they require. You can therefore always create more order whenever you wish.

Now I think you know almost as much I did when I began. Try it. Find out what it is like *really* to participate in learning. You will be surprised how often you will learn more as well.

This is the help the Socratic Methodology can give you in stopping your pupils' scores in mathematics from sliding down the SAT scales. Let us now enlarge our perspective to see what it can do to revive your society's spiritual values.

*

Science has won for us the ability to affect nature more than our ancestors would ever been able to imagine; but it has done nothing to curb our natural inclination to kill and destroy.

We would prefer to live in a world of honest, compassionate, rational people, all wanting an honest, just and fair future for their children, in which change may be achieved without violence.

This requires the ability to distinguish prejudice from reason; but it also requires our appreciation of the importance of maintaining diverse cultures.

I am indebted to Professor Murray Gell-Mann, a spectacularly innovative Nobel Laureate in Theoretical Physics, retaining an unusual concern for the rest of our world, for pointing this out. [1]

I will explain how to achieve both.

To help us we will all need a spiritual guardian.

`Not another Alfred Pennyworth, Bruce Wayne's butler, as played by British actor Michael Caine, complete with his original Cockney accent.

It must be available to children as a faculty of mind.

Most of my ex-pupils are now parents themselves. When I met some of them for their final school reunion, which usually I have avoided, they asked me to create a Facebook group *'to tell everyone in the world what you taught us in your classroom'*!

At the time, this seemed a little extravagant; but since its creation 'Children for a just, honest, and fair world' has actually gained an international following. I hope this may now increase.

What I tried to teach my pupils in my classroom was that they should never to be afraid to be honest, and to ask questions. Both of these apparently simple acts actually require considerable initiative and courage.

Their spiritual guardian should surely help here.

All major religions, and science, agree that we possess something that they define as *'the essence of identity'* (OUP); *the spiritual part; the animating, actuating cause of an individual life'* (Webster).

Rather curiously, and despite the confidence with which they agree that it exists, there is no similar agreement as to what this something actually does. Surely there should be. This is clearly not an insignificant part of any individual's life. In order to sustain identity it must sustain courage. In order to actuate and animate, it must prompt action.

Both religions and science agree to call this the soul.

In my Facebook essays, via their parents, I tell children what their soul does.

I explain that their soul is their spiritual guardian: that it helps them to be courageous and that it prompts their actions: that it does this mainly through the activity of the left side of their brain.

None of this will surprise young pupils who have already been introduced to the Socratic Methodology, whether in mathematics or in any other subject.

They will have learnt that the left brain's functions are unique: that it is uniquely able to create, retrieve, and critique information, much of which may be new to the rest of the mind.

For better or for worse - and in a moment we shall come to a fierce argument about whether better or for worse - the ability to think conceptually, to express thoughts conceptually, and therefore to speak and understand speech, has evolved mainly in the left-brain of our species.

It is true that the right side has a modest ability to create apparently audible sounds. This is how schizophrenics and mystics are believed to receive their commands. Usually it is concerned exclusively with perceiving and remembering patterns, and reproducing them when required.

The simplest of these patterns must help us to recall where we are when we wake in the morning: *"Hello sun! Hello sky! Hello trees!"* The most complex will include patterns of social behavior in which we are required to participate, or to which we must respond.

Whether they are static or active, I will call them all routines.

Almost all of human life revolves around routines.

For at least half a million years our ancestors were using their right brains to learn the routines they needed to survive: to ensure access to water, to food and shelter, to maintain social support, to defend, to kill, to travel – and, of course, to keep their living space clean.

At the very beginning of my Facebook essays I suggested that the most powerful human impulse began with a soft *schrr-schrr-schrr* of a primitive broom sweeping a floor: applying the routine called 'cleaning' to claim and identify a defined space as exclusive.

DEVELOPING THINKING SKILLS
VIA BRAIN BASED LEARNING

The right side of the brain will always demand an exclusive space for the routines by which it identifies itself. This impulse was not discovered by Hitler, or Stalin, or Mao Zedong. Thousands of years before them Joshua was ordered by his God to clear the land promised to the Hebrews by killing *'all the men and all women, young and old, the cattle, the sheep and donkeys.'* [2]

In every society of prehistory, this struggle to survive created a permanent addiction.

Once they all were found reliable, the more singular routines were customarily sanctified by their shamans or priests as being required by the command of their gods. These became the signifiers of the racial, social, religious, even the existential integrity of their people.

Once declared to be sacred, no matter if seen by later generations to be arbitrary or trivial -and, indeed, often *because* later seen to be arbitrary and trivial - they were even more urgently rehearsed as unchallengeable proof of their owners' exclusive identity, impossible to change.

Many millions of people are still subservient to their right brain's demands. They can never be persuaded to abandon the routines which provide them with their identity. If the presence of such people becomes *irritating to a greater and more ruthless power*, the only solution is to remove them completely. They cannot change themselves. This has happened before.

These are events of our history.

We have yet to learn how to preserve *'the essence, the spiritual part, the animating, actuating cause'*, projected into people's consciousness by the left brain, without it becoming an immediate irritant to the older and more ruthless power of the right brain,

Given these considerable functional differences, there is clearly great potential for conflict. Much mental anguish will result if their rivalry becomes too intense.

Much actual conflict results in the world.

So far as I know, no attempt to reconcile them has been attempted before.

Besides the advice of Professor Gell-Mann, I will also be helped by two other distinguished scholars: Professor Julian Jaynes of Princeton, and Professor Iain Gilchrist of Yale,

Both agree that this conflict is the result of evolution.

Both agree that this evolution was triggered by some huge disasters around the Mediterranean and the borders of Asia about twenty thousand years ago.

It was possibly a series of earthquakes, followed by years of drought, followed by devastating floods, followed by many centuries of wars.

Both agree that this woke an entire race of ancient Rumpelstiltskins from their three million year-long sleep. It destroyed the stability of emergent civilisations. It caused their populations to lose faith in many previously trusted routines, including the worship of many idols. Quite possibly it prepared the way for belief in one all-powerful, very jealous god.

THE LEFT SIDE OF THE BRAIN

Both agree that it accelerated the evolution of the left brain's ability to be conscious of itself, to develop new solutions to problems, and to learn to express them in more complex language.

Both agree that the result is who we are today.

They *disagree* completely whether what happened brought Paradise to an inevitable but also gentle end: the new complexity of language would certainly allow such insights as: *"Crikey, Eve, we're naked!"*, or whether it brought about an even worse catastrophe continuing to this day. [3]

In Professor Jaynes' analysis the new abilities of the left brain created modern humans. With all [THAT] this evolution may also entail (admitting that much is bad), we modern humans are a spectacular advance on our mumbling, fumbling, hardly conscious ancestors.

To the left brain's ability to question, investigate and innovate, we owe every cognitive and social advance of the past twenty thousand years. We have continued to find previously trusted routines unfounded and unnecessary: most famously encouraging Karl Marx to dismiss every religion as 'opium for the people'. Modern atheists have continued this tradition.

For Professor Gilchrist this is nothing [LESS] than a hooligan desecration of all that cultures hold sacred, a destruction of all the old, best, most trusted routines that impelled the Irish poet W.B. Yeats to write: *'The ceremony of innocence is drowned; the best lack all conviction, while the worst are full of passionate intensity.'* [4]

Dr. Gilchrist would apparently rather believe that without the interference of the left brain, human beings would have been able to create ever larger civili[z]ations in which every one played the part assigned to them by birth and social class, and which would all have remained entirely peaceful because no-one would ever have got it into his or her head to demand anything different.

This is rather like the society that Karl Marx dreamt would naturally appear once the avarice of capitalism, dominated of course by the left-brain, had been smartly knocked on head.

Unfortunately, Marx seemed not to have reali[z]ed that money is just one element of social control. The right brain needs nothing but routines. And these can impose directly by force.

A short while ago a young Muslim girl tried to demand something different in the form of a modern education for herself and other girls. She was promptly shot in the head by a young Muslim man for daring to advance 'secularism'.

It is often impossible to see how to satisfy two mutually exclusive points of view: such as this young girl's wish to be educated and her moronic assassin's determination to prevent it.

Sometimes this may require a very special expertise. I once heard an Israeli physicist explain that he had succeeded in reconciling the Genesis account that our universe was created in six days by calculating that the billions of years required by modern theory would be reduced to exactly six days simply through relativistic time shortening!

The White Queen would have made him her Astronomer Royal.

Occasionally, however, it is possible to recognize that both contain some elements of truth.

There is indeed a constant tension in all our minds between the ancient needs of the right side to create and sustain a steady picture of its world, a pattern and routine in which it can keep us safe, whilst this steady picture is under constant attack by the left brain obsessively analyzing, questioning, looking always for weakness and fault.

This has produced, in turn, an evolutionary crisis which threatens our survival as a species, and an existential crisis which prevents individual transcendence.

Here now is your hope for the future.

In an earlier examination, in his 'Quark and the Tiger', Murray Gell-Mann observes that some of us, at least historically, have been here before.

When the early Greeks thinkers, Socrates being only one of the most famous, were beginning to bring their newly discovered analytical thinking to bear on their societies' myths and rituals, the effect was not to destroy either, but rather radically to alter their significance.

Gell-Mann points out that whilst the myths were criticized, reinterpreted, even privately derided, *'the continuity of the ritual was what helped hold the society together.'* [5]

Provided that we can persuade moronic young men that they will do their own cause a very great disservice by shooting far braver young girls in the head, we must also recognize the enormous value of religions, and their many different routines, in helping to hold societies together.

But nor should the religious anathematize atheists. Their dissatisfaction with religious routines may be only dissatisfaction with religious routines. It does not mean that their soul is dead.

Quite the opposite may be true. Angels can sometimes learn from sinners: and vice-versa.

There is a wonderful story amongst Aesop's Fables of the little mouse who one day finds a lion snared in a great net of ropes. Once, out of pity for such a small whiskery creature, the lion had spared the life of the mouse. Now the mouse returns its kindness. Although the ropes are thick and hard, its teeth are sharp, and one by one it bites through enough of the knots to set the lion free.

As teachers of the Socratic Methodology, our task is somewhat similar to that of Aesop's determined little mouse.

There is no need, as we now see, to prefer the left side of the brain more than the right side; or the right side more than the left. Without the proper function of both, we would simply stop like toys whose clockwork has run down.

But, with all due respect to Dr Gilchrist, the left side is uniquely important.

It is the Grail. It is the repository of the soul.

Many young people today are deeply confused about the direction of their lives. Frightened by the freedom that beckons outside religions, some may plunge into what they are told is more fundamental, although actually it is likely to be an even more limiting routine.

Such routines are very easily manufactured. They will usually benefit some group or some persons. Usually they demand belief in ridiculous ideas which allow believers to feel unique.

Many are so disgusted, on the other hand, that the major religions are unable prove their claims to be uniquely truthful, that they decide that there is no fundamental morality.

They are as trapped by their own cynicism as the lion in its net: trapped by their lack of belief in their own minds; beset by the complexity of the world's routines which beset us all.

They would like to be free, but are as fearful of being free.

Our pupils need only to be advised to work on their own fears slowly. They have a lifetime in which to be guided by their soul to find new solutions to new and old problems, and to learn more every day of what it is to be alive.

When they have learnt enough mathematics, the teeth they need are simply the interrogatives by which any routine can be questioned.

Every mouse has many sharp little teeth. They all have names: *Who? Where? Which? How? Why? Why not? Whether? What if? Whose?* And, sharpest of all: *Cui bono?*

Given the additional interesting possibility of a new nuclear race, the most serious new and old problem now confronting us all is how to reconcile the increasingly assertive major religions with secularism and atheism: not only the different schools of Islam, the different professions of Christianities, Judaism, and, especially in the Unites States, Mormonism.

Everyone understands that this is a major problem. It is currently the hottest topic in many university departments devoted to religions, peace, and world affairs. No-one has yet to find a way to address it without immediately being accused of either being institutionally partial to one or religion or incapable of understanding any because of secret atheism.

Clever old Plato saw the solution at about the same time that Gell-Mann suggests the Athenian Greeks were beginning to renege on their right brains' identification of religious rituals as manifestations of divine truth.

Prompted by the insights of their left brains, the Athenians were beginning to treat such rituals as important to individuals, as necessarily to be respected in general: but never to be allowed to be more important than the preservation of their civil discourse and their democracy.

Please notice the US Constitution is a product of the same state of mind.

Plato noticed was that true spirituality, the foundation of all religions, requires the development of intellectual clarity, perceptual honesty, and, above all, the courage to question.

This is what his old tutor Socrates taught, and was killed for.

Plato further realized that young people can begin to learn these spiritual qualities on the way to understanding mathematics: not least because mathematics depends on these values.

The Socratic Methodology aims to help your pupils to learn how to learn mathematics more effectively and more enjoyably, engaging them to work competitively as a team.

It aims to open their minds to the intellectual freedom enshrined in the Constitution and to the spiritual values it guarantees.

It allows religions their freedom: but not to the extent that the routines important to the right brain stop the left brain from continuing to explore, to question, and, above all, to doubt.

*

Let me end my chapter with one the happiest anecdotes of my own career.

I had been working for about two months through the Methodology with one of my youngest classes when a young lad arrived unexpectedly from an ordinary English school.

He had clearly never seen any class working at any subject as mine were with me. But, after a week or so, he began to get the hang of it, was soon as active as any, and I had stopped thinking of him as needing any special attention.

After another month or so he came to my desk one day to ask if he could tell me something 'in private'.

'*Uhoh!*' I thought, imagining all kinds of horrors; but, of course, I agreed.

He waited until the rest of the class had gone and the classroom door had closed, then he leant towards me like a conspirator.

"*You know this method you've been teaching us,*" he whispered urgently, "*about reading sentences from the book aloud, then asking ourselves: What does that mean, so's we really understand it?*"

"*Yes,*" I agreed I did know it. I had been teaching it for years.

He leant, alarmingly, even closer: but by now I could feel his excitement.

I've found out" he whispered, now almost squeaking, "*I've found out: IT WORKS WITH OTHER SUBJECTS!!!*"

REFERENCES

[1]   *'The Quark and the Jaguar'*, Gell-Mann, M., 1994, p. 375.

[2]   Joshua 6.21

[3]   *The Origin of Consciousness in the Breakdown of the Bi-Cameral Mind'*, Jaynes, J. 1976; *'The Master and His Emissary'*, Gilchrist, I. 2009

[4]   '*The Second Coming'*, Yeats, W. B., 1931.

[5]   Ibid, p. 280.

In: The Nurturing of Talent, Skills and Abilities   ISBN: 978-1-62618-521-0
Editor: Michael F. Shaughnessy   © 2013 Nova Science Publishers, Inc.

Chapter 5

DEVELOPING MATHEMATICAL TALENT

*Linda E. Brody**

Johns Hopkins University, Baltimore, Maryland, US

INTRODUCTION

Galileo revolutionized scientific inquiry by noting that the language of nature is mathematics and Gauss called mathematics the queen of the sciences. In today's world, the application of mathematics to a growing number of scientific, medical, engineering, and technological fields may be more important than ever, as these are the fields that fuel society's economic engine and that can result in innovative solutions to our greatest problems. This was underscored in the report of the National Mathematics Advisory Panel (2008) which stated that "the national workforce of future years will surely have to handle quantitative concepts more fully and more deftly than at present" (p. xii). And the National Science Board, in their report *Preparing the Next Generation of STEM Innovators*, concluded that "a coherent, proactive, and sustained effort to identify and develop our nation's STEM innovators will help drive future economic prosperity and improve the quality of life for all" (National Science Board, 2010, p. 4).

The implications for educators of our increased need for talent development in mathematics and math-related fields are twofold. First, we need to strengthen our mathematics curriculum to assure that *all* students gain the knowledge and skills needed to be successful in careers that require mathematical and technological expertise. Though there have been attempts to improve math curricula by importing programs such as Singapore Math into American schools, as well as efforts by the National Council of Teachers of Mathematics to raise targeted learning standards, the United States continues to lag behind numerous other countries in mathematics and science achievement according to such measures as student performance in the Program for International Student Assessment (PISA). Currently, the Common Core State Standards Initiative is preparing to offer a more rigorous problem-solving approach to the learning of mathematics in the hope that it will prepare students to compete in our global society. Even if this initiative achieves its goals, however, it is unlikely

---

* Corresponding author: Linda E. Brody. E-mail: Lbrody@jhu.edu.

to sufficiently address the needs of students with the most advanced mathematical reasoning abilities.

We need a systematic mechanism for identifying students with the potential to excel in mathematics, and we need to provide these students with the educational programs and resources that will enhance their enjoyment of solving difficult problems and allow them to fully develop their abilities. It is this group of students that the Study of Mathematically Precocious Youth (SMPY) was founded to serve, and there is much evidence that the principles and practices SMPY developed have proven effective, and that they can help us meet the challenge of addressing the needs of mathematically talented students going forward.

THE STUDY OF MATHEMATICALLY PRECOCIOUS YOUTH (SMPY)

Julian Stanley referred to the events that led him to establish SMPY in 1971 as "serendipity" (Stanley, 2005, p. 9). At the time, Stanley was a renowned professor of psychology and research methodologist not working at all with precollege students. But he had a long history of interest in tests and measurements and some interest in giftedness that may have been influenced by his own experiences growing up with limited academic challenge so, when he was told about a young middle school student, Joe, doing amazing work in a summer university computer course, he was curious to learn more about him. To assess the extent of this young man's abilities, Stanley administered the SAT and other above-level tests, a move that was very radical at that time, and Joe scored well within the range of entering college students. After local high schools proved unwilling to accommodate his academic needs, Stanley arranged for Joe to enroll at Johns Hopkins full-time at the age of 13, where he proved highly successful as a young college student.

Soon two other students emerged to successfully follow similar paths, leaving Stanley to wonder if there might be other students with extraordinary potential languishing in lockstep educational programs. He founded SMPY "to find youths who reason exceptionally well mathematically and to provide them the special, supplemental, accelerative 'smorgasbord' of educational opportunities they sorely need and…richly deserve for their own optimal development and the good of society" (Stanley, 2005, p. 9). Note that Stanley's goal was about helping the students, but he also strongly believed that society will benefit if we cultivate the talents of our most mathematically brilliant students.

The 1970s represented a period of experimentation for SMPY, since most of what the small team of researchers piloted had never been done before. They utilized a variety of ways to assess and nurture mathematical talent. They initiated the idea of a Talent Search, where students were invited to take the SAT out-of-level, and the researchers were quite surprised when many more middle school students than they expected scored extremely well on this test designed for high school students applying to college.

Their approach was to identify students, learn more about them, try intervention strategies, evaluate the effectiveness of the strategies, and modify the approach if needed. Although radical acceleration into college had worked for Joe, they knew other options were needed for a more diverse group of mathematically talented students, and they experimented with numerous ways to accelerate and/or enrich their learning of mathematics and science. They recommended other initiatives, especially AP courses and competitions. Over time, the idea of offering a "smorgasbord of opportunities" evolved, the concept being that students should choose from a variety of options and pursue those that are most appropriate for meeting their individual needs. See Stanley, Keating, and Fox, 1974; Keating, 1976; and Benbow and Stanley, 1983a for more on SMPY's early history.

SMPY's first book was entitled *Mathematical Talent: Discovery Description, and Development* (Stanley, Keating, and Fox, 1974), which was abbreviated as MT:D[3] and represents three steps in finding and serving mathematically talented students: discovery, description, and development. Discovery pertains to systematically finding students who exhibit exceptional mathematical abilities; Description relates to finding out about their other characteristics, including psychosocial factors, that also influence decisions about educational interventions and strategies to meet students' individual needs; and Development involves developing the talents through appropriate educational strategies and services. Soon a 4th D was added for Dissemination, i.e., sharing what is learned about the students and the talent development process so that others can employ it. Later, once Talent Search programs began to also address the needs of verbally talented students, the acronym was expanded to MVT:D[4] which stands for "building on mathematical and/or verbal talent through discovery, description, development, and dissemination" (Brody and Stanley, 2005; Brody, 2009).

SMPY's initiatives were research-based from the beginning, and the results were disseminated in numerous publications. They demonstrated the predictive validity of above-level testing as a tool to identify students with exceptional mathematical abilities (e.g., Stanley, 1977/78); they assessed the concomitant abilities and affective traits of the students with strong math abilities (e.g., Fox, 1976; Haier and Denham, 1976); and they evaluated the efficacy of numerous intervention strategies, especially accelerative ones (e.g., Brody and Fox, 1980; Fox, 1974; Stanley, 1977). Gender differences in mathematical abilities and achievement was a topic that received considerable attention when the researchers became aware of large differences favoring males at the highest levels of performance in the early talent searches (Benbow and Stanley, 1980, 1983b; Fox, Brody and Tobin, 1980), differences that are much less true today (Brody, and Mills, 2005; Olszewski-Kubilius, and Lee, 2011; Wai, Cacchio, Putallaz, and Makel, 2010).

In addition to conducting their own research as they sought to identify the most effective ways to serve mathematically talented students, the SMPY researchers took time to study the literature available at that time and were influenced by what they learned. In particular, they were very conscious of Lewis Terman's (1925) findings related to the characteristics of gifted children and the value of acceleration, and were inspired by his work to launch a longitudinal study of SMPY participants (see Stanley, 1977). Other research that influenced SMPY's efforts included: Harriet Zuckerman's (1977) findings that Nobel Laureates benefitted from the accumulative advantage of one opportunity leading to another, which suggested the need for continuous opportunities for mathematically talented students; Harvey Lehman's (1953) study of the relationship between age and achievement that found that mathematicians produced their greatest work at young ages, which supported the need to accelerate students who might aspire to be great mathematicians; and the retrospective studies of eminent individuals (e.g., Cox, 1926; Goertzel, and Goertzel, 1962), which made the SMPY researchers aware of the variety of experiences that had led to developing the talents of the subjects and pointed to the importance of working with students as individuals. Since acceleration of content seemed appropriate for students with advanced mathematical skills, and yet it was quite controversial at the time, they commissioned a full review of the acceleration literature (Daurio, 1979), which they found supportive of their instincts to move advanced students quickly through the math curriculum and onto more challenging material.

A 50-year longitudinal study of SMPY participants is ongoing and being directed by Camilla Benbow and David Lubinski at Vanderbilt University. This investigation is studying the talent development and adult achievements of five cohorts of individuals, four of whom were identified through a Talent Search between 1972 and 1997, and a 5th cohort of graduate students who attended top math and science programs. Numerous publications report on the status of these groups at key intervals. Most notable are findings that show individuals at the highest levels of ability as measured by Talent Search scores in middle school outperforming those with lower scores in their adult years in earning advanced degrees and producing such creative products as publications and patents (Park, Lubinski, and Benbow 2008; Lubinski, Webb, Morelock, and Benbow, 2001; Wai, Lubinski, and Benbow, 2005). In addition to math ability predicting future achievement, the researchers found spatial ability, investigative interests, and theoretical values predictive of high levels of STEM pursuits and achievement (Shea, Lubinski, and Benbow, 2001; Wai, Lubinski, and Benbow, 2009). And special educational opportunities, of the nature recommended and/or offered by SMPY, were also found to be relevant to the talent development of these individuals (Lubinski and Benbow, 2006). These findings affirm the predictability of Talent Search above-level assessments, the relevance of other crucial factors, and the value of supplemental educational services and programs.

BLOOM'S RESEARCH ON TALENT DEVELOPMENT

Bloom's (1985) landmark study of talent development in a number of domains was published a little too late to directly influence the early development of SMPY's key principles and practices, but the findings are important in that they support what SMPY instinctively tried to do and are useful today as we grapple with providing the right opportunities to enhance talent development in mathematics. Among the groups Bloom and his colleagues studied were 20 mathematicians (19 males and one female) who had received Sloan Foundation fellowships, a mark of exceptionally high mathematical accomplishment. In looking at these individuals retrospectively, they found a pattern of talent development that proved to be similar in many ways to what they discovered about the process in other domains.

The mathematicians in Bloom's study exhibited early interest and ability in mathematics that was reinforced throughout their childhood. They typically lived with well-educated parents who strongly supported academic achievement and their children's interests in math and/or science by providing challenging activities. In general, the mathematicians' early teachers did little to advance their mathematical learning beyond the regular curriculum, but they continued to advance their knowledge of mathematics outside of school, which kept their interest in the subject high. In middle and high school, they did considerable independent work in mathematics, and many expressed the belief that their participation in extracurricular activities—math teams, other competitions, Saturday and summer enrichment programs—

played an important role in keeping math fun and providing a peer group of students with whom they could interact who shared their interests and abilities. By college and graduate school, peers, teachers, and mentors who also loved math proved essential and were more accessible.

While this group of individuals managed to garner the resources needed to achieve their extraordinary success in mathematics, one wonders how many students fail to develop their talents because they are not recognized and their needs are not met. There are clear implications from Bloom's findings that support what SMPY set out to accomplish. First, it appears that the mathematicians exhibited early signs of having unusual problem-solving abilities, suggesting that it is possible to identify talent at young ages. Furthermore, the recognition of their abilities spurred their parents to provide special learning opportunities, indicating that it is not only *possible* to identify talent but *important* to do so. The crucial role parents play in developing early skills is also evident from these histories. However, not all parents are prepared to offer what their children need, so we must provide tools to assist them; a recent attempt to help parents is the Bedtime Math blog, which poses a math problem a day that parents can do with their young children. As children get older, parents should encourage them to pursue more intensive supplemental programs and resources, but they need to be knowledgeable about what opportunities are available. Finally, it is important to advocate for schools to meet the needs of their advanced students so that all of the responsibility doesn't lie with the parents, and role models and mentors must show students how the math they love transfers to real-world careers.

SMPY's belief that out-of-school activities and programs can play a crucial role in the talent development process, not only for expanding learning but as vehicles for students to meet and interact with intellectual peers, was supported by this research, as was the crucial role played in the talent development process by significant others, i.e., by parents, other family members, peers, teachers, mentors, and role models. It was the goal of SMPY to assure that mathematically talented students get the support they need to advance their abilities at each developmental stage, and this remains the goal of the Study of Exceptional Talent (SET) today.

THE STUDY OF EXCEPTIONAL TALENT (SET)

By 1979, SMPY's initiatives were attracting large numbers of participants and there was a need to expand further to accommodate a wider geographic area. Consequently, the Center for Talented Youth (CTY) was founded at Johns Hopkins University, and similar programs were soon established at Duke University, Northwestern University, and elsewhere (see Touron, 2005). These centers continue today, conducting Talent Searches, offering a variety of academic programs and opportunities to students who excel on the Talent Search assessments, and conducting research on academically talented students. With a national network in place that provides above-level testing and advanced programs, the Talent Search centers are an important mechanism for identifying and serving students with advanced mathematical and verbal abilities (Lee, Matthews, and Olszewski-Kubilius, 2008).

Meanwhile, after establishing CTY, SMPY returned to its roots and sought to identify and work with the highest scoring students "who reason *extremely* well mathematically" and study them over time. A national search was announced for students who score 700 or above on the SAT-Math before age 13, and qualifying students were invited to take advantage of counseling opportunities and to receive information about challenging educational opportunities and resources. Though the identified students lived all over the United States, the relatively small number being served allowed for considerable personalized interaction between the staff and students.

This initiative moved to CTY as the Study of Exceptional Talent (SET) in 1991 and was named the Julian C. Stanley Study of Exceptional Talent in 2005. SET continues to identify students with exceptionally advanced reasoning abilities, to provide them with information about resources and opportunities that offer the challenge they need to achieve their full potential, and to study them over time in an effort to learn more about the talent development process (Brody, 2005; Brody, and Blackburn, 1996). In addition to directly serving the students who qualify for SET, the staff encourages others who are counseling students with advanced academic needs to adapt this approach for their own needs and situations.

Qualifying for SET

The core of the Talent Search identification model is to utilize above-grade-level specific aptitude tests to find students with advanced mathematical or verbal reasoning abilities. When this concept was first pioneered by SMPY, and the SAT was used with 12 and 13 year olds, the approach was quite radical, as identification for gifted programming was, and still is, typically based on scores on general IQ and/or age-appropriate achievement tests. The problem with using IQ tests as an identification tool is that they are too general to predict achievement in a particular domain. A frequently cited quote from Julian Stanley, before the rise in coffee prices, was that "a high IQ and fifty cents will buy you a fifty-cent cup of coffee." The point he was making is that a general ability test doesn't measure ability in specific areas, and it is necessary to assess mathematical reasoning in particular to find those students with the potential to excel specifically in mathematics. It also must be an aptitude or reasoning test, not a test of mathematical achievement. Achievement tests assess what a student already knows and, though they are important tools for placement purposes, they are not useful in reliably predicting a student's readiness to comprehend more complex content and learn at a fast pace in the future. To predict future achievement, the test content must also be above-grade level. An in-level test provides a comparison to age peers, but an above-level assessment, such as testing 12-year olds with the SAT, differentiates among high-ability students who all hit the ceiling on an in-grade test and can identify those whose abilities are advanced and thus more like that of older students.

The Talent Search programs have since expanded beyond the SAT to offer a variety of assessments to a broader age range, but they remain committed to using above-grade-level specific aptitude tests to identify students for their programs. Many years of results have shown that above-level aptitude testing consistently differentiates among students who all scored high on in-grade tests prior to entering the Talent Search; the participants spread out across the range of possible scores on the above-level test (e.g., see Barnett, Albert, and Brody, 2005). Of course, there may be individual students whose low scores on the SAT at age 12 do not fully reflect their future potential, but for groups of Talent Search participants, the predictability of this assessment for later achievement is quite amazing (e.g., see Benbow,

1992; Park, Lubinski, and Benbow, 2008). For the highest scorers, the opportunity to demonstrate the extent of their ability on a test designed for older students and without a great deal of preparation allows their precocity and potential brilliance to be noticed and addressed when it might not otherwise be.

SET identifies and serves students who score 700 or above on either the SAT-Math or Critical Reading before age 13. Approximately 80% of SET students qualify on math, especially since the SAT changed its verbal format from analogies to a test of critical reading which resulted in a verbal assessment that has proven to be very difficult for even highly precocious middle school students. Typically, students test as 12-year old 7th graders, but several students as young as age 8 have qualified for SET, and those who test after their 13th birthday can still be eligible if they earn an additional ten points above the minimum for each additional month of age. There are currently about 1200 active precollege SET members, as well as over 5,000 alumni who range from college-age to those in their mid-40s who qualified for SMPY/SET in the early 1980s. The focus of SET's services is on the precollege group, while alumni participate in follow-up studies. Some of the older SET alumni are now parents of recent SET qualifiers.

SET Counseling

After a student obtains the SAT scores required to qualify for SET, either by testing through a Talent Search or taking the SAT on their own, they are asked to fill out background questionnaires and invited to take advantage of SET's counseling services. The focus of SET's counseling is on providing advice regarding educational placement and identifying challenging resources to help students attain their goals. Consideration of a student's social and emotional development and their need to find intellectual peers is often a factor in determining recommendations.

Students may seek counseling for any number of reasons. Some really struggle with few opportunities for adequate challenge in school and seek advice about such alternatives as skipping a grade, attending boarding school, or entering college early, while others may be satisfied with their school placement but seek help finding a summer program or an internship opportunity. For the students who accelerate rapidly through their math courses, finding enough high-level math courses to keep them engaged in math throughout high school can be a challenge, though many more options exist for this today than in years past. A lot of students need help finding a mentor or advice on selecting a college. SET tries to be responsive to individual needs, with an overall goal of encouraging students to embrace challenging opportunities, as they identify and pursue their passions.

The following assumptions, which are grounded in research and/or SMPY/SET's many years of direct experience working with academically advanced students, underlie SET's counseling efforts.

- Above-grade level assessments are crucial for estimating a high-performing student's true level of ability and inform program recommendations.
- Students need to be taught at their optimal level of learning, with the pace and level adjusted as needed for their ability and achievement levels.

- Students with advanced academic abilities are at risk of failing to achieve their potential if they are not adequately challenged.
- The more talented/advanced a student is, the greater the need for a differentiated program.
- Students with advanced academic abilities vary greatly in their specific abilities, content knowledge, interests, motivation, goals, personality and learning styles, and these differences result in differing educational needs.
- School programs can be enhanced with curricular flexibility and articulation at the next level.
- Students with advanced academic abilities can increase their learning opportunities by participating in supplemental educational programs and extracurricular activities.
- Mathematically talented students, while moving ahead appropriately in mathematics, should also gain a broad background in the liberal arts.
- Students with advanced academic abilities need to be able to interact with intellectual peers who share their interests.
- Students with advanced academic abilities need access to role models and mentors who provide insight into real-world applications of learning.

In advising SET students, Talent Search test results can be used diagnostically to help in the process. Above-level test scores are particularly helpful when discussing accelerative strategies. For example, a student who is high on both the math and verbal parts of the SAT may be a candidate for grade skipping, while subject acceleration in math but not a change in grade placement may be advisable for a student who scores high on the SAT-M but much lower in verbal or reading scores. This situation applied to the brilliant mathematician Terry Tao, who astounded Julian Stanley when he scored 760 on the SAT-Math at the age of 8. Nonetheless, he scored low on the SAT-Verbal at that time (he was only 8!) so, while he accelerated in grade placement when he was older, the SAT-V test score led to a recommendation from Julian Stanley that his family proceed slow in advancing his grade placement until his verbal abilities were more developed, while still advancing him rapidly, and appropriately, in math (Muratori et al., 2006).

Of course, SAT scores are not the only factor that should be considered when helping a student make educational decisions: a student's other abilities, achievement levels, interests, motivation, goals, maturity, social needs, and available opportunities must all must be considered in choosing academic and career paths. When the first SMPY Talent Searches were Baltimore-based, the staff brought the high-scoring participants back for much additional testing of their abilities, achievement, and affective characteristics, all of which provided important information and was helpful in guiding the students. With SET students now living all over the country, even all over the world, this type of in-person testing is not realistic, though recognition of the relevance of spatial ability, particularly for STEM careers, led CTY to develop a Spatial Test Battery which is now offered as an optional Talent Search assessment (Stumpf, Mills, Brody, and Baxley, in press).

Typically, additional information about SET students is gleaned through interviews, as counselors probe interests and goals and assess the availability of resources. The goal is to match appropriate resources with the specific needs of the individual student, after considering a variety of factors in determining those needs. An important component is to involve the students themselves in any decision-making, not to work exclusively with parents.

Students' interests are especially important to consider, as SET aspires to help them define their true passions and pursue exceptional levels of achievement in those areas.

In addition to counseling students individually, SET hosts small group gatherings where members and their parents are invited to meet and interact with others who live in their area, as well as with a SET counselor. The goals are for students to meet intellectual peers with whom they might develop a relationship, for parents to be able to use each other as resources, and for communication between families and the SET office to be enhanced as a result of the attendees meeting a member of SET's counseling staff.

In addition to these individual and group efforts, SET students receive resources that inform them about educational opportunities. The *SET Precollege Newsletter* shares news about SET activities and spotlights students' achievements; *Imagine* magazine features articles by students who have participated in challenging programs, profiles role models and career fields, and lists a variety of educational resources and opportunities; and the Cogito website has goals similar to *Imagine* but uses an interactive Internet format and focuses on STEM initiatives. Building on Stanley's concept of presenting a smorgasbord of opportunities from which students should choose those that best meet their needs, these resources offer information about supplemental learning opportunities and portray peers and role models who are engaged in exciting programs.

OPTIONS FOR PROMOTING MATH TALENT DEVELOPMENT

For students whose academic programs fail to challenge them optimally, acceleration in grade placement and/or subject matter remains a viable option. Commonly recommended by SMPY as a strategy to challenge students with advanced mathematical abilities, the practice is still somewhat controversial, as critics fear negative social and emotional consequences. Nonetheless, it is probably the most researched strategy that exists for serving students with advanced academic abilities, and the results clearly support its efficacy without showing negative social or emotional effects (Colangelo, Assouline, and Gross, 2004; Kulik, 2004; Swiatek, and Benbow, 1991). In particular, early entrants to college have been studied extensively with the findings supporting the practice (Brody, Muratori, and Stanley, 2004).

Much of the fear of acceleration relates to whole grade acceleration. Though this is a highly defensible practice when used appropriately (Colangelo, Assouline, and Lupkowski-Shoplik, 2004), it is important to remember that it is only one form. Southern, Jones, and Stanley (1993) listed 17 types of acceleration, and similarly extensive lists have been generated by other researchers.

For mathematically gifted students, in particular, subject acceleration in mathematics may be necessary but perhaps is not appropriate in other subjects nor is whole grade acceleration. The good news is that the sequential nature of the math curriculum makes it exceptionally amenable to modification and to allowing students to move through it more quickly, and online, summer, and part-time college courses can provide access to math content for students who complete the regular high school math curriculum before they are ready to graduate. Studies of students who accelerated in mathematics prior to enrolling full-time in college have been positive (Kolitch, and Brody, 1992). Stanley (2000) famously wrote about "helping students learn only what they don't already know." If our goal is to keep students engaged in mathematics, it is essential that they not be required to have to relearn skills they have already mastered.

A major change from the early days of SMPY, when acceleration was one of very few options available for advanced students, is that there has been a huge growth in the number of other opportunities available to challenge mathematically talented students. It is likely that much of this growth can be credited to the efforts of SMPY and to the Talent Search programs that continue today, and whose identification practices have called attention to the exceptional abilities of large numbers of students and the need to serve them. In addition, as students have been counseled by these programs to seek challenging educational opportunities, demand may have fueled the response to create more of them.

One development has been an increase in the number of selective math and science high schools. While specialized high schools are not a new phenomenon in our country, e.g., Bronx High School of Science was founded in New York City in 1938, numerous new ones have emerged throughout the United States in recent years, including prestigious state-supported residential schools such as the Illinois Mathematics and Science Academy and the North Carolina School of Science and Mathematics that were established to bring top students from across a state together in a more rigorous learning environment. There are reportedly at least 80 schools that are members of the National Consortium of Specialized Secondary Schools of Mathematics, Science and Technology and, while they vary considerably in their level of selectivity and the nature of their programs, they have common goals in supporting the advancement of mathematical and scientific talent (see Subotnik, Tai, Rickoff, and Almarode, 2010).

Students who lack adequate challenge in their high schools may consider leaving high school and entering college early, a path that was taken by the first students Stanley worked with and that is still an option today. However, some students may be academically ready to enter college at younger-than-typical ages but not socially or emotionally ready to be completely independent as full-time college students. In recognition of students like this, a number of colleges and universities have established early college entrance programs that admit young students as a cohort and provide the additional support these students may need. This is also not a completely new idea, e.g., Bard College at Simon's Rock was established in 1964 to admit students who have not yet finished high school, but quite a few new programs have been created in recent years. As with the specialized high schools, there is variability in the specific nature of these programs, e.g., some are state-supported and others private, some commuter and others residential, and some accept students at younger ages than others (Brody, Muratori, and Stanley 2004). One of the newer programs is a bit of a hybrid between being a high school and an early college program: The Gatton Academy of Mathematics and Science in Kentucky was recently recognized by *Newsweek* as America's top high school, yet it is located on the campus of the Western Kentucky University and students typically graduate with 60 college credits.

The specialized high school and early college options described above are designed to provide students with more advanced coursework than is offered by a typical high school and to provide an environment where students can interact with their intellectual peers. For students who do not have the option of attending one of these schools, summer programs can offer similar advantages, particularly the residential summer programs that have been established specifically to serve gifted students. These programs attract students from broad geographic areas and provide environments where they can live and study with peers who share their interests and abilities. SMPY championed the idea of residential programs, and their valuable social as well as academic benefits have been well-documented (Mickenberg, and Wood, 2009a, 2009b). CTY serves over 10,000 students each summer on campuses throughout the United States with a wide variety of course offerings.

This model of serving motivated precollege students in challenging residential summer programs has been replicated by the other Talent Search programs, and numerous other colleges, universities, and organizations have developed their own versions, thus offering students many choices. For students with clear interests and abilities in math, in particular, there are excellent summer math programs such as the Ross Mathematics Program at Ohio State, which a great many mathematicians attended in their youth and credit with helping to develop their true appreciation for the beauty of mathematics, as well as newer ones like PROMYS, AwesomeMath, and MathPath. These all offer opportunities for students to work with other top students to solve challenging math problems. For those interested in doing original work in math or science, programs such as the prestigious Research Science Institute provide the option of working with a mentor. SET students typically participate in several summer programs during their middle and high school years, resulting in increased excitement about the subjects they study, an important component in compelling them to the next step in their educational path.

The mathematicians studied by Bloom attributed much significance to their involvement in competitions and local math-oriented activities, and numerous stimulating opportunities fall into this category. School-based math teams, and competitions like MATHCOUNTS, American Regions Mathematics League, and the American Mathematics Competitions, offer students the camaraderie of working with peers who also share a love of math, nurture their competitive skills to want to excel, and provide recognition for their skills. Mathematician and SMPY protégé Dr. Lenny Ng reflected that "It was the competitions that really introduced the fun side of math to me. . . . [They] also contributed quite a bit to my social life" (Muratori et al., pp. 316-317).

Students looking for local Saturday enrichment programs can sometimes find them offered by colleges in their area or by private organizations such as IDEA MATH which has weekend programs in the Boston area, or they might join a Math Circle in their community, a model for bringing students together with other mathematically talented students that was imported from Europe and is now spreading throughout the United States. Other students might use technology to discuss math online with other interested students in forums such as the one offered by the Art of Problem Solving (AoPS). These are all options that enhance knowledge and provide the interaction with peers that makes math fun.

CONCLUSION

It has been over 40 years since SMPY was established, and there is much evidence that the principles and practices it embraced are effective in promoting talent development in mathematics. The implications of what we have learned suggest that the African proverb "It takes a village to raise a child" applies specifically to developing the talents of children with special mathematical abilities. It takes parents, teachers, counselors, peers, and mentors, as well as exposure to challenging content and access to supplemental programs and resources, to provide students with the skills, knowledge, inspiration, and motivation to excel in math or a math-related field. Fortunately, the variety of programmatic options available today makes the job much easier than it was in the past.

Though the significant others in a child's life all play crucial roles, there is a subtle shift in who is primary as students grow and develop. Parents have the greatest impact in early childhood, but teachers become more relevant during the school years, out-of-school options and interaction with like-minded peers can be significant influences in the teen years, and ultimately mentors and role models show students the path toward their chosen career fields. This trajectory applies to students in any domain; for math-talented students, exposure to math activities and programs, and to people who share a love of math is key.

There is also a shift in the focus of the subject matter over time. A child must master core arithmetic skills before moving on to develop a deeper understanding of mathematical principles. The student must then learn to apply that knowledge in meaningful ways. Ultimately, if talent is developed to this level, the goal is for our most promising mathematicians and scientists to have the knowledge, skills, and creative potential to generate new mathematical ideas and/or create innovative products.

Throughout the learning process, the joy of problem-solving must be communicated, which is not possible if the emphasis is on basic skills that students have already learned. Thus, coursework must be challenging, accelerated if necessary for advanced students, and is best presented in meaningful ways and using teamwork to arrive at solutions. With the technological challenges facing society today, it is more crucial than ever that students' mathematical talents be discovered and fostered. But we have the knowledge and tools to be able to do so.

REFERENCES

Barnett, L. B., Albert, M. E. and Brody, L. E. (2005). The Center for Talented Youth talent search and academic programs. *High Ability Studies,* 16(1), 27-40.

Benbow, C. P. (1992). Academic achievement in mathematics and science of students between ages 13 and 23: Are there differences among students in the top one percent of mathematical ability? *Journal of Educational Psychology,* 84(1), 51-61.

Benbow, C. P. and Stanley, J. C. (1980). Sex differences in mathematical ability: Fact or artifact? *Science,* 210, 1262-1264.

Benbow, C. P. and Stanley, J. C. (Eds.) (1983a). *Academic precocity: Aspects of its development.* Baltimore: Johns Hopkins University Press.

Benbow, C. P. and Stanley, J. C. (1983b). Sex differences in mathematical reasoning ability: More facts. *Science,* 222, 1029-1031.

Bloom, B. S. (Ed.), (1985). *Developing talent in young people.* New York: Ballantine Books.

Brody, L. E. (2005). The Study of Exceptional Talent. *High Ability Studies,* 16 (1), 87-96.

Brody, L. E. (2009). The Johns Hopkins talent search model for identifying and developing exceptional mathematical and verbal abilities. In: L. V. Shavinina (Ed.), *International handbook on giftedness* (pp. 999-1016). New York: Springer.

Brody, L. E. and Blackburn, C. (1996). Nurturing exceptional talent: SET as a legacy of SMPY. In: C. P. Benbow and D. Lubinski (Eds.), *Intellectual talent: Psychometric and social issues* (pp. 246-265). Baltimore: Johns Hopkins University Press.

Brody, L. and Fox, L. H. (1980). An accelerative intervention program for mathematically gifted girls. In: L. H. Fox, L. Brody and D. Tobin (Eds.), *Women and the mathematical mystique* (pp. 164-178). Baltimore MD: The Johns Hopkins University Press.

Brody, L. E. and Mills, C. J. (2005). Talent search research: What have we learned? *High Ability Studies,* 16(1), 97-111.

Brody, L. E., Muratori, M. C. and Stanley, J. C. (2004). Early entrance to college: Academic, social, and emotional considerations. In: N. Colangelo, S. G. Assouline and M. U. M Gross (Eds.), *A nation deceived: How schools hold back America's brightest kids*, Vol. II (pp. 97-107). Iowa City: University of Iowa.

Brody, L. E. and Stanley, J. C. (2005). Youths who reason exceptionally well mathematically and/or verbally: Using the MVT:D[4] model to develop their talents. In: R. J. Sternberg and J. E. Davidson (Eds.), *Conceptions of giftedness* (2nd edition) (pp. 20-37). New York: Cambridge University Press.

Colangelo, N., Assouline, S. G. and Gross, M. U. M. (Eds.) (2004), *A nation deceived: How schools hold back America's brightest kids*, Vol. II. Iowa City: University of Iowa.

Colangelo, N., Assouline, S. G. and Lupkowski-Shoplik, A. E. (2004). Whole-grade Acceleration. In: N. Colangelo, S. G. Assouline and M. U. M Gross (Eds.), *A nation deceived: How schools hold back America's brightest kids*, Vol. II (pp. 77-86). Iowa City: University of Iowa.

Cox, C. M. (1926). *The early mental traits of three hundred geniuses.* Vol. II of *Genetic studies of genius*, L. M. Terman (Ed.). Stanford, CA: Stanford University Press.

Daurio, S. P. (1979). Educational enrichment versus acceleration: A review of the literature. In: W. C. George, S. J. Cohn and J. C. Stanley (Eds.), *Educating the gifted: Acceleration and enrichment* (pp. 13-63). Baltimore: Johns Hopkins University Press.

Fox, L. H. (1974). A mathematics program for fostering precocious achievement. In: J. C. Stanley, D. P. Keating and L. H. Fox (Eds.), *Mathematical talent: Discovery, description, and development* (pp. 101-125). Baltimore: Johns Hopkins University Press.

Fox, L. H. (1976). The values of gifted youth. In: D. P. Keating (Ed.), *Intellectual talent: Research and development* (pp. 273-284). Baltimore: Johns Hopkins University Press.

Fox, L. H., Brody, L. and Tobin, D. (1980). *Women and the mathematical mystique.* Baltimore: Johns Hopkins University Press.

Goertzel, V. and Goertzel, M. G. (1962). *Cradles of Eminence.* Boston: Little, Brown and Co.

Haier, R. J. and Denham, S. A. (1976). A summary profile of the nonintellectual correlates of mathematical precocity in boys and girls. In: D. P. Keating (Ed.), *Intellectual talent: Research and development* (pp. 225-241). Baltimore: Johns Hopkins University Press.

Keating, D. P. (Ed.) (1976). *Intellectual talent: Research and development.* Baltimore: Johns Hopkins University Press.

Kolitch, E. R. and Brody, L. E. (1992). Mathematics acceleration of highly talented students: An evaluation. *Gifted Child Quarterly,* 36(2), 78-86.

Kulik, J. A. (2004) Meta-analytic studies of acceleration. In: N. Colangelo, S. G. Assouline and M. U. M Gross (Eds.), *A nation deceived: How schools hold back America's brightest kids*, Vol. II (pp. 13-22). Iowa City: University of Iowa.

Lee, S-Y., Matthews, M. S. and Olszewski-Kubilius, P. (2008). A national picture of talent search and talent search educational programs. *Gifted Child Quarterly,* 52(1), 55-69.

Lehman, H. C. (1953). *Age and achievement.* Princeton, NJ: Princeton University Press.

Lubinski, D. and Benbow, C. P. (2006). Study of Mathematically Precocious Youth after 35 years: Uncovering antecedents for the development of math-science expertise. *Perspectives on Psychological Science,* 1(4), 316-345.

Lubinski, D., Webb, R. M., Morelock, M. J., and Benbow, C. P. (2001). Top 1 in 10,000: A 10-year follow-up of the profoundly gifted. *Journal of Applied Psychology,* 86, 718-729.

Mickenberg, K. and Wood, J. (2009a). *Alumni program satisfaction and benefits of CTY summer programs.* Technical Report No. 29. Baltimore: Johns Hopkins Center for Talented Youth.

Mickenberg, K. and Wood, J. (2009b). *Short-term benefits of CTY summer programs.* Technical Report No. 30. Baltimore: Johns Hopkins Center for Talented Youth.

Muratori, M., Stanley, J. C., Gross, M. U. M., Ng, L., Tao, T., Ng, J., and Tao, B. (2006). Insights from SMPY's former child prodigies: Drs. Terrence (Terry) Tao and Lenhard (Lenny) Ng reflect on their talent development. *Gifted Child Quarterly,* 50(4), 307-324.

National Mathematics Advisory Panel (2008). *Foundations for success.* Washington DC: US Department of Education.

National Science Board (2010). *Preparing the next generation of STEM innovators.* Washington DC: National Science Foundation.

Olszewski-Kubilius, P. and Lee, S-Y. (2011). Gender and other group differences in performance on off-level tests: Changes in the 21st century. *Gifted Child Quarterly,* 55 (1), 54-73.

Park, G., Lubinski, D. and Benbow, C. P. (2008) Ability differences among people who have commensurate degrees matter for scientific creativity. *Psychological Science,* 18(11), 948-952.

Shea, D. L., Lubinski, D. and Benbow, C. P. (2001). Importance of assessing spatial ability in intellectually talented young adolescents: A 20-year longitudinal study. *Journal of Educational Psychology,* 93(3), 604-614.

Southern, W. T., Jones, E. D. and Stanley, J. C. (1993). Acceleration and enrichment: The context and development of program options. In: K. A. Heller, F. J. Monks and A. H. Passow, *International handbook of research and development of giftedness and talent* (pp. 387-409). New York: Pergamon.

Stanley, J. C. (1977). Rationale of the Study of Mathematically Precocious Youth (SMPY) during its first five years of promoting educational acceleration. In: J. C. Stanley, W. C. George and C. H. Solano (Eds.), *The gifted and the creative* (pp. 75-112). Baltimore: Johns Hopkins University Press.

Stanley, J. C. (1977-78). The predictive value of the SAT for brilliant seventh and eighth graders. *College Board Review,* No. 106.

Stanley, J. C. (2000). Helping students learn only what they don't already know. *Psychology, Public Policy, and Law,* 6(1), 216-222.

Stanley, J. C. (2005). A quiet revolution: finding boys and girls who reason extremely well mathematically and/or verbally and helping them get the supplemental educational opportunities they need. *High Ability Studies,* 16 (1), 5-14.

Stanley, J. C., Keating, D. and Fox, L. H. (Eds.) (1974). *Mathematical talent: Discovery, description, and development.* Baltimore: Johns Hopkins University Press.

Stumpf, H., Mills, C. J., Brody, L. E., and Baxley, P. G. (in press). Expanding talent search procedures by including measures of spatial ability: CTY's Spatial Test Battery. *Roeper Review.*

Subotnik, R. F., Tai, R. H., Rickoff, R., and Almarode, J. (2010). Specialized public high schools of science, mathematics, and technology and the STEM pipeline: What do we know now and what will we know in 5 years? *Roeper Review,* 32(1), 7-16.

Swiatek, M. A. and Benbow, C. P. (1991). A ten-year longitudinal follow-up of ability-matched accelerated and unaccelerated gifted students. *Journal of Educational Psychology,* 83, 528-538.

Terman, L. M. (1925). *Mental and physical traits of a thousand gifted children.* Vol. I of *Genetic studies of genius,* L. M. Terman (Ed). Stanford, CA: Stanford University Press.

Touron, J. (Ed.) (2005). *The Center for Talented Youth model.* Special issue of *High Ability Studies,* 16(1).

Wai, J., Cacchio, M., Putallaz, M., and Makel, M. C. (2010). *Intelligence,* 38, 412-423.

Wai, J., Lubinski, D. and Benbow, C. P. (2005). Creativity and occupational accomplishments among intellectually precocious youths: An age 13 to age 33 longitudinal study. *Journal of Educational Psychology,* 97(3), 484-492.

Wai, J., Lubinski, D. and Benbow, C. P. (2009). Spatial ability for STEM domains: Aligning over 50 years of cumulative psychological knowledge solidifies its importance. *Journal of Educational Psychology,* 101(4), 817-835.

Zuckerman, H. (1977). *Scientific elite: Nobel laureates in the United States.* New York: Free Press.

In: The Nurturing of Talent, Skills and Abilities
Editor: Michael F. Shaughnessy

ISBN: 978-1-62618-521-0
© 2013 Nova Science Publishers, Inc.

Chapter 6

LEARN, UN-LEARN, AND RE-LEARN: DEVELOPING CRITICAL THINKING AND LEARNING SKILLS AND ABILITIES IN THE 21ST CENTURY SOCIAL STUDIES CLASSROOM

Donald C. Elder III[*]
Eastern New Mexico University, New Mexico, US

INTRODUCTION

Any list, of the greatest American films of all time, will most likely include "The Best Years of Our Lives," the 1946 Oscar winner for the Best Motion Picture. It is the story of three servicemen coming home at the end of World War II, and focuses on the problems that they have readjusting to civilian life. Although each of the veterans faces a challenge, Captain Fred Derry (portrayed in the film by Dana Andrews) has perhaps the most difficult transition of the three. He finds that the only job open to him is his old position working at the soda fountain of a local department store, and learns that his wife is unfaithful. Disheartened, he resolves to leave his home town, and start a new life.

As he is preparing to leave, however, Derry has an encounter at the local airport with the owner of a company that is building prefabricated housing units out of scrap metal salvaged from the type of airplane that he flew in during the war. Intrigued by the potential of making something useful out of an item that was deemed unnecessary in the post-war world (a description that, of course, could also be applied to him), Derry tells the owner about his military experience with the source of his building material and asks him for a job. The owner asks Derry if he knows anything about the prefabrication business, to which Derry replies that he does not. But Derry goes on to say that his time in the service did give him one skill: the ability to learn. The owner, himself a veteran of the Second World War, smiles and tells his foreman to put Derry to work.

---
[*] Email: Donald.Elder@enmu.edu

For many men belonging to what we often call "The Greatest Generation," Derry's story would be immediately recognizable. Forced by the Great Depression to leave school prematurely, many of them only gained the capacity to develop critical thinking skills only through their years in the military. Fortunately, for most American K-12 students in the 21st Century, the path towards becoming a critical thinker does not need to involve forced detours into either the work force, or the military. But that means that K-12 educators will bear almost the total responsibility for helping students attain a skill that will be increasingly necessary in a world of increasing complexity. This chapter will, for that reason, offer suggestions to educators on how best to accomplish the goal of helping students possess, like Captain Fred Derry, the ability to learn and to think critically.

Clearly, the tale of a veteran adjusting to changing conditions establishes the premise that the ability to learn is crucial to all individuals facing an uncertain future. A pragmatist might, however, suggest the limited applicability of this story to the field of Public Education. Captain Derry, after all, will seemingly need to learn only technical skills to accomplish his transition from a soda fountain employee, to a worker in the housing business. But this critique is too narrowly focused on the immediate moment of Derry accepting a new position. The particular airplane that Derry flew, according to "The Best Years of Our Lives," was the B-17 Flying Fortress, and 12,731 of them were produced during the Second World War. Even if every one of these aircraft survived the war, this means that there would be a finite amount of metal salvaged from these airplanes that Derry's company could use in the post-war world. What will happen to the business when the moment arrives that the last B-17 is torn apart?

Obviously, Captain Derry did not have to deal with that eventual reality in "The Best Years of Our Lives," but it illustrates a truism of American life: everything changes. What seems to be a revolutionary development that will stand the test of time, will be eventually overtaken and made obsolete. One need look no further back in time than the last fifty years in the realm of sound reproduction to see the validity of this assertion. Vinyl records gave way to 8-track tapes, which were then replaced by cassettes. Soon compact discs became the delivery system of choice, but soon they lost popularity to digital music devices. American history is replete with similar examples of seemingly foolproof business ventures that eventually lost their competitive edge.

A prime example of this phenomenon is Henry Ford. Ford revolutionized the American automobile industry, and at one point in time his Model-T dominated the roadways of the United States. As a result of his success, Ford became an American icon, and his public pronouncements about the issues of the day were disseminated far and wide. One of his most notable comments came in an interview in 1916, in which he said "History is more or less bunk." Ford was suggesting that there was no need for us to study the past, as we were a society that lived only in the here and now. That philosophy of disregarding the past, however, came back to haunt Ford. As other car companies sprang into existence in the 1920s, and began offering consumers a variety of choices regarding automobiles, Ford steadfastly refused to allow any deviation to the standard Model-T.

A quick glance at the history of business in America would have shown him the folly of his ways, but Ford maintained that the superior quality of the Model-T would bring consumers back to their senses and keep them buying his standard product. Finally, however, with his company facing a serious decline in sales, Ford reluctantly agreed to introduce a new vehicle, which he dubbed the Model-A. History, which he had derided only a decade before, had thus gotten the best of the great Henry Ford.

Here, then, is the true meaning of the climactic scene of "the Best Years of Our Lives." Individuals need much more than technical expertise to survive in a world of change; equally important is the ability to see comparisons and contrasts, and to recognize cause and effect. These, of course, are skills that the study of history inculcates in a learner. Although occasionally overlooked in the great scheme of things in the educational milieu, History is therefore a subject that must be taught, and taught well, to prepare individuals to face the vagaries of change in the United States of the 21st Century.

LEARNING AS A SKILL AND TALENT

Learning is, of course, a life-long journey. The process begins with birth, and continues as long as individuals remain sentient human beings. In a perfect world, the individuals find intellectual stimulation throughout their lifetimes, but realistically the best chance for them to develop learning and critical thinking skills comes during their K-12 years. But one could ask whether it is possible to utilize all thirteen of these years for those purposes. Are children too young in Kindergarten, for example, to develop skills that will make them better thinkers? At the opposite end of the spectrum, by the time they become seniors in high school, have students become too jaded to further refine their ability to learn?

Such questions are useful, for they force us to examine the nature of learning. Do age and environment, for instance, affect our intellectual capacity? Studies suggest that they do indeed play a role, but not one that precludes learning from taking place if either circumstance seems set against the individual. Whatever stage of the educational process that one examines, it is possible to develop processes that will help individuals be capable of learning, and thinking critically.

What, then, are the best ways to help students develop these skills, talents, and abilities within the context of the study of history? First and foremost, it is important to foster in students a curiosity about the past. A classic example of how crucial this inquisitiveness is comes from the last amendment to the Constitution to be ratified. This amendment, the 27th to be added, was declared in effect on May 19, 1992. Interestingly, it had been introduced over 200 years earlier in 1789 by James Madison. After the ratification of the Constitution, 12 amendments were sent to the states for their consideration. Ten of them were adopted, but the other two were not. One of those that the nation rejected, sought to limit the ability of the members of Congress to increase their salaries. It stated that "No law, varying the compensation for the services of the Senators and Representatives, shall take effect, until an election of Representatives shall have intervened." (Bernstein, 1992) Three-fourths of the states, according to the Constitution, need to ratify an amendment for it to go into effect, but only six of the thirteen states that comprised the Union in 1789 voted affirmatively on Madison's suggested modification. Because of this, the proposed amendment was never adopted, and gradually faded from the national consciousness.

All that changed in 1982. In that year, a student at the University of Texas named Gregory Watson was working on a report about another proposed Constitutional amendment that had never been ratified: The Equal Rights Amendment (ERA). First discussed as a possible amendment back in the 1920s, this was an effort to make it unconstitutional to deny women equal treatment in American life. Momentum in favor of this idea grew over the next half century, and culminated in Congress sending the ERA to the states for ratification in 1972. Congress mandated that the amendment had to be ratified by three-fourths of the states (as previously noted, the requirement specified for all amendments by the Constitution) within a seven-year period of time. If such affirmation had not taken place by the end of that time span, however, the amendment would never become a part of the Constitution. States immediately began to ratify the ERA, and soon 35 of them had given their approval to the amendment—only 3 states short of the required number.

After the initial success enjoyed by the proponents of the ERA, however, the momentum for ratification stalled. In fact, no other state would ever ratify the amendment. Moreover, some states that had originally ratified the ERA voted to rescind their approval. As the deadline for the ERA approached, Congress passed legislation that would extend the ratification period for three additional years, but even this did not save the ERA. It was officially declared to be a nullity in 1982, the year that Gregory Watson chose to make the ERA the focus of his term paper.

Clearly, Watson could have written a very effective term paper based solely on an examination of the history of the ERA. Watson, however, had an intellectual curiosity that drove him to examine the ERA within the context of the larger subject of Constitutional amendments in general. Considering the failure of the nation to ratify the ERA, Watson wondered if there were other amendments that had suffered a similar fate. This led him to the discovery of Madison's amendment from 1789.

In and of itself, this inquiry would hopefully make Watson's teachers proud. He had clearly done more than simply report on the ERA: instead, he had engaged in a comprehensive historical effort to compare and contrast what he had learned. This, of course, is one of the hallmarks of critical thinking. Obviously, Watson was demonstrating a skill that teachers hope all of their students will acquire.

Here again, if Watson had stopped his research at that point, he would have had a project that most likely would have found favor with his professor. But Watson had not yet satiated his intellectual curiosity. Instead, he delved further into the history of the amendment suggested by Madison. His study of the ERA had revealed that Congress had attached a time limit to that amendment, and he wondered if the addition to the Constitution suggested by Madison had had a similar restriction placed on it. When he examined the actual wording, however, Watson found that no expiration date had been assigned. Madison's amendment, then, was theoretically still subject to ratification.

This discovery would in all probability have secured from most educators the highest grade possible for Watson's paper, and many students at this point would simply have written up the results of their inquiry and turned it in. But there are two things that make Watson's story so remarkable and compelling. First, although today we recognize Watson's accomplishment as a shining example of authentic learning, it is interesting to note that initially his efforts did not in fact find favor with its intended audience. Indeed, his professor at the University of Texas gave Watson a C for his paper, explaining that she did not believe his assertion that Madison's amendment could still be ratified. This rejection would have caused most students to discard the paper and never think of it again. Here, however, is the second factor that makes Watson's saga noteworthy. Undaunted by the less than effusive praise he had received for his paper, Watson did not terminate his involvement with the subject of Madison's amendment. Rather, he started a campaign to have states take up and consider the document. Slowly at first, states began to see the merit of Madison's idea and started to ratify the amendment. It took ten years, but finally in 1992 the Archivist of the United States ruled that a sufficient number of states had ratified the amendment, and declared it to be in effect. What began as a routine assignment for a college student, thus ended in a very extraordinary fashion: with the ratification of a Constitutional amendment.

This story is illustrative for today's educators for two reasons. First, it provides a powerful antidote to the view commonly expressed by students that because of the size of our nation it is impossible for one person to make a difference. Put quite simply, Gregory Watson did make a difference. If he could, so can others.

But the second reason this story carries such weight is that it proves how powerful a tool critical thinking can be. Watson, using a compare-and-contrast strategy, came upon a subject that sparked in him the desire to know more about it. American educators may never have a student quite like Gregory Watson, but every year they will have students capable of achieving a greater understanding of the world they live in, if only they can be taught to ask questions pertaining to that existence.

ASKING IMPORTANT QUESTIONS

While Gregory Watson utilized critical thinking skills to effect a change for the future, others employ those capabilities to give us a better understanding of the past. A prime example of this phenomenon occurred quite recently regarding our understanding of the American involvement in South Vietnam from 1945 to 1975. Although no one knew with any certainty at the time, the nature of our nation's effort changed dramatically because of an event in 1968 known as the Tet Offensive. In January of that year, indigenous South Vietnamese known as the Viet Cong and soldiers from the North Vietnamese Army, seeking to overthrow the American-backed government of the Republic of South Vietnam, launched a nation-wide series of assaults with the goal of motivating the people of that nation to join their cause. From today's perspective, it is obvious that the campaign failed to achieve its primary goal. The citizens of the Republic of South Vietnam refused to take up arms against the government, and within months the military situation inside the country had been stabilized. To make things worse for the insurgents, American and South Vietnamese military units had inflicted devastating losses on the attackers (with an estimated 40,000 enemy combatants killed in action). Few plans in history have gone as badly awry as did the one implemented by the foes of the United States in South Vietnam in 1968.

Any student who chooses to read even a cursory account of America's role in Vietnam during the period from 1945 to 1975 will have no trouble learning these facts about the Tet Offensive. But any reputable treatment of the subject will also undoubtedly note that while the enemy campaign failed from a military point of view, it succeeded beyond the wildest hopes of the insurgents in that it started the process by which the United States would eventually end its support of the Republic of South Vietnam. How is this seeming contradiction possible? How can a military victory, ultimately result in a political defeat?

The answer to this question is lengthy and multifaceted, but in its simplest form, the explanation is that the American people lost the resolve to continue a vigorous military defense of the Republic of South Vietnam as a result of the Tet Offensive. A look at the events leading up to the Tet Offensive can help put the subject into context. First, it becomes apparent when looking at the era that American support for the military effort to help the Republic of South Vietnam had already started to erode during the months preceding that campaign. A look at that period in time reveals that American public support had begun to waver for a number of reasons, ranging from growing casualty lists to the recognition of the strain that the war was placing on the American economy.

President Lyndon Johnson sought to stop the burgeoning anti-war movement by stating that the war against the insurgents was going well and would soon be over. Spokesmen for the government, including the commander of United States forces in South Vietnam, echoed those sentiments at public appearances in late 1967. But the Tet Offensive seemed to belie that assessment. It appeared to many Americans that an enemy force supposedly on its last legs obviously had the strength to launch a nation-wide assault, and that perception cast grave doubts on the validity of Johnson's assertion. Indeed, many Americans began to ask and question critically what was truly happening in that part of the world.

One such individual was the television broadcaster Walter Cronkite. The anchor of the *CBS Nightly News*, Cronkite was one of the most respected American journalists of the post-Second World War era. As was the case with many Americans, Cronkite had been shocked by the ability of the Viet Cong and the North Vietnamese Army to launch assaults of such scope and magnitude as part of the Tet Offensive. Reviewing the reports coming from South Vietnam, Cronkite is supposed to have said "What the hell is going on over there? I thought we were winning." If those exact words did not emanate from Cronkite, they fully convey his astonishment regarding the audacious enemy offensive. He resolved to see the situation in South Vietnam for himself, and as a result he went to that region in February of 1868.

What Cronkite found in South Vietnam troubled him deeply. Travelling throughout the nation, Cronkite saw first-hand evidence of the determination of the insurgents to keep fighting until they had overthrown the American-backed government. He gradually came to the conclusion that Johnson's assessment of the situation in Southeast Asia had been, to say the least, over-optimistic. This led him to decide that, rather than simply report news about the Tet Offensive, he would offer an editorial comment regarding his assessment of the situation. Accordingly, on February 27, 1868, Cronkite publicly declared on his nightly news program that the United States was "mired in stalemate" in South Vietnam. He went on to suggest that the only sensible course of action for the United States was to negotiate a settlement of the conflict, rather than seek an ultimate victory.

In today's day and age, Cronkite's action is regarded as the turning point in our nation's involvement in Southeast Asia. Prior to Cronkite's broadcast, it appeared that Lyndon Johnson would be able to keep the nation committed to the goal of militarily protecting an independent, democratic Republic of South Vietnam. But Johnson, watching Cronkite deliver his pessimistic editorial on that day in February of 1968, instantaneously recognized that he no longer had the political capital necessary to achieve that goal. After Cronkite's broadcast ended, Johnson turned away from the television set he was watching and said "If I've lost Walter Cronkite, I've lost Middle America."

In the days that followed, Johnson began to put into motion a plan that would initiate a dialog with the insurgents in Southeast Asia. These talks, it was hoped, would lead to a peace settlement for the region. Johnson soon realized that his efforts to develop a meaningful discussion with the insurgents would require an all-consuming time commitment on his part, and he knew that this meant trouble for him politically. Johnson was up for re-election in 1968, and by the end of February, he was aware of the fact that he would face challenges from both political parties as part of that process. Believing that bringing peace to Southeast Asia was more important than his political future, Johnson decided to announce on March 31st, 1968, that he would not seek re-election that fall.

This is an incredibly powerful story of, again, how one person's stand on an issue affected American history. By this account, a president of the United States changed an American policy because a broadcast journalist brought to his attention the reality that the populace no longer supported that goal. Any US History textbook that claims to accurately depict that era will undoubtedly reference this event, a coverage that seems quite warranted by the facts. And Americans living in the 21st Century will have no trouble accepting the veracity of this account, as we have seen how much influence broadcast journalists have on shaping the popular perception of political issues facing our nation. When the fact that Lyndon Johnson was known to have intently paid attention to how networks covered the American effort in Southeast Asia—he had, for example, installed three television sets in the Oval Office so that he could simultaneously monitor the nightly news broadcasts—its seems absolutely certain that Cronkite could indeed have changed the course of history.

Within the past decade, however, a number of historians and journalists have begun to question this widely-held popular view of the events that took place in those critical months in 1968. Some wondered, for example, if Johnson's dramatic announcement on March 31st that he would not seek re-election had been solely based on his realization that negotiations with the insurgents would be time consuming. After all, these skeptics noted, Jimmy Carter had chosen to actively seek re-election in 1980 while simultaneously attempting to secure the release of our hostages being held in Iran. These quizzical individuals turned to those of Johnson's closest advisors who were still living, and asked if they felt that it was possible Johnson had made up his mind not to run based on his pending involvement in the negotiation process. When asked this question, a number of Johnson's inner circle said that Johnson had already told them privately that he would not seek re-election weeks before Cronkite's broadcast. Johnson's health, they revealed, had been failing him for some time, and he worried that he might not survive another four years in the White House. That, more than anything, had already convinced him even before the Tet Offensive to eschew a second campaign for the presidency. These statements, coming years after Johnson's decision, may be a reinvention of the past, but they provided the first suggestion that the accepted version of America's change of course in Southeast Asia may be faulty.

This discovery opened up the entire subject of Cronkite's famous broadcast for further review. Researchers soon discovered a fact that cast even more doubt on the widely held view regarding the broadcast's importance: Johnson had not actually seen the broadcast on February 27, 1968. It turned out that Johnson had been at a birthday party that evening for his good friend John Connally, the governor of Texas. And back in the days before it was possible to record programs and watch them later, this meant that Johnson had no chance to view the program that night when he returned to the White House. More investigation led researchers to theorize that Johnson had never seen the broadcast, or at the very least had only watched a clip of it at some later date.

While this evidence seemed to cast aspersions on the accepted view of Cronkite's influence, some historians still maintained that the broadcast could have still had the effect popularly assigned to it. Perhaps, they suggested, it was after seeing a clip of Cronkite's broadcast or reading a transcript of it that Johnson uttered his memorable words. In this manner, the broadcast could still have affected Johnson's decision.

At this point, opinion among the experts was still fairly evenly divided on the veracity of the assumption that Cronkite's broadcast had forced Lyndon Johnson to reevaluate America's course of action in Southeast Asia. But there was one final, crucial bit of vital information regarding this disagreement yet to be revealed. Surprisingly, no one had looked closely at who had heard Johnson's words and recorded them. Researchers and historians began to delve into the past, and found that the first reference to this statement came from a man by the name of George Christian. Christian served in 1968 as Lyndon Johnson's press secretary, and the revelation of his role seemed initially to lend credence to the accuracy of the quote. Who better than a press secretary, it was argued, to be at Johnson's side when he said those fateful words?

This could have ended the discussion about the accuracy of the quote, but others chose not to let the matter drop. They found, upon further review, that Christian had quoted Johnson for the first time in 1979, over a decade after the words would have been spoken. Furthermore, Christian had asserted that Johnson had said these words in the Oval Office immediately after Johnson had witnessed Cronkite's broadcast. Clearly, this is a troubling aspect to those examining the subject from an unbiased point of view. If Christian was wrong about where and when Johnson delivered his famous words, could he be wrong about the words themselves?

A look at Johnson's actions immediately after Cronkite's editorial comment seems to suggest that the doubters may indeed be correct, or at least have a valid point. In the days after the broadcast, Johnson publicly gave no hint of any doubts about the rectitude of his policy vis-à-vis Southeast Asia. Rather, his speeches in early March argued that a strong prosecution of the war could result in outright victory. "We shall and we are going to win" is a fairly typical example of what Johnson said in those days. In light of this, it hardly seems likely that Johnson had decided that all was lost in Vietnam because of Walter Cronkite.

Given this information, what does actually explain Johnson's decision to seek a negotiated settlement in Southeast Asia? A closer investigation suggests that Johnson changed his mind because of two meetings that he had in March about America's course of action in that region. The first meeting was with the Chairman of the Joint Chiefs of Staff, US Army General Earle Wheeler. At that conference, Wheeler urged the president to call into service 205,000 US Army reservists to help bolster American forces deployed around the world. Johnson was taken aback by this request, recognizing that such an action would seem to many Americans to be an admission that the military effort to save the Republic of South Vietnam would require an escalation of the conflict. Unfortunately for Johnson, word of this request leaked out, and the public drew the exact conclusion that Johnson had feared. Polls soon indicated that for the first time a majority of Americans regarded the decision to send combat troops to South Vietnam to have been a mistake.

This turn of events was deeply troubling to Johnson, but from his perspective things only got worse a few days later. Johnson's new secretary of defense, Clark Clifford, asked a group of Americans who helped shape public opinion (i.e. business, religious, and educational leaders) to attend a conference at the White House to discuss American involvement in Southeast Asia. In the past, these individuals had supported Johnson's course of action in that region, but at that March meeting they almost to a man told Johnson that he could no longer seek a military solution to the situation there. While fuming privately at how these individuals (dubbed "The Wise Men" by the American press corps) had betrayed him, Johnson soon recognized that his hopes for a peace settlement predicated on American success on the battlefield had evaporated.

This realization was troubling to Johnson because of the state of affairs within his own political party. Minnesota Senator Eugene McCarthy was already a candidate for the Democratic presidential nomination, promising that if elected he would end American involvement in Southeast Asia. On March 16, 1968, New York Senator Robert F. Kennedy (President John F. Kennedy's younger brother) also entered the race. He, like McCarthy, ran as an anti-war candidate. Johnson at last realized that the only way to possibly salvage any hope for a viable Republic of South Vietnam was to seek a negotiated settlement before either of these men could be elected on a peace platform. For this reason, then, Johnson chose to focus his efforts on trying to diplomatically secure the preservation of an independent Republic of South Vietnam before either McCarthy or Kennedy could obviate that possibility by unilaterally withdrawing from the region.

This sequence of events provides a much better explanation of Johnson's public announcement on March 31st, 1968 than does the theory that Walter Cronkite's broadcast alone altered American history. While it is possible that evidence hitherto unseen may someday tip the scales back in favor of the view currently found in many textbooks, it seems logical to assume that five years from now, students in America's schools will read a much different explanation in their textbooks of Johnson's decision to seek a negotiated settlement in Southeast Asia.

Our gradually evolving understanding of what prompted a major change of course in American history regarding Vietnam demonstrates a number of elements that are crucial to critical thinking. First, an individual seeking to understand the past has to be willing to challenge popularly held views regarding an event. Just as historians, journalists, and researchers refused to accept at face value a widely held interpretation of why our strategy in that far off portion of the world was radically altered in 1968, a critical thinker will always be willing to ask contrarian questions about comfortable assumptions and investigate the actual historical records. This story also proves that a critical thinker examines the origins of a story before accepting its validity at face value. And finally, a study of Johnson's decision to seek a negotiated settlement in Southeast Asia (ironically, Johnson died the day before the treaty finalizing this arrangement was signed in 1973) shows why a proper appreciation of cause-and-effect is such an important goal for a critical thinker to strive for.

CONCLUSION

The United States in the 21st century is a nation in a continual state of flux. No aspect of American society is immune from the effects of the phenomenon of change. We find it increasingly difficult to keep abreast of new developments, and risk becoming a people who feel overwhelmed by the complexities of modern life. Interestingly, this possibility was foreseen over 40 years ago by a writer named Alvin Toffler. He recognized during the 1960s that the rate of technological change was rapidly increasing, and began to believe that this would eventually create a disconnect for those unable to nimbly respond to the changing conditions in America. To help citizens be better able to cope with this reality, he wrote a book that he titled *Future Shock*. In it, he painted a grim picture of the fate that awaited those that could not adapt to the changes taking place around them. The book was a best seller, and remains in print to this day.

While most Americans in today's day and age remember—if they recall anything about *Future Shock*—the book's dire forecast, few seem to remember that Toffler offered suggestions for how individuals could cope with the changing landscape. Not surprisingly, Toffler felt that public education represented the best hope for a better future. In his book, and in his subsequent writings, Toffler asserted that revising school curricula to help students be more effective thinkers offered a way for our nation to survive and even flourish in an age where the only constant was change. Although there is some debate today about the actual words that he used, he is generally credited with making the uncannily accurate observation that "The illiterate of the 21st century will not be those who cannot read and write, but those who cannot learn, unlearn, and relearn." (Ferguson, 2012) For this reason, it is imperative that those educators entrusted with the responsibility of giving instruction in the realm of the Social studies heed these words every time they enter the classroom.

Thus, from these historical vignettes, we can see the importance of deep exploration and deep examination of printed as well as verbal records and the need to examine events in historical context. Furthermore, we have addressed the impact that one person may have on events as well as the impact that one media representative may have on not only national events, but events literally around the world.

Teachers need to be able to teach the deep examination of events, using primary as well as secondary sources and employ different viewpoints and perspectives. Teachers must teach the skills of comparing and contrasting, evaluating, questioning, reflecting and delving into historical issues, as well as working historians reflecting on sometimes unresolved past events. One individual armed with the proper research tools, critical thinking abilities, and higher order thinking skills can indeed make a difference in this ever changing world, and be increasingly prepared to be a part of future historical generations.

REFERENCES

Bernstein, R. B. (1992)."The Sleeper Wakes: The History of the Twenty-Seventh Amendment." *Fordham Law Review* 61 (December).

Ferguson, R. (2012). "Alvin Toffler on Learning." You Tube.

In: The Nurturing of Talent, Skills and Abilities
Editor: Michael F. Shaughnessy

ISBN: 978-1-62618-521-0
© 2013 Nova Science Publishers, Inc.

Chapter 7

BACK TO THE FUTURE: WHAT WE ALREADY KNOW ABOUT CRITICAL THINKING AND SCIENCE EDUCATION

*Jerry Everhart**

Eastern New Mexico University, Portales,
Roosevelt County, New Mexico, US

INTRODUCTION

The United States is in the midst of reassessing inter-related societal and educational priorities. A new national conversation about educational reform is in it's early stages and focuses on the reverse of thirty-five years of questionable practices that have marginalized critical thinking and, consequently, undermined preparation of students entering science, technology, engineering, and mathematics-intensive (STEM) careers. Historians will view the second decade on the twenty-first century as a transitional time linking a post-Cold War malaise to a new age of scientific enlightenment -- possibly. The need to assess and solve a cadre of challenges as world hunger, climate change, disease, and energy acquisition dictates more emphasis on problem solving and critical thought. The United States' ability to deal with pressing problems has been masked over the last four decades. Due to epic strides in technology, space exploration, food science, medicine, and energy, the public has taken innovation for granted. These technological advancements are the products of Cold War investments in education and they are dissipating as aging scientists exit the workforce. Since 1980, little attention or effort has been made to re-staff research labs, university science departments, and the teacher profession. Consequently, deficits exist in most areas of scientific research. If cohorts of scientists require 20 years to develop (public school, undergraduate plus graduate programs), new and immediate investments into science education might not yield a full complement of scientists until 2030. The United States must quickly rejuvenate the scientific community, incentivize STEM career paths, reform

* Corresponding author: Jerry Everhart. E-mail: Jerry.Everhart@enmu.edu.

curricula, and re-tool teachers, and, unfortunately in the interim, "poach" significant numbers of scientists from other countries until greater numbers of competent scientists become available. Re-tooling schools and universities is a matter of re-instituting well documented practices of the past to meet goals in the future. This chapter explores historical benchmarks, past and current practices, and strategies necessary to produce and develop the next generation of critical thinkers and scientists.

REVERSAL OF FORTUNE

Teachers, aided by the federal funding, NURTURED children on hefty doses of science and mathematics during the cold war era that spanned 1945 to the late 1970s. As Detante subsided and the Berlin Wall and all it signified collapsed, President Ronald Reagan did little to shore up education in the 1980s. Though taken quite seriously by the education community, A Nation at Risk (1983) was a political document used to justify substantial changes in priorities during the subsequent 30 years. A Nation at Risk became the precursor to, and justification for, charter schools, school choice, increased control of the K-12 curricula, and attacks on teacher preparation programs. Decisions regarding allocation of resources, ultimately, dismantled the Cold War emphasis on science while refocusing attention on President Reagan's "Back to Basics" -- a political movement neither substantiated by research nor endorsed by educators. Unsuccessfully, educators made valid arguments that elimination of monies that supported instructional materials, professional development for teachers, and supplemental experiences as summer institutes, science camps, and internships would result in reduced interest in math, science, and engineering careers. School science curricula for K-12 fared no better in the subsequent three administrations and 20 years. President George W. Bush's "No Child Left Behind" (continued by the Obama administration) completed the dismantlement of science education by stressing testing versus learning, reducing mathematics to computational mechanics, and has eliminated critical thinking and higher order thinking from public education.

Persistent myths about mathematics and science education in the United States exist that hinder the nation's ability to re-tool schools. Since the mid-1970s, several international measures have been employed that rank nations in math and science. Despite the annual rhetoric that accompanies the release of international ranking, data indicate that the United States has always received a position in the middle of the ranking in mathematics and science -- not at the top. The public (and politicians) have concluded a loss of status among nations that never occurred. The disparity between the United States' unprecedented innovation and productivity (especially in areas of mathematics, science, and technology) and national ranking has lead to imposition of reforms that were unwarranted. If one examines that disparity with something other than a political lens, a reasonable conclusion might be that some unique elements of the educational system may account for the nation's long history of scientific successes...as problem solving, questioning the status quo, and critical thinking. Could features that made the United States educational system unique among nations be lost in an attempt to improve numerical rank on standardized tests? Recent reforms in math and science education have fundamentally stripped problem solving and critical thinking from the curricula.

Several questions must be answered before significant reforms can be instituted to change the course of weakened math and science education that would lead to STEM careers and a truly scientifically literate citizenry. Whether the United States is able to recover from mislaid priorities of the last 40 years may have little to do with science content, but more to do with cultural factors that have shifted. Two interrelated questions arise as the country assesses options linked to the future of STEM -- the status of science education, and whether critical thinking, problem solving, and even scientific thinking can be re-integrated into school curricula. Does the United States still value science education and critical thought? Does the United States remember how to prepare critical thinkers and scientists?

Although STEM-related language is re-emerging in educational, corporate, and political discourse -- little evidence of any shift in priorities is evident if one examines time allotment for science education in schools, funding, and teacher preparation. Decreases in the number of hours that science is taught in schools indicate an "optionality" of the subject matter. Finite funding appears available for packaged reading programs and related teacher professional development versus strengthening science programs. Marginalization of science in schools may be symptomatic of the more troubling debate between lay groups and the science community. Facts and preponderance of data on some facets of science have become subject to re-interpretation by politicians, corporate groups, and the clergy; these interests are averse to critical examination of subject matter linked to evolution, climate change, and earth history. Fundamental to critical thinking, these vocal and politically-connected groups want to eliminate discourse on these subjects in public schools. In attempt to discredit or undermine all science research, oppositional groups cite niche research as chemoluminescent jellyfish, shrimp on treadmills, and robots that fold towels; trivialization of science makes the ability to question (i.e. critical thought) less important.

In stark contrast, educational programs of the 1960s and 70s touted the value of questioning, testing, assessing, and concluding. A variety of well-researched programs were available that stressed the importance of critical thinking, science processes, and hands-on instruction. Affectionately referred to as the "alphabet soup" by science educators, some of the more enduring programs included Science- A Process Approach (SAPA), Science Curriculum Improvement Study (SCIS), Biological Sciences Curriculum Study (BSCS), Conceptually Oriented Project in Elementary Education (COPES), Elementary Science Studies (ESS), and Full Option Science Studies (FOSS) among many others. These programs are noteworthy, not for nostalgia for the past, because they dominated science curricula and demonstrated the nation's commitment to critical thinking. They stimulated students engendering passion for science, nurturing a persistence for uncovering facts, coaching and refining inductive and deductive reasoning, and fostering curiosity about the world around them -- the underpinning for pursuit of career paths in science. Few comparable resources exist in today's schools.

In the mid-1970s, the United States tracked innovation in education through the National Diffusion Network (NDN). Funded by Congress and operated under the Office of Education, the agency maintained extensive files on programs that contributed to the educational knowledge base. Each program collected data, underwent a rigorous panel review, and if "validated", wound up in the NDN's "Programs that Work" annual publication. During the Network's last year of operation, one-half of validated programs dealt with cognitive skills, mathematics, and science. The NDN fell victim to "Contract for America"-related budget reductions in 1995.

Dissemination of information on successful programs today is less systematic; educators are dependent upon academic journals, blogs, social media, published video documentation, and private foundation publications for spreading the word about programs that work. Considering budget reductions, questionable educational reforms, and devaluation of science in the public sphere -- it is easy to conclude that despite the growing need for critical thinkers, science education has yet to reach a level of prominence comparable to the late twentieth century.

TWO CASE STUDIES

Good examples of programs that advocate critical thinking and sound science education do exist. These cases exemplify good work that promotes critical thinking, passion for science, intellectual curiosity, and the persistence needed in the pursuit of STEM-oriented careers. San Jose State University (California) has instituted two programs to develop critical thinking skills in their science majors program. Funded by a private foundation, the Department of Biological Sciences' freshmen are participating in a curriculum reform that guides and informs students in their transition to becoming scientists. All of the students in the program intend to pursue careers in science despite that more than 40% self-report less than stellar pre-college, "No Child Left Behind" preparation. Students are highly motivated and want to be scientists. Biology faculty have modernized the curriculum -- strengthening the content by shifting from a nomenclature-oriented curriculum to a highly interdisciplinary approach characterized by team teaching, simulations, and hand-on activities with complementary laboratories that contain some open-ended investigations. Undergraduates are responsible for research commonly associated with graduate-level courses. Well trained laboratory instructors guide their students through authentic research experiences that employ the scientific method; some lab reports take the form of formal posters that parallel experiences that practicing scientists might have at professional conferences. With emphasis on critical thinking, students routinely engage in labs that require posing their own questions, establishing procedures, controlling variables, and collecting data. Some lab reports take the form of formal posters that parallel experiences that practicing scientists might have at professional conferences. Faculty stress process; students hone critical and systematic thinking, communications, collaboration, and problem solving. In surveys, eighty-four percent of program participants stated that their involvement has further confirmed their commitment to become a research scientist or medical doctor. Students stress the role of thinking critically about biology as faculty help make connections between seemingly disparate concepts as electrophoresis and the plant population studies on hills outside the city.

Another model program at San Jose State University pairs upper division science majors with mentor faculty. The intent of the collaboration is to fast-track the induction process with emphasis on critical thinking, risk-taking, persistence, collaboration, and skills development. A select group, admitted to the program by interview, work beside faculty in chemistry, biology, and forensic science laboratories. Students move through a four-step process on their route to becoming scientists; each step includes honing critical thinking skills.

Steps include: 1) awareness; 2) participation; 3) induction; and 4) maturation. With critical thinking is the primary measure of progress through the four steps, students learn about research, standards, and expectations (step 1); commit to laboratory routines and processes learning persistence, curiosity, and passion (step 2); students become a contributing member of the lab -- asking questions and posing their own questions (step 3); and students become experts in their field sharing knowledge at professional meetings and co-authoring articles in refereed journals (step 4).

Employing a natualistic approach, faculty gradually turn over responsibilities to students while creating conditions where students exercise critical thinking skills -- much as a working scientist would in his/her own lab. Inevitably, students attain high degrees of confidence in their analytical abilities, attain a high degree of proficiency using scientific methodologies, contribute directly to the on-going research, publish and present, and pursue advanced degrees at other noteworthy institutions. The student researchers express a high degree of satisfaction with the program and cite self-efficacy in critical thinking as a major contributor to their continuing success.

Broad commitment for critical thinking, institutional support, and well-prepared faculty are features of the second noteworthy case. In the early 1990s, science educators in North Carolina engaged in a multi-year research program to determine whether students could achieve using traditional measures if critical thinking skills became the primary focus in sixth grade science classrooms. Seven districts with more than sixty teachers representing all level of expertise participated from across the state. Meeting in summer institutes, teachers examined their own practices and agreed on instructional methods that promoted critical thinking in children.

With emphasis on inductive and deductive reasoning as tools for understanding the world, teachers established eight broad science questions that would drive the entire year of instruction; they developed lesson plans that would lead students through the process of uncovering facts, experimenting, assessing value, and explaining concepts.

Teachers were eager to begin the program, but they were unsure whether their students would perform as well as their counterparts not in the research program; in fear of possibly lowering district averages, participating teachers asked that their children's standardized test scores be disaggregated from those of the district. The North Carolina Department of Public Instruction denied the research program's request, but agreed to provide data on how the experimental program students performed in comparison to traditional students. The program proceeded as planned. Using textbooks as supplements only, teachers posed a single science question, facilitated daily activities, and offered support as students' questions arose in roughly six-week increments. Students uncovered information, designed experiments, conducted research, and used innovative strategies to share what they learned. Much of what the children learned seemed incidental to the question under consideration and many lessons transformed into interdisciplinary investigations. Not incidental to the process designed by the North Carolina teachers were strong connections among understanding, logic, and well-reasoned analysis. Students were engaged, productive, and "owned" the information that they developed over time.

At the end of the first year of critical thinking-oriented instruction, the student participants performed as well or better than non-experimental students statewide on standardized tests. Teachers noted their own satisfaction as teacher-facilitators and endorsed the new methodology. Teachers believed students were better prepared making stronger connections among scientific principles and they left the experience asking, "Why limit students to only what the teacher knows and what textbooks offer?"

BACK TO THE FUTURE

The American zeitgeist for innovation, questioning the status quo, and scientific research is not lost, but merely obscured by four decades of poor societal, political, and educational decisions. An ill-prepared workforce along with a host of medical, environmental, and energy challenges will force a change-of-course in science education beginning with a shift backward to critical thinking. Whether the United States remains sixteenth of thirty worldwide in math and science on standardized tests, ultimately, will not alter the nation's ability to lead; learning from the past and making informed decisions about future reforms must begin soon lest another generation is left under- or undeveloped in critical thinking skills and scientific thought processes.

If critical thinking is to regain a role in modern education, fundamental change must occur in all levels of education. Using past successes as a blueprint for reforming curriculum and instruction -- especially in the discipline of science, educators must employ five strategies.

Contextualize Content and Engage Students

Although the mechanics of critical thinking may be undisputed, critical thinking without context is little more than a mental exercise or game. Students must think deeply about the world around them. They must be invited to think interdisciplinarily, experiment, question accepted information, and draw their own conclusions.

Even though this form of education is difficult to measure on standardized tests and political factors may bring pressures to bear, critical thinking will yield, as it has in the past, bountiful results. Students will own those results and the generative nature of understanding will result in another era of invention and growth. Any deficiency or vacancy in STEM careers will be resolved if science is embraced once more by the public. Schools should mirror the balance between content knowledge and process skills found in most STEM careers.

Encourage Curiosity through Questioning

Most parents are amused, and sometimes annoyed, at the number of questions generated by their children. Questioning, in conjunction with observation, is the child's best avenue for learning about the world. Persistence of questioning is curiosity -- a highly prized characteristic among all fields and occupations.

Likely, a legacy of human evolution, questioning is a venue for transferring important information inter-generationally and is the first step in evaluation -- the higher order of thought. Through direct instruction, simulation, and experimentation, children learn that not all questions yield the same type and quality of information.

As critical thinkers, youth must have a forum in which they can continue to ask questions and science is founded on such inquiry. Possibly the most distinct feature of American schools pre-1980s was emphasis given to student-driven investigation.

Look beyond Textbooks

Textbooks play a different role in a critical thinking program. Since critical thinking is interdisciplinary and non-linear, traditional texts are useful as guides. Publishers would be responsible for more than the perfunctory, introductory chapters that describe the scientific method and ways of knowing about the world.

Unlike present day texts, content and suggested activities will be conceptually aligned with forms of inquiry and critical thought. Like the North Carolina case earlier in this chapter, students uncover information in the context of answering questions; present day texts advocate critical analysis, yet advocate classroom activities with single approaches and single solutions. Since critical thinking engages and contextualizes, publishers must become more agile and tailor issues and content to meet local and regional interests versus targeting the interests of the largest market.

Affirm That Thought Requires Time

Inherently, instruction that integrates critical thinking strategies require more time than traditional teaching. Students must reflect, gather information, weigh the value of that information, and form conclusions. Time intensive reflection upon conditions and one's own interests, biases, and priorities are critical thinking corollaries. Additional time for science must accompany curricular reforms.

Since context is key to critical thought, high-interest science should be elevated to the top of elementary and secondary school curricula; in a critical thinking curriculum, reading and mathematics are subsumed under the sciences. Essential qualities of successful scientists can only be developed with adequate time. Curiosity, persistence, and passion for content co-develops as students achieve flow. Similar to San Jose State University's students, classes must guide children through stages where critical thinking skills are introduced, developed, and mature.

Reflection upon conditions and one's own interests, biases, and priorities are critical thinking corollaries. Contemplative processes require a delay in formulation of conclusions. Critical thinkers weigh possibilities and employ alternative lenses in order to arrive at the "best" solution. To paraphrase John Locke, the laborious pursuit of new ideas transmutes thought into useful information; higher order thinking requires time. Responding to the questions as "Why?" and "Of what value is this information?" poses different challenges than simple regurgitation of facts. If schools are being charged with producing scientists they would be remiss if attention was paid solely to factual content. Rarely is science linked to immediate gratification. Scientists' toil over questions and development of new information is rarely instantaneous.

Barriers arise in experimental processes, data collection, and contradictory conclusions. Execution of an experiment once is not enough; scientific validity is attainable only if experiments can be replicated. Good scientists know this, teach this, and practice these methods in their own laboratories. If persistence is integral to critical thinking -- time to attempt and fail and attempt and succeed is necessary.

Nurture Institutional Commitment

Federal, state, and local agencies can demonstrate their commitment to critical thinking by re-instating adequate funding, encouraging innovation in schools, return scheduling and some curricular decisions to teachers, and re-establishing venues for programs that work to share their successes. Leadership must incentivize pursuit of STEM career paths through setting goals, funding research, and re-tooling practicing teachers and teacher preparation programs.

Funding must precede, not follow, any commitment for educational reform. Programs that have served the educational community well in the past should be re-instated as the National Diffusion Network, Eisenhower funds for professional development, and many disbanded "Title" programs and budgetry decisions linked to the Elementary and Secondary Education Act (as ESEA Title IV-C, increases in class size). These programs were good investments in promotion and documentation of innovation in education. Although critical thinking-based programs are not new -- the ideas are fresh to the incoming generation of teachers charged with teaching cognitive skills to children.

Although the current cohort of practicing teachers are products of the Cold War, critical thinking era -- many are aging and retiring; college graduates of the class of 1980 are exiting the workforce and are being replaced with novices that have known only "Back to Basics" and "No Child Left Behind" forms of schooling.

Critical thinking skills deserve the same commitment of time and resources in teacher preparation afforded reading and mathematics. Changes in teacher education followed by intensive professional development and summer institutes are needed to improve questioning skills, question-driven instruction, and creation of instructional settings with procedures conducive to critical thinking.

CONCLUSION

Does the United States still value science education and critical thought? Based purely on educational policies of the last forty years, the answer is unclear. Distribution of resources suggests that the nation has yet to reverse direction away from prescriptive, fact-driven regimens towards open-ended, generative instruction that was the hallmark of American education in the twentieth century. If more enlightened politicians and administrators do not re-direct the current path of education policy, social and commercial demands will. Such a change of course will be labor-intensive and costly. Derek Bok, two-term president of Harvard University, noted, "If you think that education is expensive, try ignorance." No guarantees exist on investments made in education and institutional shifts toward difficult-to-measure intangibles such as critical thinking are fraught with challenges. The nation does remember how to prepare critical thinkers. A framework for change is available in lessons learned in the not distant past.

In: The Nurturing of Talent, Skills and Abilities
Editor: Michael F. Shaughnessy

ISBN: 978-1-62618-521-0
© 2013 Nova Science Publishers, Inc.

Chapter 8

DEVELOPING PHILOSOPHICAL THINKING SKILLS AND ABILITIES

Gerard Casey[*]

University College Dublin, Ireland

ABSTRACT

If you were to ask what skills and abilities and training people in a particular trade or profession might require the answer would be reasonably clear in many cases, for example, for lawyers, engineers, doctors, or train drivers. While the skills, abilities and training will necessarily differ among these various fields of endeavor, there is one thing, one negative thing, they all have in common; whatever it may be that goes towards the making of a good lawyer is not itself a legal matter; what engineering is and what makes a good engineer is not an engineering matter. The same holds for medicine, history, psychology and so on; and what literature is and what makes a good writer is a literary question only inasmuch as someone is likely to write about it. However vague and porous the boundaries constitutive of such disciplines may be, these boundaries are drawn from the outside, not the inside. There is, however, one discipline, one field of study, one intellectual enterprise—it's hard to use a name which isn't in some respect question-begging—for which this is not true. Yes, you've guessed it: it's philosophy. What philosophy *is* is itself a philosophical question. (see Nagel, p. 3 but see also Rorty 1984, p. 79) Indeed, whether there is in fact any such thing as philosophy is itself a philosophical question. This intellectual incestuousness and resultant intellectual vertigo is characteristic of the philosophical enterprise. There is a joke, old but good, which goes something like this. A would-be student comes to the Philosophy stand at the University's open day and asks the philosopher sitting at the table, "What's Philosophy?" He replies, somewhat uncomfortably—philosophers hate this question!—"Well, it's the discipline that asks questions such as 'Who am I?', "Where have we come from?', 'Where are we going?'—that's Philosophy." The student looks quizzically at our philosopher and remarks, "Philosophy? Sounds more like amnesia to me!" *In ioco, veritas*—many a true word spoken in jest. Philosophy often comes across to non-philosophers as the activity conducted by intellectually high-grade and expensively

---

[*] E-mail: gerard.casey@ucd.ie

trained amnesiacs. How can philosophers ask such embarrassingly basic and obvious questions with a straight face?

Given what appears to be the intellectually incestuous character of philosophy, how is one supposed to go about figuring out what skills and abilities philosophers ought to have or develop in order to be the best in their field? Matters can't possibly be as vague and indeterminate as our joke suggests, can they? Let's go to a respectable source for illumination. Harvard's Department of Philosophy website says, "Philosophy is the systematic and critical study of fundamental questions that arise both in everyday life and through the practice of other disciplines." That's some help—not a lot, but some. What would those questions be? "Some of these questions concern the nature of reality: Is there an external world? What is the relationship between the physical and the mental? Does God exist?" (Harvard University, Department of Philosophy) Well, that still leaves us uncomfortably close to our joke territory. What other kinds of questions might philosophy seek to answer? "Do we act freely? Where do our moral obligations come from? How do we construct just political states?" With this second set of questions we seem to be moving towards more practical concerns though perhaps only relatively speaking. Any other questions? Well, yes. "Other [questions] concern the nature and extent of our knowledge: What is it to know something rather than merely believe it? Does all of our knowledge come from sensory experience? Are there limits to knowledge?" Is that it? No. Here's the final batch of questions. "And still other [questions] concern the foundations and implications of other disciplines: What is a scientific explanation? What is the status of evolutionary theory versus creationism? Does the possibility of genetic cloning alter our conception of self? Do the results of quantum mechanics force us to view our relations to objects differently?"

So much for the questions. Does philosophy offer any answers? Even lawyers don't just ask questions; they occasionally give us answers, expensive answers, to be sure, but answers nonetheless. So too with physicists, biologists, chemists, and even psychologists, though we may perhaps get more answers than we can handle from them. The Harvard Department of Philosophy appears strangely reticent to present us with possible answers to the extensive list of questions it has compiled. Instead, it seems to prefer to concentrate on procedural matters. "The aim in Philosophy is not to master a body of facts, so much as think clearly and sharply through any set of facts. Towards that end, philosophy students are trained to read critically, analyze and assess arguments, discern hidden assumption, construct logically tight arguments, and express themselves clearly and precisely in both speech and writing." (Harvard University, Department of Philosophy) There can be no doubt that the ability to read critically and to assess arguments and so on are skills well worth having for philosophers. But others can also benefit from acquiring these skills, a point the authors of the website immediately go on to concede: "These formidable talents can be applied to philosophical issues as well as others, and philosophy students excel in fields as varied as law, business, medicine, journalism, and politics."

The acquisition of critical skills (even if we are not quite sure what those skills are) is very much motherhood and apple pie stuff—who is not in favor of a more widespread distribution of such skills? What is most significant, I think, in the Harvard webpage is its assertion that "the aim of Philosophy is not to master a body of facts...". A cynical observer might be inclined to think that this is so, if it is so, largely because there is no philosophical body of facts to master. One is reminded of the passage in the BBC TV series *Blackadder* in which, in a scene set during a general election, Edmund Blackadder tells a reporter from *The Country Gentleman's Pig Fertilizer Gazette*, "we in the Adder Party are going to fight this campaign on issues, not personalities." "Why is that?" asks the reporter innocently, to which Blackadder responds, "Because our candidate doesn't have a personality". (Curtis & Elton)

The most radical approach to take to the "what is philosophy?" question is to deny the very possibility of philosophy or reluctantly to accept its existence but take it to be an essentially pointless enterprise such as the form of cognitive neurosis D. G. Garan would have us believe it is. (Garan, p. 432) Garan's reason for thinking this is that he believes philosophy to be characterized by a search for "complete cognitive satisfactions in themselves" not merely the problem-solving or need satisfaction that is the province of other more specific forms of knowledge and such complete cognitive satisfaction, he thinks, is intrinsically impossible. While one might be tempted to reject Garan's negative judgement out of hand, there is some prima facie evidence that seems to support it. Assuming for the purposes of this chapter that there is such an intellectual enterprise as philosophy—a big assumption—the subsidiary matter of what philosophy is becomes a derivative philosophical question and, until we have some idea of what the answer to that question is going to be, we are going to find it hard to identify the skills and abilities needed for it.

* * * * *

Why does it seem as if philosophy has made no progress since its beginnings some 2,500 years ago? Philosophers seem to discuss the same issues over and over again with no discernible evidence of progress. Is this because the questions it raises are astoundingly difficult so that the best minds that have ever lived have been unable to answer them; or is it, rather, that they are simply unanswerable, like the question "How heavy is green?" The difficulty in answering this question comes not from its extraordinary depth but from its quite ordinary and total lack of meaning! It lacks the more or less clear and distinct horizon of intelligibility that normal questions are surrounded by. Suppose I were to ask you, "What time is it?" and you were to respond "six feet three inches!" I would be at a loss to understand not what you said, which in its own way is perfectly intelligible, but why you said it and, more to the point, how it is supposed to constitute an answer to my question. It's neither right nor wrong—it just doesn't seem to be the kind of response I was looking for when I asked the question. If, on the other hand, you were to respond, "It's half past spring" I would be less puzzled but inclined to think your love for poetry was infecting your common sense. This response is 'sort of' "kind of" an answer—after all, Spring is a division of time, albeit a crude division—so this response is just on the borderline of comprehensibility. If you were to respond "It's 3.57 p.m." even if it were actually 4.15 p.m., your response would clearly be an answer to my question. We can see, then, that a question, as it were, stands at the center of a circle—responses outside the circumference or horizon of the question are not answers at all; responses in the vicinity of the circumference are 'sort of' answers, and responses clearly within the circle's circumference are unambiguously answers, right or wrong as the case may be.

When one turns to philosophy, matters become more complex. "What does it mean to be?" "Does existence precede essence or essence precede existence?" "What is time?" 'Is morality in any way objective or is it merely a projection of our desires?"—these are the kinds of questions philosophy asks, plus all the other questions that grace the pages of the

Harvard Department of Philosophy's webpage that I mentioned above. It is very difficult to discern the horizon of comprehensibility surrounding such questions so as to be able to say clearly what is, what isn't and what might just be an answer.

Even if we come to locate a set of answers within the horizons of our circles, our problems have hardly begun. How are we to tell which of the possible answers to such questions, if any, are correct? What criteria of judgement are to be employed in judging such matters? Even more fundamentally, isn't it the case that the establishment of any such criteria will be—you know what's coming—philosophically contested? In the case of most questions, we have a fairly clear idea of what falls outside the realm of possible answers and what falls inside—What size bed can we get into this room? What's the best cure for a headache?—but the problem with philosophical questions is that what counts as evidence is often itself philosophically questionable so that there appears to be no neutral standpoint, no objective standard, no indisputable evidence that can be used to get you to an answer.

In his four (yes, four) volume trilogy, *The Hitchhiker's Guide to the Galaxy*, Douglas Adams plays comic havoc with the logic of question and answer. In Adams's book, the answer to the question of Life, the Universe and Everything is 42! If that's the answer, what exactly was the question? Was it "What do you get when you multiply 7 x 6?" or "How many sheep are left in a field if you start with fifty and eight are abducted by aliens?" Hardly! What then? The truth, when finally revealed, is that "the Question and the Answer are mutually exclusive. Knowledge of one logically precludes knowledge of the other. It is impossible that both can ever be known about the same Universe." (Adams, p. 588) The question of Life, the Universe and Everything is at the center of a circle that has no circumference; the answer is constituted by a circumference with no center. If this is a prototype of a philosophical question, it is no wonder that many people experience severe cognitive bewilderment when they first encounter philosophy—concepts, ideas, notions all start to spin in dizzying fashion, giving point to Garan's characterization of philosophy as a form of neurosis.

* * * * *

If philosophy is just a grandiose obsessive-compulsive disorder then the question of what skills and abilities are required to be expert at it is easily answered. Contract a non-life-threatening neurosis, add to it a penchant for clever critical analysis, and you're halfway there. It perhaps goes without saying that most philosophers do not subscribe to the idea that philosophers are academic neurotics (Wittgenstein is perhaps the exception) so, from their perspective, what is it that goes into the making of an outstanding philosophical practitioner?

In the contemporary academic world, there are two major approaches or traditions regarding the study, teaching and practice of philosophy with, needless to say, countless sub-varieties, and consequently at least two ways in which to characterize the skills and abilities required to be the very best in the field. On the one hand, there are those who value precision, argument, analysis, rigor, sharpness of focus above all else—let's call them analytic philosophers—and there are those who tend to favor depth and breadth in the matters with which they concern themselves together with a predilection for the historical exegesis of those whom they regard as the great philosophers, with perhaps somewhat less concern for precision, argument and rigor than for what one might call vision or insight—let's call them continental philosophers. These names that I have given the adherents of these traditions are not chosen at random but reflect for the most part the terms many practicing philosophers today use to describe themselves. However, as you might expect, as with most things in philosophy, the exhaustiveness, exclusivity and appropriateness of this division, the names attached to it, and whether or not a given philosopher belongs to one or the other or neither are all highly contested matters.

This philosophical division finds institutional expression in many universities with most philosophy departments being largely comprised exclusively of either analytic philosophers or continental philosophers, with relatively few departments containing representatives of both or, at most, a token few. Those who don't identify explicitly with either side of this division can find themselves placed in an uncomfortable institutional position. To characterize things in this way is to paint with a very broad brush but it will do as a starting point, if a crude one, for the discussion below.

Analytic philosophers do, from time to time, read the works of older philosophers but to the extent that they read the very old rather than the more recent thinkers they tend to do so as a way of finding material that is pertinent to their immediate contemporary analytic concerns. This substantially ahistorical approach to the history of philosophy is perhaps encapsulated in the claim by Mitchell Green that "…you can have a philosophical mind without knowing much about which famous philosopher held what theory at what time. What makes famous philosophers famous is their stunning exercise of philosophical skill; but just as you can be a superb chess player without studying the techniques of the masters of the past, you can develop philosophical skill without consulting the history of the field." (Green, p. 2) Well, this is not perhaps quite as obviously true as Green would have us believe, not least because we are left somewhat in the dark as to what kinds of philosophical skills famous philosophers are stunning at exercising. The best possible example to support Green's sweeping statement would perhaps be the that of the Austro-English philosopher Ludwig Wittgenstein who was— no disrespect intended—something of a philosophical ignoramus while yet managing to be one of the most significant philosophers of the 20th century, in the view of some, *the* most significant 20th century philosopher. But very few of us are Wittgensteins in the making and it would be foolish to subscribe, even if unwittingly, to the fallacy of the undistributed middle along these lines: "Wittgenstein, a great philosopher, was someone who knew very little of philosophy's history; I know very little of philosophy's history, therefore I too must be a great philosopher."

The more purely formal a discipline, the more likely it is that someone can make worthwhile contributions to it at an early age and without much acquaintance with its history or tradition. As examples of this, I have in mind mathematics, music and, a la Green, chess. But even though largely formal, such enterprises are not entirely formal so that, for example, I can think of very few first rate chess players who have become so without studying the games of other players. Capablanca is, perhaps, the chess player who best fits Green's account but Capablanca was a chess erratic in much the same way that Wittgenstein was an erratic in philosophy. Whatever may be the case with relatively formal disciplines, it seems to me that it would be the exception rather than the rule that one would make worthwhile contributions to the materially rich disciplines of history, philosophy or literature (Rimbaud is perhaps the Capablanca/Wittgenstein of French poetry) without an extensive knowledge of their traditions and their literature.

If there is one thing analytic philosophers are agreed upon, it is the central importance of argument to philosophy and, consequently, the central importance of acquiring the necessary skill in this area. "Philosophy" writes Willem deVries, "is an argumentative discipline; your professional life will be spent mostly in taking issue with what others say and defending your claims against attack. If you are uncomfortable in a discipline the fundamental structures of which are adversarial and in which collaboration is unusual, a career in it may not end up suiting you, however much you love philosophy." (deVries, no date)

Analytic philosophy, with its emphasis on argumentative techniques, on analysis, on counter-argument and counter-example can easily turn into a form of dialectical arm-wrestling. Plato commented that those who are young tend to regard philosophy as a kind of game and that there was a danger that they would use their infatuation with logic and dialectic for simply destructive purposes, like young puppies with a doll. (Plato, 539b; see Casey, pp. 247-248) The old, by contrast, "would not want to take part in such folly" but would "converse in order to discover the truth rather than…merely playing and contradicting for play. (Plato, 539c) Aristotle, too, believed that the young lacked the necessary experience for the study of ethics and politics, youth in this context being a matter of psychic development and not simply a matter of chronology: "Whether he is young in years or immature in character makes no difference; for his deficiency is not a matter of time but of living and of pursuing all his interests under the influence of his emotions." (Aristotle,1094b29-1095a10) "The basic fact which gives rise to Plato's and Aristotle's misgivings is that the data of philosophy are our lived experiences and that youth lacks the necessary depth of experience on which to reflect philosophically. There is therefore a danger that philosophy will become for them simply a kind of conceptual geometry, an intellectual game that fails to connect with real life." (Casey, p. 248) Looked at from the outside, analytic philosophy can appear to be an essentially juvenile and shallow enterprise, conducted by philosophers possessed of the secret of eternal intellectual youth.

We have already seen that the Harvard Department of Philosophy places a premium on critical reading, the analysis and assessment of arguments, the detection of hidden assumptions in philosophical texts, the ability to construct tight logical arguments, and clarity and precision in language and in this it is at one with its fellow analytic Departments. The University of Michigan's Department of Philosophy webpage, continuing in the same vein as Harvard's, remarks that "learning to state one's position clearly, without ambiguity, and to set out systematically the considerations for and against it, is the key to writing a good philosophy paper, and most courses will encourage this skill." (University of Michigan, Department of Philosophy) This skill, of course, is no recent invention but goes back all the way to the foundation of the university when it was practically invented de novo by Peter Abelard in the 11th century. In his treatise *Sic et Non* (This Way and Not This Way), Abelard began the tradition of the critical assessment of the authoritative Christian Scriptures, setting out apparently contradictory passages side by side so that the apparent contradictions might be resolved by the power of human reason. This scholastic method, once elaborated, was then applied to other authoritative sources such as Aristotle in philosophy and the *Digest* and *Institutes* of Justinian in law. Over the centuries, the elaboration of this method seemingly for its own sake, especially the drawing of distinctions without any corresponding differences, brought it into disrepute. As should be obvious, this method, in modern guise, is heavily favored by analytic philosophers who, like their medieval scholastic predecessors, are often accused of logic chopping or arguing simply for the sake of arguing and of drawing distinctions that make little or no difference. Analytic philosophy—philosophy *tout court* for much of the Anglophone world—has become ever more technical and the problems it deals with are ever more peripheral to and remote from the 'big questions' from which philosophy started. "With the exception of a handful of lone wolves like Karl Jaspers, Jean-Paul Sartre and George Santayana," one author notes, "modern philosophy has retreated from the hurly-burly of everyday life to concern itself with technical issues of ever more esoteric import. In Europe the taste was for logical positivism and phenomenology, in the United States for symbolic logic, pragmatism or abstruse philosophy of science, while Britain retreated into the inane and scholastic cul-de-sac of linguistic philosophy." (McLynn, p. xiii) McLynn's comment, though remarkably dated in its specific references for a book written in 2010, is nonetheless substantially correct in its overall bearing.

Continental Philosophy is often characterized (or caricatured, if you prefer) as being obsessed with content to the virtual exclusion of form or structure and as manifesting a less than positive attitude to logic and argument, preferring instead the declamatory, edifying and naked assertion. (see Rorty 1981a, 1981b and 1984) There is a common perception, common among analytic philosophers at least, that continental philosophy is concerned with articulating the great vision, the grand narrative, and is more interested in edification than in truth. Rorty remarks that "philosophy professors in France and German have...more interest in the philosophers I call 'edifying' and in sweeping historical narratives than their British and American colleagues." (Rorty 1984, p. 87) As an example of such a narrative, Rorty instances Habermas's then-recent lectures on modernism and postmodernism at the College de France, saying of them that "The idea of getting straight on the contemporary philosophical scene by retelling a story that starts with Hegel and runs up through Nietzsche and Weber and Heidegger to Foucault would not occur to most Anglo-Saxon philosophers". (Rorty 1984, p. 98) I would say that it is not so much a matter of its not occurring to Anglo-Saxon philosophers as its not being considered by them a philosophical matter at all. There can be no doubt that the continental philosopher's concern with 'big' questions fits comfortably with the stereotypical view of philosophy as sketched at the start of this chapter in the "sounds more like amnesia" joke. But, as very quickly becomes evident, in order to answer these big questions, the discussion needs to shift sideways to consider other issues and, frequently, shift again and yet again until eventually, a process of radical peripheralization has taken place and now the questions being discussed appear to have little or no relevance to the original point of departure. A glance at some of the literature will show this to be so.

In the end, a philosophy would seem to require two essential dimensions. First, it must have some characteristic, distinct and comprehensive 'take' on 'God, man and the world', a distinct vision, if you like of what it is to be human, what the essential constitution of the world is and how all this relates to the transcendent, if there is any such realm. While this 'take' might be necessary for philosophy, it cannot be sufficient, not least because it shares this approach with religion, among other things. For philosophy to be philosophy, then it must not only have some distinctive and comprehensive 'take' on reality but it must have some systematic approach to investigating that reality and a broadly rational approach to articulating it. "Philosophy...has traditionally concerned itself with a relatively explicit and systematic attempt to formulate a scheme of beliefs that provide a general explanation of the meaning of reality and of its bearing on the significance of man in relation to that reality. And since philosophers increasingly tried to save their theories from sheer arbitrariness, they also developed a strong interest in arguments for their views..." (Hackett, pp. 12-13) These cursory comments are not meant to provide a simple-minded reconciliation of the two major philosophical schools that exist today, merely to indicate in the largest possible way, what, historically and thematically, philosophy has been and is.

* * * * *

Given what I have said, is it going to be simply impossible to indicate those skills that an intending graduate student in philosophy should have or acquire? To put my cards on the table, I believe, as indicated just now, that philosophy has two dimensions that are individually necessary and jointly sufficient to make an outstanding philosopher. These are a philosophy motor and a philosophy vision. The motor of philosophy is argument, construed as broadly as possible as the supplying of reasons, in principle available to all, for whatever claims are being made. Anyone can make claims; anyone else can simply deny them. Only claims backed by argument are philosophically pertinent. It follows, then, that a highly developed skill in logic, both formal and, perhaps even more pertinently, informal, is essential to the mastery of this aspect of philosophy. The vision that first-rate philosophy requires is a distinct personal approach to the fundamental recurring questions bearing on the transcendent, the human and the world in which we live.

Let me see if I can explain a little more clearly what I mean by this. Consider the world of classical music. One of the benefits of modern recording techniques is that it has made available to us a vast quantity of music that up to now was accessible only to those who could read music scores or who were lucky enough to have access to rare and sporadic live performances. Nowadays, the music of pretty much any composer of any note at all can be found in some recorded version or other. For music lovers, this is a wonderful situation to find themselves in but it has served to underscore something that many have long suspected. Among the legion of forgotten composers, there are very few who deserve to be unforgotten. Most of the great composers in the classical music canon are characterized not only by their technical skill but also by the fact that each has a distinctive 'voice' that music lovers come to know and love. I have in mind here composers such as Sibelius, Bruckner, Mahler, Shostakovich whose stature no one can doubt (among the musical greats, Tchaikovsky is perhaps the most prominent of the great composers whose 'voice' can sometime threaten to overwhelm his technique) and among the undeservedly neglected who should be unforgotten, a composer such as Franz Berwald. On the other hand, the world is oversupplied with highly competent and technical gifted composers who fail to combine their excellent techniques with a distinctive 'voice'. Their music is well made, enjoyable and eminently forgettable.

To apply this to philosophy: Reason, logic and argument—philosophical technique—just by itself can easily allow philosophy to degenerate into a scholastic form of logic chopping, as it did in the late Middle Ages and as it sometimes, perhaps all too frequently, does today; on the other hand, focusing on the 'big' questions without subjecting them to the rigors of argument easily lends itself to the production of skeleton-free quasi-intellectual rhapsody, the kind of thing that one finds in those works that provide a target for those who like to lampoon the intellectually pretentious. One calls to mind the spectacular spoof article written by Alan Sokal that was published in the mid-90s, entitled "Transgressing the Boundaries" whose subtitle,"Towards a Transformative Hermeneutics of Quantum Gravity" should, perhaps, have given rise to suspicion. (Sokal, passim).

The skills of the motor of philosophy can be taught, acquired and perfected; the ability to achieve a vision of philosophy cannot be taught. The only thing that teachers of philosophy can do in this respect is to encourage and not to destroy any nascent philosophical superstar. Philosophy graduate programs aim to provide a comprehensive technical training in philosophy and they are devised to produce competent practitioners of philosophy. As already mentioned, some universities will provide a mainly analytical training, some a continental training, and yet others will situate the more technical elements of their training in an historical context. However well devised such programs might be and however inspirational their teachers, it would be as foolish to expect that such programs will routinely produce an Aristotle, a Berkeley, or a Descartes as it would be to expect Schools of Music to routinely produce a Bach, a Beethoven, a Brahms or a Bruckner. There is no technique or method of training yet discovered that is capable of doing this in any field. Rorty remarks that there are "about as many edifying philosophers in a century as there [are] great and original poets or revolutionary scientific theories—perhaps one or two, if the century [is] lucky." (Rorty 1984, p. 84)

And so to practicalities. What does a would-be graduate student need to do to get into a good PhD program? What will such a student be expected to do once in a program? I can't guarantee the universal applicability of what I'm about to say but I believe it to be a reasonably accurate portrait of the professional philosophical scene. To have a chance of admission to a good program in a good university, you will need to be at or near the top of your undergraduate class, with very good grades—probably a minimum of 3.8 GPA in systems that use that classification or a First Class Honours or a High 2:1 in the British system and systems derived from it. A good writing sample is essential to any viable application. In today's extremely competitive environment (deVries notes that in 2004-5, NYU received 253 applications for 7 places and accepted 11) the closer to being publishable your writing sample is, the better. For North American universities, a strong GRE score is essential and as the GRE is increasingly being used by other university systems, that makes a good score in this test increasingly important. Admission committees can use your GRE score in different ways but one obvious one is to make a minimum score a necessary condition for further consideration so that all candidates falling below that level will immediately be eliminated. Your letters of reference must be enthusiastic but enthusiasm by itself will carry little weight unless the reference exhibits a real and evidence-based knowledge of your achievements and potential and speaks to these in some detail. A knowledge of the cultural context from which references come and the cultural context to which they are going is useful. Given their reputation for hyperbole, deserved or otherwise, West Atlantic references may well have to be partially discounted while, given their propensity for the use of litotes or meiosis, East Atlantic ones may need to be upgraded via a hermeneutics of self-deprecation.

Once you are accepted into a graduate program, what then? It hardly needs to be said that the more substantial a knowledge you have of philosophy before you arrive the better. To have read, in whole or in part, some or all of the works of Plato, Aristotle, Cicero, Marcus Aurelius, Augustine, Aquinas, Descartes, Hobbes, Locke, Hume, Mill and Nietzsche (to mention just some among the classics) and, among the moderns and contemporaries, for example, Nozick, Husserl, Parfit, Heidegger, Kripke, Chalmers, Searle and Putnam cannot but contribute to a successful graduate school career. Most graduate schools will require you to take a significant amount of courses distributed across a number of broad areas—epistemology, metaphysics, practical philosophy, and so on. In analytic schools, the satisfactory completion of a course in Logic at an intermediate level is normally a minimal requirement. Many programs will also require you to have or to acquire a reading competence in French and German and, if your research requires it, Latin or Greek. When you have completed your coursework, you will need to prepare for writing your dissertation. This sometimes takes the form of preparing a bibliography of the fundamental primary and most significant secondary works in the area in which your dissertation is located (philosophy of religion, metaphysics, or whatever) on which you will then be examined. Only when all this has been done, will you move on to the actual writing of your thesis upon the completion of which comes your final examination, the *viva voce*. And then you can start looking for an academic position!

*****

Philosophy is an intellectually incestuous discipline. The criteria it employs and the evidence it adduces are, in large part, internal to the inquiry itself in contrast, let us say, to chemistry, whose theories have to meet the demands of a reality exterior to chemical theories. That makes it difficult to say with either ease or certainty what skills a philosopher should have. Despite this, the great philosophers exhibit both a distinctive vision of reality in all its aspects—metaphysical, epistemological, ethical—together with an ability to give a rationally persuasive account of this vision. The latter ability—in its guise as logic and argument—is something that can be acquired and improved through education and, together with some measure of acquaintance with the thoughts of the great philosophers, constitutes the substance of a graduate school education; the former ability, as a species of native genius, can only be encouraged or discouraged; it cannot be taught. While there can be many competent and insightful practitioners of philosophy at any given time, Richard Rorty is right in thinking that if we produce one or two 'edifying' philosophers every hundred years or so, we are doing well.

REFERENCES

Adams, D. (2002 [1979-84]). *The Hitchhiker's Guide to the Galaxy: The Trilogy of Four*. London: Pan Macmillan.

Aristotle. (1962). *Nichomachean Ethics* (trans. M. Ostwald). Indianapolis: Bobbs-Merrill Educational Publishing.

Casey, G. (2009). Teaching Philosophy to the Gifted Young. *Gifted Education International*, 25, 246-258.

Curtis, R.& Elton, B. (1987). Dish and Dishonesty. *Blackadder the Third*. London: BBC1.

deVries, W. (No Year). Graduate Study in Philosophy. Retrieved 22 September, 2012, from http://www.unh.edu/philosophy/media/pdfs/Graduate-StudyAdvice.pdf

Garan, D. G. (1975). *The Key to the Sciences of Man: The 'Impossible' Relativity of Value Reactions*. New York: Philosophical Library.

Green, M. S. (2006). *Engaging Philosophy: A Brief Introduction*. Indianapolis: Hackett Publishing Company.

Hackett, S. C. (1979). *Oriental Philosophy: A Westerner's Guide to Eastern Thought*. Madison, Wisconsin: University of Wisconsin Press.

Harvard University, Department of Philosophy. (2012). Why Philosophy? Retrieved 29 September 2012, from http://www.fas.harvard.edu/~phildept/undergradprogram_-whyphilosophy.html

McLynn, F. (2010). *Marcus Aurelius: Warrior, Philosopher, Emperor*. London: Vintage.

Nagel, T. (2012). *Mind & Cosmos: Why the Materialist Neo-Darwinian Conception of Nature is almost certainly Wrong*. Oxford: Oxford University Press.

Plato. (1974). *The Republic* (trans. G. M. A. Grube). Indianapolis: Hackett Publishing Company.

Rorty, R. (1981a). *Philosophy and the Mirror of Nature*. Princeton: New Jersey: Princeton University Press.

Rorty, R. (1981b). Zür Lage der Gegenwarsphilosophie in den USA. *Analyse & Kritik*, 3, 3-2.

Rorty, R. (1984). A Reply to Six Critics. *Analyse & Kritik*, 6, 78-98.

Sokal, A. D. (1996). Transgressing the Boundaries: Towards a Transformative Hermeneutics of Quantum Gravity. *Social Text*, 46/47, 217-252. Retrieved 19 October, 2012, from http://www.physics.nyu.edu/sokal/transgress_v2/transgress_v2_singlefile.html.

University of Michigan, Department of Philosophy.(2012). Techniques and Tools of Philosophy. Retrieved 20 September, 2012, from http://www.lsa.umich.edu/philosophy/-undergraduate/techniquesandtoolsofphilosophy_ci

In: The Nurturing of Talent, Skills and Abilities ISBN: 978-1-62618-521-0
Editor: Michael F. Shaughnessy © 2013 Nova Science Publishers, Inc.

Chapter 9

SUPPORTING SOCIAL AND EMOTIONAL DEVELOPMENT OF GIFTED CHILDREN AND ADOLESCENTS

Lisa Rivero[*]
Milwaukee School of Engineering

SUPPORTING SOCIAL AND EMOTIONAL DEVELOPMENT OF GIFTED CHILDREN AND ADOLESCENTS

What do gifted children and adolescents need?

Many people answer this question by addressing academic needs, such as appropriate intellectual challenge or opportunities for college preparatory courses. The main goal, then, becomes giving gifted students the academic skills necessary to do well in school, to get good, if not perfect, grades and, ultimately, for many of them, to gain acceptance into top-tier universities.

However, our brightest students also have social and emotional needs that, while not always different in kind from those of their classmates, are often complicated by what it means to be gifted. When those needs are not met, and when children and teenagers do not have the skills necessary to face everyday social-emotional challenges and developmental crises, not only can their academic progress be jeopardized, but their life-span development may be affected.

Just what do we mean by "gifted," and how are the social and emotional needs of gifted children and adolescents any different, if at all, from those of other students?

---

[*] E-mail: lisarivero@sbcglobal.net.

GIFTED, SOCIALLY AND EMOTIONALLY

Defining giftedness is not a task for the faint of heart. Even the National Association for Gifted Children (NAGC) admits that there is "no universally agreed upon answer" to the question of just what giftedness is, and that the concepts of giftedness, intelligence, and talent "are fluid" and "may look different in different contexts and cultures" (2008). NAGC's own proposed definition is as follows:

> Gifted individuals are those who demonstrate outstanding levels of aptitude (defined as an exceptional ability to reason and learn) or competence (documented performance or achievement in top 10% or rarer) in one or more domains. Domains include any structured area of activity with its own symbol system (e.g., mathematics, music, language) and/or set of sensorimotor skills (e.g., painting, dance, sports). (NAGC, 2008)

The U. S. federal government defines gifted and talent youth as those who "give evidence of high achievement capability in areas such as intellectual, creative, artistic, or leadership capacity, or in specific academic fields, and who need services or activities not ordinarily provided by the school in order to fully develop those capabilities" (U.S. Department of Education, 2004, Section 9101.22). Several individual states use their own variations of the federal definition to identify students for gifted programming, and a debate continues as to the role that talent plays in giftedness, to what extent talent and giftedness differ or intersect, and even whether the word "gifted" has outlived its usefulness (Webb, Gore, Amend & DeVries, 2008).

Almost none of these perspectives, however, speaks primarily or seriously to the social and emotional experiences and needs of the gifted. While most people are familiar with giftedness as a function of high intelligence, identified primarily through IQ tests, fewer may know of a definition proposed in 1991 by a group of parents, teachers, and advocates concerned with what they saw as an overemphasis on the role of high achievement in the identification of gifted children. The Columbus Group (who met in Columbus, Ohio) saw giftedness primarily through the lens of asynchronous (uneven or out-of-step) development:Giftedness is asynchronous development in which advanced cognitive abilities and heightened intensity combine to create inner experiences and awareness that are qualitatively different from the norm. This asynchrony increases with higher intellectual capacity. The uniqueness of the gifted renders them particularly vulnerable and requires modifications in parenting, teaching and counseling in order for them to develop optimally. (Morelock, 1996, p. 8)

For the purpose of a discussion of social and emotional development, the Columbus Group's definition comes closest to addressing advanced intellectual ability combined with intensity of experience, while also acknowledging the sense of differentness felt by many gifted children and adults.

The international non-profit organization Supporting Emotional Needs of the Gifted (SENG) also focuses on social and affective components of giftedness[1]. SENG was created

---

[1] As a matter of disclaimer, at the time of writing this chapter, the author is a member of SENG's Board of Directors.

in response to the suicide of a gifted seventeen-year-old college student, whose parents contacted psychologist James T. Webb in search of programs that addressed the emotional needs of children like their son (Webb, 2008). While SENG does not put forth its own definition of giftedness, its mission statement is "to empower families and communities to guide gifted and talented individuals to reach their goals: intellectually, physically, emotionally, socially, and spiritually" (SENG, 2012).

GROWING UP, SOCIALLY AND EMOTIONALLY

Regardless of how we identify gifted students, their social and emotional development and needs are, in many ways, not very different from those of other children. For example, the nonprofit organization ZERO TO THREE (2012) defines social-emotional wellness for infants and toddlers as "the developing capacity to experience and regulate emotions, form secure relationships, and explore and learn—all in the context of the child's family, community and cultural background" (para. 2), a definition that most would agree holds for children of all ability levels.

We can also consider Erik Erikson's eight stages of psychosocial development, each of which is defined by a choice or crisis that must be resolved before we can move to the next stage (Erikson, 1993):

Birth to age 1 or 2: Basic Trust vs. Basic Mistrust
Early childhood (ages 2-3): Autonomy vs. Shame
Preschool (ages 3-5): Initiative vs. Guilt
Childhood (ages 6-11): Competence vs. Inferiority
Adolescence (ages 12-20): Identity vs. Role Confusion
Early adulthood (ages 20-40): Intimacy vs. Isolation
Middle adulthood (ages 40-65): Generativity vs. Stagnation
Ages 65 to death: Integrity vs. Despair

Erikson proposed that adolescents, for example, are "primarily concerned with what they appear to be in the eyes of others as compared with what they feel they are, and with the question of how to connect" their previously learned "roles and skills" with new and future roles and careers (p. 261). Adolescence is a time when "a future within reach becomes part of the conscious life plan" (p. 306). It is also a time of extremes: a struggle between idealism and elitism, potential overidentification "with the heroes of cliques and crowds," and a need to define oneself through belonging and comparing oneself to groups (p. 262). Jeffrey Arnett (2004) has argued that what Erikson called an occasional prolonged adolescence is more common now than ever before, as more young people go to college and are dependent on their parents for a longer period of time, leading to a new stage: emerging adulthood (ages 18 to the mid-twenties).

Arnett argues that, in the 21st century, the question of identity is resolved in emerging adulthood rather than in adolescence. However long the period of identity formation lasts, the needs of this stage go well beyond getting good grades or constructing the perfect university application.

ASYNCHRONOUS DEVELOPMENT

Erikson's first five stages provide a general framework by which to understand the psychosocial developmental for all children, regardless of how intelligent they are. A complicating factor for the gifted, what can require "modifications in parenting, teaching and counseling" (Morelock, 1996, p. 8), is asynchrony—the fact that gifted youth often mature in different areas at different rates, as Tracy Cross (2001) explains:

> Parents, teachers, and counselors should be aware that an individual gifted child may be affected by the psychosocial crisis at earlier ages than Erikson believed. Adults should realize that some gifted children have an intellectual ability to understand the world years ahead of their chronological age but have the emotional development typical of their same-age peers. (p. 54)

Sally Reis and Joseph Renzulli (2004) offer a different perspective on asynchronous development. Their overview of the research found that gifted children's ability to manage their emotional experience, rather than typical for their age, is "often more mature than expected for chronological age," and "some talented children are advanced in understanding their own emotions and demonstrate compassion, moral sensitivity, loyalty, and courage that can set them apart from their peers" (p. 122).

Stephanie Tolan (2007), co-author with James T. Webb and Elizabeth Meckstroth of the seminal book, *Guiding the Gifted Child*, reminds us of yet another potential area of asynchrony: sexual development. While their bodies may develop "on schedule," their cognitive understanding of what is going on in their bodies may be far ahead of age peers, and their emotional experience of puberty on another plane altogether.

Returning to Erikson, we can now see how asynchronous development can complicate the search for identity. Gifted children may begin to think about their long-term futures well before their classmates do, especially if they have been academically accelerated or enter college early. Because their roles can be more varied and complex than those of children who have fewer interests or talents, finding one or two groups in which to hone their identity is more difficult. Miraca Gross (1998) explains how giftedness in children complicates the usual stages of development:

> [M]any of the behaviors, attitudes and needs which are characteristic of adolescence appear in intellectually gifted children in the middle or later years of childhood. The psychosocial drives towards identity, autonomy, intimacy and achievement can be expected to intensify earlier in intellectually gifted children than in children of average ability, and intensification of these drives can increase the feeling of salience–even alienation–in the gifted young person who is already aware that she is different. (para. 15)

What, then, can adults expect from gifted children in terms of stages of development? Because gifted children are a heterogeneous group, with variations in intellectual ability, interests, and personality (Reis & Sullivan, 2008), there is no single developmental timetable or theory to which parents and teachers can turn to know what to expect or when to expect it.

The lesson we can draw is that our usual expectations of how and when children should development may not be appropriate for any given gifted child or adolescent, especially when we consider the "intensification" they bring to their development.

INTENSITY: A TALE OF TWO STUDENTS

I teach at a four-year engineering college, where the students are highly intelligent and driven, with a particular aptitude in science and math, and a tendency to focus passionately on their interests, in and out of the classroom. Even within this population, however, there are noticeable differences in students' intensity, an intangible quality that is, nonetheless, often instantly recognizable.

Consider two of my technical composition students this term: let's call them Jeremy and Robert. Both are extremely bright and capable. Both attend class regularly and do the work on time. But Jeremy is clearly going through the motions, concerned enough about his grades to take care to meet all of the requirements and to complete any extra credit I assign, even when he doesn't need it, yet not engaged by the material in any way (that I can see) that extends beyond the class.

Robert, on the other hand, won't let go of a concept until he understands it, regardless of whether he does well on an exam. He stays after class to follow up with questions, but forgets to turn in his extra credit assignment. His final paper, while well written, is longer than I had assigned and pushes the scope of what he realistically had time to research. When he gives his oral presentation, he rises on his toes with excitement as he talks about his chosen topic, and his eyes never turn off.

I would never presume to say that Jeremy is not gifted or to assume that if he isn't intensely interested in my class, he shows passion and engagement in no other areas of his life. However, Robert's obvious intensity, combined with his intelligence and ability, sets him apart from most other students in a way I can only think of as "gifted."

Mary-Elaine Jacobsen (2000), author of *The Gifted Adult*, describes intensity as "increased arousal," the "result of a sensory, neural, and emotional network that is more receptive and more responsive," that shows itself as "verbal agility, excitability, a strong sense of humor, exceptional concentration, empathy, emotional sensitivity, and high energy" (p. 258). This intensity complicates social and emotional development of the gifted, regardless of individual levels of achievement.

INTENSITY AS EXCITABILITY

One theory that has been discussed in recent years to help to explain the social-emotional experience of gifted children and adults is Kazimierz Dabrowski's (1964, 1967) Theory of Positive Disintegration. It is important to note that Dabrowski, a Polish psychologist and psychiatrist, did not intend his work to be a theory of giftedness, nor was he writing solely or necessarily about gifted individuals. However, teachers, researchers, and parents have found that much of his theory fits their experience of what it is like to "grow up gifted."

While Dabrowski's theory is far too complex to explore in detail here, his main idea is that people have varying degrees of potential for personal development, for which he outlined five levels. Those with a high potential for personal growth move through the levels as a result of positive disintegration, which is a breaking down of existing psychological structures to make way for a more conscious creation of one's personality. The lowest level of development and the highest level are both "integrated" levels, free from internal conflict, the difference being that the first level, primary integration, is a thoughtless integration, where one has no internal struggles because one does not recognize or acknowledge "what should be." The fifth level, secondary integration, occurs rarely, and is the result of a consciously created personality through periods of positive disintegration (Dabrowski, 1967).

Cheryl Ackerman (2009) describes several ways in which Dabrowski's Theory of Positive Disintegration differs from many other stage theories. For example, whereas many other theorists, such as Piaget and Erikson, tied their stages to specific age ranges, Dabrowski's theory is "unrelated to physical maturation" (p. 82). Personal growth and development, for Dabrowski, hinges as much on emotional growth and development as on intellectual, social, and physical growth. Also, integral to Dabrowski's theory is the view that inner conflict, including the conflict inherent in many forms of psychoneuroses and mental illness, is a necessary catalyst for personal growth and for the development of one's personality (Ackerman, 2009).

Dabrowski proposed that people who have the potential for advanced development have what he called "overexcitabilities," what Dabrowski expert Sal Mendaglio describes as a "heritable property of the central nervous system that produces greater than expected responses to internal and external stimuli" (Mendaglio). This is very similar to the description Jacobsen (2000) gives for "intensity." The five overexcitabilities (also referred to here as "OEs" or "excitabilities" or "intensities") are emotional OE, intellectual OE, imaginational OE, sensual OE, and psychomotor OE.

Dabrowski (1967) found that individuals with higher emotional and imaginational excitabilities were the most prone to the process of positive disintegration and to personality development (p. 148). In young children, however, intensity or excitability can seem more of a challenge than an advantage—both for the children and for the adults who care for and teach them—shown by these descriptions of OEs, adapted from Michael P. Piechowski's *'Mellow Out' They Say. If I Only Could. Intensities and Sensitivities of the Young and Bright* (2006):

- Emotional OE: Feelings and emotions intensified, strong physical reactions to emotions, capacity for strong attachments and deep relationships
- Intellectual OE: Intensified activity of the mind, passion for probing questions and problem solving, reflective thought
- Imaginational OE: Capacity for living in a world of fantasy, spontaneous imagery as an expression of emotional tension, low tolerance of boredom
- Sensual OE: Enhanced sensory and aesthetic pleasure, sensual expression of emotional tension
- Psychomotor OE: Surplus of energy, physical expression of emotional tension

Excitabilities can make children look and feel out of step with age peers who take life more in stride or who behave in ways that meet common expectations for their age and grade. For example, a young child who is emotionally excitable may, while watching a school play of Peter and the Wolf, identify so strongly with the characters that he begins to cry, which is compounded by feelings of shame when he is escorted out of the room by a teacher. Or a highly imaginative young girl may have difficulty disengaging from the world she has created in her mind long enough to complete math worksheets.

In social relationships, as well, excitabilities can pose challenges. Excitable children are often seen as too talkative, too sensitive, too curious, too "in their heads," or too active for usual childhood friendships and activities.

Even as these children mature into greater self-awareness and self-control, they do not grow out of their intense natures. In adults, emotional excitability "produces states of agitation and depression, sympathy for or dislike of oneself and the world, dissatisfaction with oneself and the environment, strangeness in relation to oneself and the environment, and feelings of inferiority or superiority" (Dabrowski, 1967, p. 61). Dabrowski wrote that the presence of excitabilities is "a sign that one's adaptability to the environment is disturbed" (p. 61), which, in his view, is a positive indication of the potential for personal growth. Consider the often quoted definition of insanity: Doing the same thing over and over again, but expecting different results. Overexcitabilities prod us to see and to do things differently, because we know not to expect different results, as our adaptions to the environment no longer work or satisfy.

It is important for adults who work with gifted children to understand the role that overexcitabilities may play in future personal development, so as to avoid either coddling children for their extreme feelings and behaviors, or punishing them unfairly. While it is true that excitable children and adults do not choose their inner intensity, they can learn early and in appropriate ways how to understand and, eventually, manage themselves. One effective way to begin to teach children about their personality responsibility is for adults to talk, in natural ways, about their own struggles and successes with managing intensity. Suppose, for example, that a mother chooses to leave a favorite library story time early because her young son's extreme reactions were interruptive. At some point on the way home, or after he calms down, she could tell him about her own memories of feeling "too much" to be able to participate in group activities, and of how she eventually learned to keep from saying everything she thought, and to feel her excitement on the inside, without always having to show it on the outside.

At the same time, parents and teachers should realize that what is normal and even healthy for gifted children in terms of feeling and behavior is often different from what we think of as normal in general, especially when we consider giftedness in terms of the Columbus Group definition of asynchronous development. As Leslie Sword (2003) writes, "Heightened sensitivity to things that happen in the world is a normal response for gifted children" (Emotional Immaturity or Emotional Intensity? section 6, para. 5). If adults view this normal response as something to be "cured" or fixed rather than understood and managed, gifted children can easily "see their own intense inner experiences as evidence that something is wrong with them" (Sword, 2003, Emotional Immaturity or Emotional Intensity? section 6, para. 9). Using the above example, rather than expect that her child sit quietly without any assistance, since "all the other children can," the mother could offer him an activity to occupy his hands and active mind, such as a notebook or sketchbook on which he can "take notes" so as to remember his questions for later. They could even have practice story times at home as he figures out how to contain his enthusiasm for short periods of time.

While a normal part of life for those with high developmental potential, overexcitabilities should never be used as an excuse for inappropriate behavior that a child can control (although it is difficult to know, at times, what truly is within a child's control). OEs should also not be equated with giftedness, however useful they might be in informal identification of gifted children.   Intellectual excitability is not the same as what most researchers understand as intelligence, and, in fact, some excitabilities (psychomotor and sensual), when present without the other three, may be a hindrance rather than a necessary component of advanced development (Mendaglio, 2012).

Overexcitabilities are only one part of Dabrowski's theory, and their value rests in their role in the development of personality.   Even more important to understand is that gifted children as defined by IQ tests may or may not be on a Dabrowskian path of personal development.

Remember that Dabrowski strove to offer a "comprehensive theory of personality" rather than a theory of giftedness (Mendaglio, 2012).   This is not to say that Dabrowski can't inform our understanding of gifted children and adults, only to caution that we not make OE's a shorthand for giftedness.

VULNERABLE, SOCIALLY AND EMOTIONALLY

In addition to their asynchronous development and intensity, gifted children and adolescents can be vulnerable in a number of other ways, three of which we will discuss here briefly: perfectionism, underachievement, and multipotentiality (Reis & Renzulli, 2004).

Empirical research has not concluded in what ways or even whether gifted children experience perfectionism more than other children, in part because of the lack of a single definition of what it means to be a perfectionist.   In groups of parents and teachers of gifted children, however, perfectionism is a perennial topic of discussion and concern.   Because the "urge to perfect" may be an innate aspect of giftedness (Jacobsen, 2000), adults can be careful not to criticize children for being perfectionists or to view perfectionism as necessarily unhealthy (Schuler, 2002). Some researchers, for example, distinguish between adaptive perfectionists, who consciously strive toward high goals, and maladaptive perfectionists, who feel that they can never be good enough (Wang, Fu & Rice, 2012).

Underachievement, like perfectionism, suffers from a lack of clear definition (Hoover-Schultz, 2005).   However, in general, children underachieve when they consistently fail to perform at levels of which they are capable.   Underachievement is "one of the most pervasive problems affecting gifted and talented students," and it can follow adolescents into adulthood (Reis & Renzulli, p. 121).

Multipotentiality refers to having high ability in several areas and the potential to excel in more than one career or endeavor.   Children and teenagers with multipotentiality can find it difficult to manage their time, to make choices that limit activities they love, and, ultimately, to choose a major and career.   Like perfectionism and underachievement, multipotentiality is a struggle for many adults as well as children.

SOCIAL AND EMOTIONAL DEVELOPMENT: HOW PARENTS AND TEACHERS CAN HELP

Complexity is a hallmark of giftedness, and no single set of guidelines will work for every gifted child. However, parents, teachers, and other adults who work and live with children and teenagers can keep in mind the following general suggestions:

Throw away your expectations of what is normal. Focus instead on what seems normal for a particular child. Even more, keep in mind that what is normal for that child can change from year to year, or circumstance to circumstance. David Willings, for example, found that some creatively gifted children can be extroverted in some situations, but introverted in others (1980).

Accept difficult emotions. When children express what we think of as negative emotions, such as anger or jealousy, adults can take a mental step back before instinctively trying to "fix" the feeling. Sal Mendaglio reminds us that emotions "are critical in Dabrowski's theory," and that all emotions, "especially negative emotions, are the forces of development—negative emotions drive personality development. Development rests with the transformative power of intense negative emotions" (Shaughnessy, 2010, para. 7). Mendaglio urges parents and other adults to accept the experience of all emotions in children, even when addressing how those emotions can be appropriately expressed.

Teach children how to set their own goals and schedules. Dominique Morisano and Bruce Shore urge adults to teach gifted children skills of personal goal setting as a possible intervention for underachievement. They remind us of the "important difference" between adults' goals for children and children's goals they set for themselves, and that "placing too much emphasis on academic performance can lead to perfectionistic tendencies" (p. 255). Adults can use scaffolding as a way to help students not to reach too high, too wide, or too low with their goals. An important aspect of goal setting in today's hyper-connected world involves striking a balance with use of technology, as William Powers (2010) reminds us in *Hamlet's Blackberry: Building a Good Life in the Digital Age*. Powers writes of the importance of "gaps," or cushions of time—harder and harder to come by—between practical experiences and any meaning we pull from them (p. 27). Teaching children such social-emotional skills as how to schedule gaps in their busy days prepares them not only for college, but for life.

Use media and technology in creative ways to support social and emotional development. Tracy Cross (2004) suggests that rather than viewing technology solely as an isolating influence, we use it creatively to provide social and emotional support for gifted students:

> [C]ommunicating with others via technology requires a modest degree of skill. Typing, navigating the Internet, word processing, composing, analyzing, and generally expressing one's thoughts and feelings are skills that can be enhanced using these forms of communication. All these examples are indicative of skills that can lead to an increasing sense of agency and positive self-concept. (p. 16)

For adults who are uncomfortable with technology, the chance to learn alongside (or from) the child also offers an opportunity to model life-long learning and risk taking.

Support children's interests. Because gifted children and adolescents are often defined by their potential for academic success, adults can be tempted to be more supportive of interests that lead to achievement in the classroom than interests that have no place in a standard curriculum, or that do not seem to lead to practical careers. However, Dabrowski (1967) argued that our peculiar and special interests, those that seem to come as gifts to us rather than our choosing them, regardless of whether they are in our areas of greatest talent, play a vital role in helping us to understand ourselves and our world, and in the creation of a mature personality.

Value process as well as product. For gifted children, especially at the beginning stages of learning a skill or subject area, success in the sense of products often comes quickly, with seemingly little effort. Think of a verbally gifted youngster whose "product" is being able to read several grade levels above age peers, without conscious effort on her part, or a musically talented child who breezes through early piano lessons to much acclaim at his first recital, even though other piano students practiced longer and harder. If adults praise the child for the reading or the piano performance, they are setting the stage for a fixed mindset, which Carol Dweck (2007) has found leads to avoidance of challenge and the belief that one's abilities cannot be developed. A better approach is to acknowledge and encourage process, effort, and intellectual risk-taking, especially when they lead to less than perfect products and other results.

Model and teach self-management. An unexpected benefit for adults who consider carefully how best to support the social and emotional development, needs, and skills of gifted youth, is that their own social and emotional skills improve in the process. Because we do not grow out of gifted intensity, gifted adults can, on a daily basis, offer children an example of what it means to work to understand and manage excitability. When possible, share stories of not only when you have controlled expression of explosive feelings, but, even more important, when you did not, what you learned from the experience, and how you forgave yourself and moved on.

We all would do well to remember that much of the social and emotional growth children and teenagers need happens outside the classroom, in their homes, with their friends, with their parents and other adults, and in moments of solitude. And, unlike knowing how to score well on a standardized test, social and emotional needs do not diminish with adulthood. There is no final exam, only the next lesson.

REFERENCES

Ackerman, C. (2009). The essential elements of Dabrowski's theory of positive disintegration and how they are connected. Roeper Review, 31(2), 81-95.

Arnett, J. (2004). The winding road from the late teens through the twenties. New York: Oxford University Press.

atia D Cross, T. (2001). Gifted children and Erikson's theory of psychosocial development. Gifted Child Today, 24(1), 54.

Cross, T. (2004). Technology and the unseen world of gifted students. Roeper Review, 27(4), 14-15,63

Dabrowski, K. (1967). Personality-shaping through positive disintegration. Boston: Little Brown & Co.

Dabrowski, K. (1964). Positive disintegration. Boston: Little Brown & Co.

Dweck, C. (2007). Mindset: The new psychology of success. New York: Ballantine Books.

Erikson, E. H. (1993). Identity and the life cycle (Reissue ed.). New York: Norton & Company.

Gross, M. (1998). The "me" behind the mask: Intellectually gifted students and the search for identity. Roeper Review, 20, 167-173. Retrieved October 31, 2012, from http://www.sengifted.org/archives/articles/the-me-behind-the-mask-intellectually-gifted students-and-the-search-for-identity

Hoover-Schultz, B. (2005). Gifted underachievement: oxymoron or educational enigma? Gifted Child Today. 28 (2), 46-49.

Jacobsen, M. E. (2000). The gifted adult: A revolutionary guide for liberating everyday genius. New York: Ballantine Books.

Mendaglio, S. (2012). Overexcitabilities and giftedness research: A call for a paradigm shift. Journal for the Education of the Gifted, 35, 207-219.

Morelock, M. J. (1996). On the nature of giftedness and talent: Imposing order on chaos. Roeper Review, 19(1), 4-12.

National Association for Gifted Children (NAGC). (2008). What is giftedness? Retrieved October 31, 2012, from http://nagc.org/index.aspx?id=57

Piechowski, M. (2006). "Mellow out," they say. If I only could: Intensities and sensitivities of the young and bright. Madison, WI: Yunasa Books.

Powers, W. (2010). Hamlet's Blackberry: A practical philosophy for building a good life in the digital age. New York: HarperCollins.

Reis, S. M. & Renzulli, J. S. (2004). Current research on the social and emotional development of gifted and talented students: good news and future possibilities. Psychology in the Schools. 41 (1), 119-130.

Reis, S.M. & Sullivan, E.E. (2008). Characteristics of gifted learners: consistently varied; refreshingly diverse. In F. Karnes & S. Bean (Eds.), Methods and materials for teaching the gifted, (pp. 3-36). Waco, TX: Prufrock Press.

Schuler, P. (2002). Perfectionism in gifted children and adolescents. In M. Neihart, S. M. Reis, N. M. Robinson, & S. M. Moon (Eds.). The social and emotional development of gifted children (pp. 71-79). Waco, Texas: Prufrock Press.

Shaughnessy, M. F. (2010). An interview with Sal Mendaglio: About meeting the emotional needs of gifted children and adolescents. Supporting the Emotional Needs of the Gifted. Retrieved October 31, 2012, http://www.sengifted.org/archives/articles/an-interview-with-sal-mendaglio-about-meeting-the-emotional-needs-of-gifted-children-and-adolescents

Supporting Emotional Needs of the Gifted (SENG). (2012). Mission/vision. Retrieved October 31, 2012, from http://www.sengifted.org/about-seng/missionvision

Sword, L. (2003). Gifted children: Emotionally immature or emotionally intense? Davidson Institute for Talent Development. Retrieved October 31, 2012, from http://www.davidsongifted.org/db/Articles_id_10241.aspx

Tolan, S. (2007). Sex and the highly gifted adolescent. Retrieved November 26, 2009, from www.stephanietolan.com/hg_adolescent.htm

U.S. Department of Education (2004). Elementary and secondary education: Title IX — general provisions. Retrieved October 31, 2012, from http://www2.ed.gov/policy/elsec/-leg/esea02/pg107.html.

Wang, K. T., Fu, C. C. & Rice, K. G. (2012). Perfectionism in gifted students: Moderating effects of goal orientation and contingent self-worth. School Psychology Quarterly, 27, 96-108.

Webb, J. T. (2008). SENG's 25th anniversary conference: Reflections on SENG's history. Supporting Emotional Needs of the Gifted. Retrieved October 31, 2012, from http://www.sengifted.org/archives/articles/sengs-25th-anniversary-conference-reflections-on-sengs-history

Webb, J. T., Gore, J. L., Amend, E. R., & DeVries, A. R. (2007). A parent's guide to gifted children. Scottsdale, AZ: Great Potential Press.

Willings, D. (1980). The creatively gifted: Recognizing and developing the creative personality. Cambridge: Woodhead-Faulkner.

ZERO TO THREE (2012). Tips for promoting social-emotional development. Retrieved October 31, 2012, from http://www.zerotothree.org/child-development/social-emotional-development/tips-for-promoting-social-emotional-development.html

In: The Nurturing of Talent, Skills and Abilities
Editor: Michael F. Shaughnessy

ISBN: 978-1-62618-521-0
© 2013 Nova Science Publishers, Inc.

Chapter 10

DEVELOPMENT AND NURTURANCE OF GIFTEDNESS

Roya Klingner

Global Center for Gifted and Talented Children
in Freising, Germany

All around the world there are children, who are different from the average children in their age group. This group of children has to deal with normality and their differences will accompany them from beginning to the end of their life.

As a former gifted child, I can feel, understand, and work with passion for children, who are different and we call them gifted kids.

This chapter centers on the following topics:

1. Definition of Giftedness from an international perspective
2. Why is development of talents and potential important for our society in the 21st century?
3. How can we nurture Giftedness in our bright kids best?
4. Development and Nurture of Giftedness in different countries

1. DEFINITION OF GIFTEDNESS FROM AN INTERNATIONAL PERSPECTIVE

For centuries, the psychologists have dealt with the topic of giftedness and so far they have yet to agree on a common definition.

There is still no unity in using a correct designation for gifted kids. Do we call them bright kids or gifted kids and what about high potential or high ability kids? Whatever we call them for me those kids are just stars. My whole life, I have wanted to help them and in my eyes they are little shining stars. The identification of gifted children depends on more than just a theoretical basis of the definition of giftedness or talent. It also requires interviews with parents, teachers, and the child itself.

Tina was a very happy gifted child full of power, emotion and energy. She came into the first grade in a regular school with a young teacher, who had never heard about those high potential kids. The teacher was only supposed to do school curriculum and practice all theoretical stuff that she had learned before. For example, all kids were supposed to raise their hands if they wanted to answer. When the teacher noticed Tina was able to answer all her questions, but most of the time did not raise her hand before answering, the teacher began to ignore her and sometimes punished her by sending her into a corner all alone. After a year, Tina slowly turned into a very quiet and introverted child. Her teacher was proud that she had changed the Tina into a "normal" average child. This is sad reality and happens in many schools around the world. Our bright kids, our shining stars are smothered this way. Incredible!

The Models of Giftedness by Heller, The Munich Model of Giftedness (MMG) (2001) and Gagné's Differentiated Model of Giftedness and Talent (The DMGT 2.0) (2012), see figure 1, are shown below.

The Munich Model of Giftedness (MMG) was created by Prof. Kurt Heller. It conceptualizes giftedness as a multifactorized ability construct within a network of non-cognitive (e.g. motivation, interests, self-concept, control expectations) and social moderators which are related to the giftedness factors (predictors) and the exceptional performance areas (criterion variables).

Gagné's Differentiated Model of Giftedness and Talent (The DMGT 2.0) proposes a clear distinction between the two most basic concepts in the field of gifted education. Gagné differentiates clearly between gifts (natural abilities) and talents (systematically developed from gifts). I believe Gagné's model is very helpful for the development of talent in schools. The importance of fate in his model might be difficult to understand, but it should not be underrated.

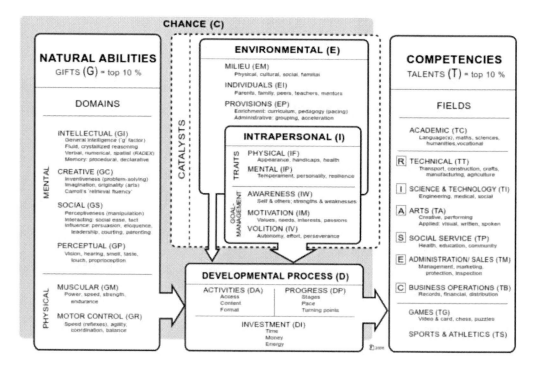

Figure 1. Gagné's Differentiated Model of Giftedness and Talent (The DMGT 2.0) (2012).

Here is another definition of giftedness from the Netherlands:

"A gifted person is a fast and clever thinker, who can manage complex things. Autonomous, curious and driven. A sensitive and emotional human being, living intensively. He or she is enjoying creating things."

'Hoogbegaafd Dat zie je zò!', from Maud Kooijman and co, a definition from 20 experts on giftedness

Even though there still is no unified definition for giftedness, I believe that giftedness is a genetic trait influenced by its environment, which needs support and education to develop it to its fullest.

2. WHY IS DEVELOPMENT OF TALENTS AND POTENTIAL IMPORTANT FOR OUR SOCIETY IN THE 21ST CENTURY?

Gifted kids are important for creative thinking, solving problems, being innovative. Because of that our society should be more interested to develop their potential for more performance. Society should take care of their emotional needs as well but are they really interested to give attention to this area? This is the reason for many of the problems and complaints of parents with gifted children. As long as our society accepts and supports them our gifted kids usually have fewer problems.

We do not need to be gifted in order to help and support gifted children but we should learn the skills of the 21st century and understand the learning style and personality of gifted children.

Another important factor is the exchange of knowledge and experiences with other gifted educators globally. Through the use of modern technology this becomes easier today. We have developed a program for gifted educators for giving them the opportunity to attend presentations of their peers in a virtual environment. This event, the Global Virtual Meeting, takes place once a month in SecondLife^{TM}. One of our speakers in 2012 was Professor Francois Gagné. He created an avatar and gave a presentation about his model and answered questions from the audience afterwards.

3. HOW CAN WE NURTURE GIFTEDNESS IN OUR BRIGHT CHILDREN BEST?

The fact is that we need a group of scientists to understand and support their special needs. Gifted and bright kids need a group of the following scientists: a medical doctor, a psychologist, a pedagogue, a sociologist, and a personal mentor to support their interests (in many cases parents fill this part).

We know that many highly able kids have more than one interest area and therefore they need more than one mentor for education and development of their competences and potentials in their life but our school system is not able to fulfill this kind of one to one teaching. In many countries of the world, our gifted kids are left behind in school. The main problem is inadequate teacher training.

Consulting parents, workshop and lectures for teachers, networking between gifted educators around the world and sharing experiences, organizing out of school activities for gifted kids to follow their interest, ...

Diversity is the key of best practice to develop giftedness and creativity.

But we also have to figure out the way to help them finding their balance and thus support them to develop not just their talents but also values and personality.

There are so many ways to develop gifts and potentials, but it is our duty to consider the interests and wishes of the children in the program, as well, instead of focusing on performance only. Most importantly never forget besides being gifted, they are still children, with high emotional needs!

4. DEVELOPMENT AND NURTURE OF GIFTEDNESS IN DIFFERENT COUNTRIES

Gifted programs in different countries are best described by those who apply them in their country. Therefore I asked specialists from different countries to describe the development of giftedness in their country. All of them are specialists in gifted education and have several years of experience working with gifted children.

I would like to thank them for their willingness to help with this article.

4.1. Development and Nurturance of Giftedness in Vietnam

Nga Giap Binh
Hanoi National University of Education, Vietnam

1. Some Information of Gifted Education in Vietnam

Gifted education in Vietnam initiatives started with national competitions in main subjects such as mathematics and literature from the beginning of the 1960s. From 1965, the first "special mathematics classes" were established (Nguyen, 2011). After the war (1975) until now, there have been expansions of special subjects, such as physics, chemistry, literature, foreign languages, biology, geography, informatics and history, in parallel with the setting up of selective schools nationwide. From the 1990s onwards, the concepts and models of selective schools in primary and lower secondary levels have been banned in order to avoid young learners' "overloading". However, the "special classes" in these school levels still exist to meet the needs of gifted children and their parents. Officially, there are 76 selective high schools, including 9 gifted "schools within schools" in the universities and other models, with about 50,000 gifted students, account for 1.74% of same age peers in national schools (Nguyen, 2009).

The first national conference on gifted education in Vietnam was organized on the 14th of September 2007 in Hai Phong City. The main aim of the conference was to review the development of Vietnamese gifted education over 42 years, and to identify innovative directions for further developments. For the first time, a systematic organization was proposed, not only for the development of gifted education, but also for a more efficient operation of the whole educational mechanism, through all levels, from kindergarten up to tertiary education. Based on preliminary developments of the first conference on gifted education, on the 26th of December 2009, the second conference was held in Nam Dinh City with the participation of over 60 schools for gifted students in Vietnam. Several proposals were submitted with the purpose of building and upgrading school systems in Vietnam to better equip gifted students with high technology and modern infrastructure. A preparation plan for the next 10-15 years of future developments was designed. It was mentioned in the documents that full and well-rounded developments of students needed to be paid attention to, to ensure that students were fully prepared for the challenges of the 21st century, the century of technology. Additionally, teachers from schools for gifted students are required to frequently upgrade their knowledge, expertise and methodology to keep up with current trends (Nguyen T.M.P, 2011). With regard to teacher training and practicing at the university level, the first faculty on this issue is the faculty of Special Education in the Hanoi National University of Education, but up to now the gifted education subjects are still in progress.

In several cases, schools for gifted learners concentrate only on the preparation of exams for their students. They aim to achieve high results in competition rather than in knowledge, and thus do not pay sufficient attention to remaining subjects at schools. Consequently the lack of understanding knowledge in other subjects is not a surprising phenomenon. Students are forced to spend their time studying only specialized subjects instead of those required by the national curricula. That leads to the fact that students in gifted schools, though at a very high level in their specialized subjects, have limited knowledge in other domains in schools (Mai Minh, 2009). This is a dangerous situation where well-rounded developments are required from future generations of the nation.

The quality of gifted education is also of serious concern. Though gifted students receive many international awards and scholarships from prestigious universities around the world, they lack essential skills for critical thinking, creative thinking, original research, and creative problem-solving skills (Mai Minh, 2009). These skills have been proved to be of significant importance for students in this fast changing world. If these students are to become scientists in the future, these skills are undoubtedly essential for their future careers. Furthermore, to achieve high accomplishments in any stage of their lives, gifted students need to be equipped with these skills. Further training in this area should be addressed as quickly as possible in the current context of globalization.

There are some impeded factors to Vietnam gifted education. Firstly, there is a popular belief in Vietnam that good for all is better than the good for some. This means that the differentiated curriculum for gifted learners have not been developed strongly until now. Although there are the recommendations in teaching gifted students in several specific subjects, the teachers of those gifted classes still have had to find their own way to design the curriculum for their high able students.

Secondly, by referencing the so-called international models which are not truly for gifted students in Vietnam, several selective schools wind up with a lack of systematic approach.

Thirdly, most of gifted students and teachers have been extremely worried about the university entrance examination, and therefore have spent a large amount of time in practicing those lower skill levels (Minh Kim, 2011).

Currently, Vietnam plans to spend VND 2.31 trillion (USD 118.6 million) towards the development of its gifted high schools system: Specifically, about VND 624 billion (USD 32 million) will be spent on professional development. By 2020 each city or province will have at least one gifted high school. The number of students who attend gifted high schools in a city or province accounts for about 2% of the total number of high school students in that area. The country also has set a goal that by 2015, all gifted high schools across Vietnam will reach a national standard. (Dantri.vn, 2010)

2. Perspectives and the Future of Talent Development

In the current situation, talent development in Vietnam mostly concentrates on intellectual giftedness. It is expected that in the next few years, provisions for gifted students in many other fields rather than in only the academic domain will be catered to. Furthermore, identification of gifted students in rural and remote areas, especially among the group of minority ethnic students, imposes critical issues. Rising awareness of the identification issues in rural and mountainous areas is essential to create the favorable conditions for gifted students to grow. As the global economy is moving towards the knowledge economy, it is vital to realize that the talents of our children are precious treasures of the nation and that these talents should be nurtured (Nguyen T.M.P, 2011). To do this, the author is developing a model for gifted education in Vietnam called the Hanoi Tower Model of Excellence (HTME). Like other multidimensional models of high ability (Gardner, 1983; Heller and Ziegler, 2001a; Heller, 2010; Sternberg and Powell, 1982), it is implemented in Vietnam as a project in Education funded by World Bank (Teaching, Research Innovation Grant –TRIG).

Using the Hanoi Tower Model of Excellence to Guide Instruction

The various theories of ability that were formulated during the first half of the twentieth century are of limited value to educators because they do not allow teachers to match instructional approaches and learning assessments to abilities. For example, the Stanford-Binet-5 or the Wechsler Intelligence Scale for Children – IV, are designed to rank students according to how they score rather than to assess how they think, their basic educational use is to determine eligibility for programs for the gifted and talented, learning disabled, and mentally retarded. What sets the HTME apart is the belief in a broad view of Minds that not only determine the gifted and talented (by creating psychological profiles of extraordinarily intellectually gifted children, young people, as well as adults) but also inform instructional practice and improve student performance. Table 1 describes each aspect of mind and provides examples of the kind of person who best represents each one.

Based on the HTME, we propose a teaching and assessment model. We suggest that for any grade level and for any subject, teaching and assessment can be designed to emphasize some or all types of ability. To take into account individual differences, instruction and assessment should involve all abilities. At some point, each student has an opportunity to excel because the task and related test match the student's ability. Notice that we do not suggest that all instruction and assessment match a student's dominant ability.

Some attempts need to be made to strengthen abilities that are relatively weak. We believe that teacher should use the HTME as a framework for devising alternative ways to teach subject matter. Some children learn a subject best when it is presented in a particular format or emphasizes a particular type of ability, whereas other children learn well when the subject is taught under different conditions (Checkley, 1997).

Table 1. The aspects of mind and illustrated examples

Mind	Core Components: f{intellectual powers}	End States
Logical-mathematical	Sensitivity to, and capacity to discern, logical or numerical patterns; ability to handle long chains of reasoning	Scientist Mathematician
Spatial	Capacities to perceive the visual-spatial world accurately and to perform transformations on one's initial perceptions	Sculptor Navigator
Distributed	Abilities related to creating artificial intelligence, to be sensitive to, or have the capacity for new technology, media	Programmer Designer
Naturalist	Ability to recognize and classify the numerous plants and animals of one's environment and their relationships on a logical, justifiable basic; talent of caring for, taming, and interacting with various living creatures	Botanist Entomologist
Existential	Ability to be sensitive to, or have the capacity for, conceptualizing or tackling deeper or larger questions about human existence	Leader Astrologer
Bodily-kinesthetic	Abilities to control one's body movements and handle objects skillfully	Dancer Athlete
Musical	Abilities to produce and appreciate rhythm, pitch, and timbre; appreciation of the forms of musical expression	Violinist Composer
Linguistic	Sensitivity to the sounds, rhythms, and meanings of words; sensitivity to the different functions of language	Poet Journalist
Intrapersonal	Access to one's own feelings and the ability to discriminate among them and draw on them to guide behavior; knowledge of one's own strengths, weaknesses, desires, and intelligences	Person with detailed, accurate self-knowledge
Interpersonal	Capacities to discern and respond appropriately to the moods, temperaments, motivations, and desires of other people	Therapist Salesperson

f = Memory → Thought → Imagination → Intelligence → Creativity → Wisdom

Note. The factor f one important concept in mathematics is function composition.

The HTME should lead to increased transfer of learning to out-of-school settings. Because it helps students mentally represent ideas in multiple ways, they are likely to develop a better understanding of the topic and be able to use that knowledge in everyday life. For the same reason, we also suggest that learning in out-of-school settings should lead to increased transfer of learning in school subjects. For example, musical mind – both listening to music and taking music lessons – have been shown to have a positive relationship with scores on a variety of cognitive measures (Schellenberg, 2006a). Listening to music that one enjoys enhances performance on a variety of cognitive performance measures for both adults and children. For preschool-age children, listening to music enhances creativity (Schellenberg, 2006b).

How can teacher apply HTME to teaching? We now know 10 aspects of mind (Logical-mathematical, Spatial, Distributed, Naturalist, Existential, Bodily-kinesthetic, Musical, Linguistic, Intrapersonal, and Interpersonal), assuming that each of them has 6 hierarchies of intellectual powers: memory, thought, imagination, intelligence, creativity, and wisdom called f {intellectual powers} (see table 1). We have 10 x 6 = 60 alternatively possible ways to teach students to enable their potential. The teaching methods of teacher should focus on how to develop their memory, how to develop their thought, how to develop their imagination, how to develop their intelligence, how to develop their creativity, and how to develop their wisdom in the future.

Using the Hanoi Tower Model of Excellence to Study Development

Regarding talent development, the approach of HTME is focused on the child "to be" or "the future child", rather than on "the present child" or what he/she is like at this moment. American researchers are constantly seeking to discover how the child came to be what he/she is; we in Vietnam are striving to discover not how the child came to be what he/she is, but how he/she can become what he/she not yet is *Children are not only children but also developing adults*". Because of this focus, the emphasis in the HTME's paradigm is on the higher level of the developing mind (cognition) or what the child will be in time. What we need is a way to study the different level of information processing that occurs between the current state and tomorrow's state. We study the child as new concepts or skills emerge. We design the hints, prompts, materials, clues, interactions, and other assistance to reveal not just what the child learns but how the child learns (Elena et al, 2007). A child is given a novel learning task, and we monitor which elements of the context are used by the child. Furthermore, we use technology to enhance the developing mind.

Using Technology to Develop Mind

Various technology tools may strengthen different minds. Technology education can support higher-level thinking such as metaphorical and analogical thinking; it provides students opportunities to "think outside the box" and develop their cognitive capabilities (Lewis, 2005).

Technology has an important role to play in fostering the development of mind. For example, computer programs allow students who can not read music or play an instrument to create musical compositions. With hypermedia, the learner can explore facts, concepts, or knowledge domains and immediately traverse to interesting links or appealing presentation formats. Most websites use hypermedia, and so do computerized encyclopedias and many other types of educational software. Programs that make it easy to do concept mapping, flowcharts, photo editing, and three-dimensional imaging are closely tied to visual-spatial mind. Idea generation and prewriting software tools, such as Sunbuddy Writer, Imagination Express, and Thinking Creatively with Picture LONGA, can assist linguistic mind. Computer programming with tools such as LOGO or the programming language of Visual Basic might help students' problem-solving and logical-mathematical mind. Clearly, there are many technology tools for all the aspects of mind that were described in the HTME.

As a teacher, these tools allow you a great deal of flexibility. With the many options that hypermedia applications offer, you can allow students to choose ways of learning that match their own strongest abilities, or you can have students use software that helps them improve in areas in which they are weak.

4.2. Development and Nurturance of Giftedness in Australia

Derrin Cramer
Gifted Education Consultant by Thinking Ahead in Australia

Australia is a vast continent and the population of just 22 million people is thinly spread. While the majority is clustered in the capital cities, 40% of Australians live in cities of less than 1 million people, and a little over 1 in 10 lives in rural areas, with many being several hours drive from the nearest population centre. Australia is now one of the most multicultural countries. A quarter of Australians were born overseas and our citizens arrive from more than 50 countries.

Each of these aspects of our country and culture has an impact on the development and nurturance of giftedness in Australia. Not only are some families with children isolated and far from resources or opportunities for the development of their potential, the characteristics which are valued by different cultural groups vary and while some seek recognition for academic ability, others shy from opportunities, even when they are identified and opportunities are available. The problem is especially apparent with our small indigenous population who, although they comprise 2.3% of our students, are not readily identified with traditional testing methods.

Since 1988, there have been two national level Government inquiries into the Education of Gifted and Talented Students. The second concluded that gifted children have special needs within the education system and noted *"that for many their needs are not being met; and many suffer underachievement, boredom, frustration and psychological distress as a result".* (Foreword).

It went on to note that an estimated 75% of gifted students are underachieving (performing below their level of potential).[1] Sadly, the situation has not changed very much since then and many of our gifted children continue to go through school without being identified and, as a result, their talents and capabilities remain largely undeveloped. Many do indeed suffer distress due to the educational, emotional and social deprivation as suggested by the report.

Perhaps part of the reason is that the 'Tall Poppy Syndrome' (a term used in Australia, New Zealand, Canada and the UK to express resentment or 'cut down' the achievements or talents of those who stand out from their peers) is deeply embedded in the Australian psyche, contributing to our seeming lack of willingness to identify and develop the talents of our brightest young minds.

---

[1] Submissions made to, and the recommendations of the Senate Select Committee on the Education of Gifted and Talented Children can be found in *The Education of Gifted Children. Collins, J. (Chair). 2001* Canberra: Commonwealth of Australia.

Education is the responsibility of individual states and territories within Australia resulting in variations in the age at which students begin and complete their school years, as well as the opportunities available to students. A consistent approach to the identification, nurturance and development of talent is further complicated by the existence of three school systems-Government, Independent and Catholic - within each state and territory. While some systems within some states do have a Policy document regarding gifted students, this is inconsistent and there remains no national requirement to identify or nurture giftedness in students. The introduction of a National Curriculum in 2013 may be a first step towards a more consistent approach but parents and educators have expressed concerns that this new curriculum makes no mention or provision for gifted students in Australia.

While the opportunities available in Independent and Catholic schools can vary considerably depending on priorities, some State Government Departments' of Education have made opportunities available with a limited number of selective entry high school programs available in some states. Opportunities during the Primary School years remain more limited although gifted classes or pull-out enrichment programs are offered in states in the final years of primary school, with places offered based on the results of selection testing.

Technological advancements are helping to reduce the distance for gifted students in rural areas with some online courses now becoming available for gifted students in regional and remote areas, allowing them to meet online and work on collaborative projects with other like minds.

The vast majority of teachers in Australian schools have little or no training in giftedness. Only two universities in Australia include a required unit on gifted students in their pre-service teacher training. 2 Psychologists, whether working in schools or in private practice also qualify without any requirement for training in the area of giftedness. A consequence of this situation is that parents frequently find they are the most knowledgeable party at advocacy meetings at schools, but often feel they are the least heard. An increasing number of families with gifted children are choosing to home educate their children when they find the system unresponsive to their child's learning needs or they are unable to find an appropriate 'fit' for their child.

While there is no doubt Australia has some passionate educators who truly bring giftedness to light in their students, the nurturance and development of giftedness and talent in this country remains patchy and limited, despite our gifted children being are our greatest and most valuable natural resource.

4.3. Development and Nurturance of Giftedness in Mexico

Ingrid Dallal Fratz, M.A.
Director of Ingennios Illuminare in Mexico

Mexico has often been called "the land of contrasts" because of the national tendency to combine the ancient with the modern in many human endeavors; this description aptly describes the national educational system in general, as it does, the Special Education efforts towards the gifted.

---

[2] Taylor, T., Milton, M. "Preparation for teaching gifted students: An investigation into university courses in Australia" *Australasian Journal of Gifted Education* Vol 15 (1) June 2006.

In very concrete terms, the official institutions still privilege the students of federal schools, at times including the private schools, evaluating their academic performance grade average and, at many points, good behavior in the classroom. Selected children from all over the country have an annual breakfast with the President of Mexico and, increasingly, they are given scholarships that the government and some private foundations hope will keep good students in schools for a longer time.

The majority of programs take such measures as sufficient and small numbers of students trickle down to receive the opportunity of psychological and educational testing in an environment where the Intelligence Quotient reigns supreme. There are federal, state and local public and private institutions that offer "programs": essentially, follow-up, some form of scholarship or stimuli, some special classes and lots of publicity. The admission fee is an IQ of 130 or more.

In recent years, there have been small numbers of specialists in the theory and practice of discovering, defining and assisting gifted individuals. These few specialists despair because their professional qualifications cannot be translated into official documents since their training is not offered in Mexico, but their efforts have begun to have an impact in Mexican society as they become known through the social media and results of individual care handling can become known to general public.

These specialists are advocating for a new paradigm, shifting from the quantitative to the qualitative approach where horizontal acceleration is preferred to grade skipping. Electronic media makes this possible and gifted children are developing a three dimensional neurological network instead of memorizing facts that do not create enough connections for them to embrace their gifts and talents in a productive environment.

Such environment fights change because it means "thinking out of the box" or daring to move to autonomous development of what is still considered abnormal, causing fear of leaving their comfort zone.

Mexico, land of contrasts, is definitely part of the fight to give gifted children better opportunities.

4.4. Development and Nurturance of Giftedness in Iran

In Iran: development of rules and regulations is done by the Islamic Parliament, Higher Council of Education and the Cabinet. According to the article 30 of the IRI Constitution the government is obliged to provide all citizens with free education up to the end of secondary school and must expand free higher education to the extent required by the country for attaining self-sufficiency. Under article education should be gratuitous. Some of the rules and regulations approved by the authorized bodies in this regard are presented in the appendix.

Compulsory schooling is 5 years at present which covers 6 to 10 year old children.

According to the Third Five Year Development Plan it will cover 6to 13 year old children which will improve compulsory schooling to 8 years. In order to improve the quality of educational activities, the assessment system which is one of the effective factors in teaching/learning process has been revised.

There are many reasons why this reform was made, some of which are outlined as: the previous system was based on traditional, non-scientific and ineffective methods. The actual usage of the finding in the real life was neglected and there was overemphasis on a great deal of knowledge.

In their form process some objectives like, matching the assessment methods with scientific findings, increasing the efficiency and effectiveness of school teachings and students active participation in teaching -learning process were taken into consideration.

The I.R. of Iran has been trying hard, during the recent years, to increase the enrollment rate, in other words, to increase schooling chances for various groups of people regardless of their gender, age, tribal and ethnic diversities , In this regard the priority has been focused on the education of school age (6-10 year old) children. It has taken efficient measures and practical strategies in the framework of the country's second development plan to achieve this main objective.

All schools of gifted and talented students in Iran are supported completely by Iranian Ministry of Education and there is a special budget for these educational centers. Educational material and curriculum are much different from ordinary education in the country and gifted students are supposed to pass many laboratory and theoretical subjects in school. At the end of each year more than 90% of Ir5anian talented students are enrolled in high level public universities and continue their study under the supervision of Talented Students System there.

4.5. Development and Nurturance of Giftedness in Germany

Germany is a federal state where each of the 16 federal countries has the right to do its own school politics.

So, it is not possible to describe in a few words what is going on with gifted education in Germany. The way gifted education is implemented in the German school system varies within the 16 federal states. Therefore, gifted education in Germany can only be evaluated by keeping the state-by-state difference in mind. While in some states giftedness is explicitly addressed in educational policy other states reference appropriate measures for extra support of gifted pupils. These support measures are (but not limited to) early enrolment to primary school, grade skipping, the revolving door policy, and the freedom for students to attend upper level classes. In most states schools provide parents and students with psychological services.

Cooperation with universities across the country is yet another resource and area of support in the giftedness community. Summer camps, private consulting organizations and specialized courses are available to educators, the gifted and their parents, however these services can be costly and therefore not equally accessible and available to everybody.

Talented students in Germany have the possibility to participate in state and countrywide competitions. Upon identification, children have the possibility to enter primary school before the age of six, given the condition that they can fully integrate into school life and are cognitively, physically and socially competent. Parents have to provide expert evaluations for an early in school admission, whereas grade skipping may only require teacher recommendations, student motivation and grades. Additionally psychological examinations may be conducted but are not necessary.

REFERENCES

Checkley, K. (1997) *The First Seven...and the Eighth: A Conversation with Howard Gardner.* Educational Leadership, Vol. 55, No. 1. September 1997.

Dantri.vn. (2010). Ministry of Education overhauling gifted programmes in high schools. Retrieved from http://www1.dtinews.vn/news/education.

Elena Bodrova and Deborah J. Leong (2007). *Tools of the mind: the Vygotskian approach to early childhood education,* 2nd Edition. Merrill Prentice Hall: Books.

Gagné, F. (2005). From gifts to talents: The DMGT as a developmental model. In R.J. Sternberg and J.E. Davidson (Eds.), conceptions of giftedness (2nd ed, pp. 98-120). Cambridge, UK: Cambridge University Press.

Gardner, H. (1983). *Frames of mind: The theory of multiple intelligences.* New York: Basic Books.

Heller, K. A. (2004). Identification of gifted and talented students. *Psychology science*, 46, 302-323.

Heller, K. A. (2010). The Munich Model of Giftedness and Talent. In Heller, K. A. and Ziegler, A (Eds.), *Talent-Expertise-Excellence, Vol.6* (pp. 3-12). Munich Studies of Giftedness. LIT Verlag.

Heller, K. A. and Ziegler, A. (2001a). Attributional Retraining: A Classroom-Integrated Model for Nurturing Talents in Mathematics and the Sciences. In N. Colangelo and S.G. Assouline (Eds.), *Talent Development, Vol. IV* (pp. 205-217). Scottsdale, AZ: Great Potential (Gifted Psychology) Press.

Lewis,T. (2005). Coming to terms with engineering design as content. *Journal of Technology Education, 16*(2), 37-54 Lubart, T.I (2000-2001).

Mai Minh (2009). Speech on the Conference on gifted schools in Vietnam in 15/09/2007m. Retrieved from http://vietbao.vn/Giao-duc/Hieu-dung-ve-truong-chuyen/30197279/202/.

Minh Kim, 2011 Gifted Education - Vietnam and international perspectives Retrieved from http://www.1vietnamedu.com/2011/06/gifted.

Nguyen, H. (2009). Selective schools will be the role models of nationwide schools in the future (in Vietnamese).Vietnam Education and Times. Retrieved from http://www.gdtd. vn/channel/2741/200912/Truong-THPT-chuyen-se-la-mau-hinh-tuong-lai-cua-cac-truong-THPT-1920322/.

Nguyen, T. M. P. (2011). Gifted education in Vietnam throughout history. Talent Development Around the World. Retrieved from http://worldtalent.fundetal.org/libros/ver_libro.php?IDlibro=7.

Pfeiffer,S.I. (2008). Handbook of Giftedness in Children. Psychoeducational Theory, research,and Best Practices. Springer Science+Business Media, LLC.

Schellenberg E. G. (2006a). Exposure to music: The truth about the consequences. In G. E. McPherson (ed.), *The Child as Musician* (pp. 111-134). Oxford: Oxford University Press.

Schellenberg E. G. (2006b). Long-term positive associations between music lessons and IQ. *Journal of Educational Psychology*, 98, pp. 457-468.

Sternberg, R. J., and Powell, J. S. (1982). Theories of intelligence. In R. J. Sternberg (Ed.), *Handbook of human intelligence* (pp. 975-1005). New York: Cambridge University Press.

Steven I. Pfeiffer (2008). handbook of Giftedness in Children. Psychoeducational Theory, research, and Best Practices. Springer Science+Business Media, LLC.

In: The Nurturing of Talent, Skills and Abilities   ISBN: 978-1-62618-521-0
Editor: Michael F. Shaughnessy   © 2013 Nova Science Publishers, Inc.

Chapter 11

IN THE DEVELOPMENT OF CREATIVE THINKING, METAPHORS MATTER

John Baer[*]

Rider University, Lawrenceville, NJ, US

Almost everyone interested in promoting creativity acknowledges that creativity and intelligence are not at all the same things. That is not to say that intelligence is not a part of creativity. Experts might argue about just how large or small a part it is, but once we agree that people are generally more creative than other animals, we've also agreed that intelligence plays *some* role. But even those who argue that it is relatively important part (such as the once widely held view that creativity and intelligence are correlated up to an IQ of 120, but not beyond) still recognize that creativity and intelligence are fundamentally different things (Kaufman, 2009).

But then our thinking gets sloppy and -- often without realizing it -- many of us slip into using intelligence as a metaphor, a model, a template for how we think about creativity. This is a serious a problem, because creativity and intelligence really are fundamentally different processes, even though they may impact and sometimes require each other. (To see how using correlated traits as metaphors for one another can be problematic, consider this analogy: Being slender and being a good long distance runner are attributes that are mutually supportive -- it's easier to run long distances if one is slender, and running long distances might lead to becoming more slender -- but these are still fundamentally different things. What we know about weight loss and gain will not serve as a very useful guide for thinking about long distance running, and vice versa. Similarly, making lots of money and buying expensive cars are probably correlated, but what we know about buying expensive cars would not be a good model for thinking about how to increase one's income.)

A better metaphor for creativity is expertise, although not in the most obvious way. Expertise, like intelligence, is associated with (and often necessary for) creativity, but even though one needs some degree of expertise to be creative in a field at the highest levels, one can have abundant expertise and still not be at all creative. In this sense, creativity and

---

[*] E-mail: baer@rider.edu.

expertise have a parallel relationship with the relationship between intelligence and creativity. Intelligence and expertise are both correlated with creativity, and both are believed by many to support creative thinking.

The similarity between creativity and expertise is actually much deeper than one simply serving the other, however. The connection I want to draw on is much more foundational, and it is essential to understand that foundation if one wants to nurture and develop creative thinking. It has to do with the domain specificity of both expertise and creativity.

We often say things like "Jane is intelligent," with no further clarification. But we don't simply say "Jane is an expert." In the latter case, we need to specify the area of her expertise (e.g., "Jane is an expert in art history," "Jane is an expert polo player," or "Jane is an expert statistician"). No one is an all-around expert (although some people may have expertise in many areas, of course) the way some people are simply intelligent. We may recognize that even intelligence has components (and some might even argue about just how independent those components are of one another, but that is a debate for another day). For today, I am simply using the ways we typically talk and think about intelligence and expertise as tools to help us understand how we think -- and how we *should* think -- about creativity.

So can we say "Jane is creative" without further clarification? People do this all the time, but that's a mistake. Jane may be creative, but it's unlikely that she is generally creative in all or even most of the things she does or might do. She's probably creative in some things and not in others. Does this seem like nit-picking? Let me explain why it's not, and why that distinction matters for anyone interested in promoting creativity.

Putting aside arguments about what IQ tests actually measure, we know two things about IQ scores: (1) they are correlated with performance in many domains and (b) if you score high on one IQ test, you are extremely likely to score high on other IQ tests (Neisser, Boodoo, Bouchard, Boykin, Brody, Ceci, Halpern, Loehlin, Perloff, Sternberg, and Urbina, 1996). This means that there's something domain general about whatever it is that IQ tests measure. Speaking of a person as intelligent therefore makes sense: It means that a person so identified has abilities of the kind measured by IQ tests that are significantly above average and that, on a wide range of tasks from diverse domains, the person is likely to do comparatively well on most of those tasks. If someone is intelligent, then it is reasonable to assume that they will have abilities in quite a few unrelated areas. This is true whether one equates intelligence with IQ tests or not. It's a fairly general skill or set of skills that are useful in many very different areas.

Expertise doesn't work that way. Calling someone an expert doesn't really make sense unless their domain (or domains) of expertise is specified in some way. Even when people have expertise in several domains, one still needs to identify those domains. Otherwise, it would be impossible to understand what it means to call someone an expert. I need people with different kinds of expertise to fix my car, teach me calculus, or set my broken bone. Expertise varies widely by domain. Knowing that someone is an expert in California wines doesn't lead one to assume that person will also be an expert in accounting, ice hockey, or modern dance.

So which is creativity more like, expertise or intelligence? Thinking about creativity the way we think about expertise is more accurate because both are highly domain specific. Just as someone may be an expert in more than one field, someone may be creative in more than one area, but neither creativity nor expertise generalize broadly across domains. This has been born out in numerous studies looking at the actual creative products produced by people in different domains. The creativity of the stories participants write is unrelated to the creativity of the collages, math puzzles, and other artifacts they create. Average correlations are just a little higher than zero, especially if one first removes variance attributable to intelligence and access to educational opportunities1 (Baer, 1993, 1996, 1998b, 2010, 2011a, 2011b).

Does this matter? Yes, because it influences both how we assess creativity and how we try to nurture it.

Efforts to assess creativity have been plagued by supposedly domain-general divergent-thinking tests like the Torrance Tests of Creative Thinking, although even Torrance knew his tests were measuring domain-specific skills. He created two different versions of his eponymous test, one that used verbal tasks and another that used visual tasks, and found that scores on the two tests were unrelated -- they had a correlation of just .06 (Crammond, Matthews-Morgan, Bandalos, and Zuo, 2005) -- so they *could not* be measuring a single skill or set of skills. These tests were -- and still are -- measuring two entirely different things. Because these tests have been used in so many psychological studies of creativity, much of what we think we know about creativity may be based on invalid data because the obtained results might be true only for one specific type of creativity (and the results might have been entirely different had the other Torrance Test been used). These tests have also been widely used in selection for gifted/talented programs -- programs that have, in turn, often suffered because by assuming creativity was domain general, these programs often wasted students' time with supposedly content-free divergent thinking exercises (like brainstorming unusual uses for bricks) that really only develop divergent-thinking skill in limited domains (Baer, 2011a, 2011b).

Think for a minute how we build muscles. Does it matter the content of the exercises -- whether they employ our biceps or our quadriceps or some other muscles? Of course it matters. To increase one's physical strength, it would be crazy to suggest doing only one kind

---

[1] The domain specificity of creativity (and the evidence that creativity in different domains is essentially uncorrelated) does not mean that there will not be some people who are creative in many domains. This is something of a red herring that often confuses readers new to the specificity-generality debate. Domain specificity argues that we should *expect* to find a few creative artists who are also creative musicians, and a few creative teachers who are also creative poets; we just shouldn't expect to find a general correlation between the levels of creativity observed across different domains. The existence of polymaths does nothing to disprove domain specificity. Similarly, the many geniuses who failed to find even modest success in other fields do not disprove domain generality, because most geniuses commit to one field and are simply unable to give as much attention and effort and time to any other pursuit (Kaufman, Beghetto, and Baer, 2010; Kaufman, Beghetto, Baer, and Ivcevic, 2010).

Here's an analogy: someone can speak several languages and also be a fast runner, and yet these can remain distinct domains with distinct underlying abilities required for success. A person who is creative in two domains doesn't demonstrate that creativity is domain general any more than a fast runner who speaks multiple languages demonstrates that running and language acquisition rely on the same basic abilities. Only if *most* fast runners spoke multiple languages (and most slow runners few) would this demonstrate a linkage between the two abilities. If the two skills are unrelated, then one would expect some fast runners to speak multiple languages and some to be monolingual — which is exactly what we observe.

In the same way, if creativity is domain specific, then one would *expect* some people to be highly creative in more than one domain. Domain specificity doesn't predict that people will be creative in only a single domain. It says only that the skills, knowledge, aptitudes, or talents underlying creativity in different domains are different, and for this reason creativity in one domain does not predict creativity in other domains. Assuming that such domain-based creativity-relevant talents are randomly distributed, one would *expect* that a few people would be creative in many domains, that some people would be creative in several domains, and that some others would be creative in few domains or none, based on a normal distribution of unrelated abilities. So the presence of a few da Vincis does not disprove domain specificity. It is *exactly* what domain specificity predicts.

of exercise. To increase overall strength one must do many *different kinds* of exercises, each designed to strengthen different sets of muscles. Exercising one muscle will strengthen that muscle, not *all* of one's muscles. Because creativity is domain specific, the same is true of creativity training: One must do many different kinds of exercises if one wishes to strengthen many different creative-thinking "muscles."

The same is true when we think about the acquisition of expertise, of course. Because we know that expertise is domain-specific, we know it matters the kinds of education or training needed to develop expertise in a domain. Learning about Japanese history will help develop expertise in that area, but will do nothing for one's expertise in calculus or piano tuning or auto repair.

If creativity were domain general, there would be essentially a single set of creative-thinking muscles that one could use with any problem, and many creativity trainers -- seduced, perhaps, by the intelligence metaphor -- operate in this way. If this were true it would make creativity training much easier (just as it would make muscle building so much easier if there were a single set of muscles to exercise), and this is perhaps one very seductive (but unfortunately misleading) attraction of domain-general theories of creativity: If they *were* true, they would allow training shortcuts. Because creativity is domain specific, however, training creativity must be more like building muscles or developing expertise. If one's goal is to enhance creativity in many domains, then creativity-training exercises need to come from a wide variety of domains (just as we must provide a broad general education if we want students to acquire modest levels of expertise in many areas; teaching them lots of mathematics is a good thing, but it won't improve their understanding of history or philosophy).

There are times when one would want to focus on just one type of creative thinking "muscles," of course. If one's goal is to increase creativity in just one domain, such as one might want to do in a gifted program focusing on a single discipline (such as a program in dance, poetry, math, etc.), then it would be appropriate for all of the creativity-training exercises to come from the particular domain of special interest. This also parallels what we would do if we wanted students to acquire expertise in a single domain. In such a case, all (or at least most) of their studies should be in content related to that area. If one wants to increase creative-thinking skills (or expertise) in many domains, however, one needs to use a wide range of domains in training.

Here's an example that shows how the intelligence metaphor causes problems in creativity training. Divergent thinking is probably the most widely taught and practiced skill (or set of skills) designed to promote creativity. Divergent thinking is generally understood to mean the process of thinking of many different possible solutions, answers, or responses to a problem, question, or prompt. Divergent thinking is no longer commonly conceptualized as Guilford originally did, as a variety of distinct skills. It is instead often thought of as a general, all-purpose kind of thinking that many people believe to be involved in creativity of all kinds and at all levels. (Divergent thinking should not be confused with brainstorming, by the way, although they are related. Brainstorming is a technique that *encourages* divergent thinking. Brainstorming is just one of many possible ways to produce divergent thinking, however.)

There is something intuitively appealing about the notion of divergent thinking, and I believe there really is something important in this concept. The problem is that divergent thinking may not refer to one type of thinking, but to many *completely different* types of thinking that only seem similar from the outside, as it were -- to an observer -- while on the inside (as cognitive processes) these various discrete and cognitively unrelated skills may have little or no connection or overlap. Just as the various things a painter and a poet and a pre-school problem-solver might do as they go about their work can all be called creative, even though the thought processes, materials, and tools they use to produce poems and paintings and problem solutions may be completely dissimilar, so it is with divergent thinking.

If divergent thinking were a single process, then a student could apply whatever divergent thinking skill she might have in any area on *any* target or problem, no matter how different the discipline or content. But that's not how divergent thinking works. It's not like a content-free computer subroutine that can simply be taken out of one program and dropped into another program doing a totally different task. Thinking of unusual uses for a brick, unusual recipes for a soufflé, and unusual ways to solve an equation are vastly different skills. If we didn't give them all a shared label (such as creative or divergent thinking), there would be little reason to think of them as related. But calling things by the same name does not confer upon them shared properties. It may cause us to *think* of them as similar, however, even if they are not. (This might be why we tend to think more favorably of people who share our name, or who simply have the same first letter in their name. Completely arbitrary and random similarities, even when we know they are arbitrary and random, lead us to see connections that aren't really there. But a similarity in name doesn't make John from Baltimore any more like me than Michael from Philadelphia, even though I happen to share a name with John. Ditto for divergent thinking in poetry, divergent thinking in painting, and divergent thinking in physics.)

As already noted, the leading developer of divergent thinking tests, Paul Torrance, demonstrated this himself. He created two different versions of his now widely used tests and found there was almost no correlation between scores on these two tests of divergent thinking -- 0.06, which is essentially zero. This showed that the two sets of divergent thinking skill were completely unrelated. Divergent thinking is not one skill. It is many *completely different* sets of skills. Even the creator of the most widely used tests of divergent thinking knew that. Unfortunately, that message has gotten lost over the years. Many well-intentioned people who want to teach and nurture and promote creativity forget this and act as if divergent thinking were some readily transferable, domain-transcending, all-purpose general skill.

Teaching divergent thinking as a way to promote creativity is fine, but if in doing so one assumes that creativity is, like intelligence, domain-general, then much effort may be unintentionally wasted. If creativity were domain-general, then in choosing divergent-thinking exercises for training it wouldn't matter the content of those exercises. If divergent thinking were one skill that supported creative thinking in general, then any exercise that increased divergent thinking skill in any domain would increase divergent thinking skill in all domains. But unfortunately, research shows that is not true. Studies in which domain-specific divergent-thinking skills were practiced and developed in one domain did indeed who increased creativity in that domain -- but *only* in that domain. This training had no effect on creative performance in other areas (Baer, 1996, 2010).

Here's another example of how using the domain-general metaphor of intelligence when thinking about creativity misleads many people. There is much evidence (Amabile, 1983, 1996) that intrinsic motivation (doing something that one finds interesting or personally meaningful) leads to higher levels of creativity than extrinsic motivation (doing something in order to earn a reward or in anticipation of having one's work evaluated -- to get a good grade). That seems to make sense, and there is evidence that this is the case (admittedly somewhat disputed evidence -- the truth, as usual, is both complicated and nuanced; see Baer, 1997, 1998a; Eisenberger and Cameron, 1996; Eisenberger and Shanock, 2003; Eisenberger and Rhoades, 2001).

But is intrinsic motivation really a single thing, or is it a multitude of things that (once again) only *seem* related when looked at from the outside? Does one's interest in poetry have anything to do with one's interest (or disinterest) in gardening? Can the same personal satisfaction that motivates a person to create a beautiful piece of music be used by that person to develop an interesting lesson plan or solve a challenging mechanical puzzle? Or is it not more likely that what we call intrinsic motivation describes not one but many completely different kinds of motivation? As with divergent thinking, intrinsic motivation might be an interesting idea relevant to different kinds of creative thinking, but thinking about it as a general, domain-transcending thing is misleading. (It's also a little silly, isn't it? Does anyone really think motivation is fungible in this way, that it can be moved around and applied wherever one might need it? It would certainly make teaching easier. One could simply direct a student who loves kickball to apply that motivation to his study of fractions. But motivation, like creativity, isn't like intelligence. It's like expertise: domain specific.)

This doesn't mean that divergent thinking and intrinsic motivation don't matter. It does mean that even though having intrinsic motivation and divergent thinking in one domain may make a person more creative in that domain, this says nothing about their creativity in other domains -- and this, in turn, has major implications for how we should nurture creative mindsets and teach creative-thinking skills.

I am not suggesting that we discard concepts like divergent thinking and intrinsic motivation when we think about creativity. When theorists lump together very domain-specific skills like being able to come up with lots of interesting and unusual ways to use a brick, many original ways to choreograph a dance, and many elaborate ways to link several discrete cosmological events -- things that require completely different underlying skills -- into an abstract concept and label it something (divergent thinking in this case), that can be very useful. It allows us to see connections that are not obvious, and this metaphorical connection might help us look at some phenomenon in new and possibly interesting and productive ways. It might, for example, help us see that a technique originally designed to come up with new advertising ideas -- group brainstorming -- could also help administrators solve a scheduling problem, help teachers find ways to reach challenging students, or help architects discover new ways to construct living spaces, although as with all metaphors, we need to be careful. Brainstorming might work well in some areas and situations and not others. The erratic results of studies of group brainstorming -- sometimes it produces creative ideas, but sometimes it appears to hinder creativity -- suggests this might in fact be the case (Diehl and Stroebe, 1991; Mullen, Johnson, and Salas, 1991; Nijstad, Stroebe, and Lodewijkx, 2003; Rickards, 1999).

The problem is that such metaphorical and tenuous connections can all too easily be reified as actual unified abilities, when in fact they may have no underlying cognitive similarities at all. Once this step has been taken, the slippery slope cascades into programs, tests, and theories that, although based initially on nothing more than a loose metaphorical connection, come to have realities (and constituencies) all their own -- false realities and sometimes well-entrenched constituencies that can turn a potentially helpful metaphor into dogmatic thinking, thinking that impedes rather than facilitates progress in understanding complex phenomena like creativity.

Because it is the mostly widely taught creative-thinking skill, the primary example I have used in this chapter is the teaching of divergent thinking, but the same processes are true of many other skills, traits or attributes often linked to creativity. Other things like openness to experience, intrinsic motivation, and content knowledge are also all very domain-specific, and all have been shown in *some* domains and contexts to promote creativity. But one cannot use much of one's knowledge of pre-Columbian pottery to solve a Rubik's Cube, fix a bug in a computer program, or a write a haiku. Nor can a person readily transfer her interest in writing haiku to learning about pre-Columbian pottery, and one may not be equally open to new experiences in the areas of writing computer code and writing haiku.

Like divergent thinking, many other attributes or abilities related to creativity (e.g., intrinsic motivation, openness to experience, and content knowledge) are very domain-specific. The fact that we can find some interesting (and possibly useful) similarities in these ideas should not confuse us into thinking that these are modules that operate in the same ways in all content domains and can be transferred freely among them. I don't doubt that the constructs of intrinsic motivation, openness to experience, content knowledge, and divergent thinking can be useful to creativity researchers, theorists, and trainers, but only if they are careful not to forget that these are all very domain-specific in their actual manifestations. When we make the mistake of thinking about these skills and attributes the way we think about intelligence, we tend to conflate many domain-specific skills and attributes. This is more likely to cloud our understanding of how creativity works than to clarify its mystery.

As the saying goes, "Complex problems have simple, easy-to-understand, wrong answers." Understanding creativity is certainly a complex problem, and the ways we think about creativity influence the choices we make in teaching, nurturing, and promoting creativity. Metaphors matter because they shape and direct our thinking and decision-making. Thinking about creativity the way we think of expertise (and *not* thinking about it the way we think about intelligence) will lead to a better understanding of creativity and better decisions about how to recognize and develop it.

REFERENCES

Amabile, T. M. (1983). *The social psychology of creativity*. New York: Springer-Verlag.

Amabile, T. M. (1996). *Creativity in context: Update to the social psychology of creativity*. Boulder, CO: Westview.

Baer, J. (1993). *Creativity and divergent thinking: A task-specific approach* . Hillsdale, NJ: Lawrence Erlbaum Associates.

Baer, J. (1996). The effects of task-specific divergent-thinking training. *Journal of Creative Behavior, 30*, 183-187.

Baer, J. (1997). Gender differences in the effects of anticipated evaluation on creativity. *Creativity Research Journal, 10*, 25-31.

Baer, J. (1998a). Gender differences in the effects of extrinsic motivation on creativity. *Journal of Creative Behavior, 32*, 18-37.

Baer, J. (1998b). The case for domain specificity in creativity. *Creativity Research Journal*, *11*, 173-177.

Baer, J. (2010). Is creativity domain specific? In J. C. Kaufman and R. J. Sternberg (Eds.), *Cambridge handbook of creativity* (pp. 321-341. Cambridge University Press.

Baer, J. (2011a). How divergent thinking tests mislead us: Are the Torrance Tests still relevant in the 21st century? *Psychology of Aesthetics, Creativity, and the Arts, 5,* 309-313.

Baer, J. (2011b). Why grand theories of creativity distort, distract, and disappoint. *International Journal of Creativity and Problem Solving, 21(1).* 73-100.

Crammond, B., Matthews-Morgan, J., Bandalos, D., and Zuo, L. (2005). A report on the 40-year follow-up of the Torrance Tests of Creative Thinking. Gifted Child Quarterly, 49, 283-291.

Diehl, M., and Stroebe, W. (1991). Productivity loss in idea-generating groups: tracking down the blocking effect. *Journal of Personality and Social Psychology, 61,* 392-403.

Eisenberger, R., and Cameron, J. (1996). Detrimental effects of reward: Reality or Myth? *American Psychologist*, 51, 1153-1166.

Eisenberger, R., and Shanock, L. (2003). Rewards, Intrinsic Motivation, and Creativity: A Case Study of Conceptual and Methodological Isolation. *Creativity Research Journal*, 15, 121-130.

Eisenberger, R., and Rhoades, L. (2001). Incremental effects of reward on creativity. *Journal of Personality and Social Psychology*, 81, 728-741.

Kaufman, J. C. (2009). *Creativity 101.* New York: Springer.

Kaufman, J. C., Beghetto, R. A., and Baer, J. (2010). Finding young Paul Robesons: The search for creative polymaths. In D. D. Preiss and R. J. Sternberg (Eds.), *Innovations in educational psychology: Perspectives on learning, teaching, and human development* (pp. 141-162). New York: Springer.

Kaufman, J. C., Beghetto, R. A., Baer, J., and Ivcevic, Z. (2010). Creativity polymathy: What Benjamin Franklin can teach your kindergartener. *Learning and Individual Differences, 20,* 380–387.

Mullen, B., Johnson, C., and Salas, E. (1991). Productivity loss in brainstorming groups: a meta-analytic integration. *Basic and Applied Social Psychology. 12,* 3-23.

Neisser, U., Boodoo, G., Bouchard, T. J., Boykin, A. W., Brody, N., Ceci, S. J., Halpern, D. F., Loehlin, J. C., Perloff, R., Sternberg, R. J. and Urbina, S. (1996). Intelligence: Knowns and unknowns. *American Psychologist*, 51, 77-101.

Nijstad, B. A., Stroebe, W., and Lodewijkx, H. F. M. (2003). Production blocking and idea generation: Does blocking interfere with cognitive processes? *Journal of Experimental Social Psychology, 39,* 531-548.

Rickards, T. (1999) Brainstorming. In M Runco and S Pritzker (Eds.), *Encyclopedia of Creativity, Vol. 1* (pp. 219-228). San Diego: Academic Press.

In: The Nurturing of Talent, Skills and Abilities
Editor: Michael F. Shaughnessy

ISBN: 978-1-62618-521-0
© 2013 Nova Science Publishers, Inc.

Chapter 12

HOW TO PARENT CHESS TALENT: CLASSIC AND MODERN STORIES

Kenneth A. Kiewra[*] *and Amanda L. Witte*

Department of Educational Psychology,
University of Nebraska-Lincoln,
Lincoln, Nebraska, US

We stand in awe of talent and its outgrowth: a Mozart concerto, a Picasso painting, a Whitman poem, or a Federer forehand. Investigations into how such talent develops began inconspicuously with Benjamin Bloom's (1985) book *Developing Talent in Young People*. Today, talent investigations and writings are in full bloom. Recently, several books exploring talent development have dotted bestseller lists including Malcolm Gladwell's (2008) *Outliers* and Geoff Colvin's (2008) *Talent is Overrated*. Research and popular writings on talent development have focused primarily on four key components: an early start, practice, mentoring, and motivation. Simply put, budding stars access the road to talent development early, usually in their own homes (Bloom, 1985), practice arduously for 10 or more years (Ericsson, 2002; Gardner, 1997), study with top mentors and coaches who hone technique and cultivate style (Colvin, 2008), and possess strong motivation, a rage to learn (Winner, 2000). What contemporary talent experts have largely missed, however, is the vital role that parents also play in talent development. One of Bloom's initial conclusions was that it is never enough for a child to commit to a talent area; parents must do so as well. And, Anders Ericsson, the foremost authority on talent development, declared recently that parenting is the frontier of talent development research (see Colvin, 2008, p. 204).

The purpose of this study, then, was to uncover and describe the roles that parents play in the development of their children's chess talent. We chose to investigate chess for three reasons. First, chess is one of three recognized domains where supreme talent can develop at a young age and child prodigies are evident (Gardner, 1997). Second, chess has an objective rating system based on tournament play that makes it easy to judge player strength (Gobet and Charness, 2006). Third, the first author has personal experience as the father of a top-

---
[*] Correspondence concerning this chapter should be addressed to Kenneth Kiewra, Department of Educational Psychology, University of Nebraska-Lincoln, Lincoln NE 68588-0345. E-mail: kkiewra1@unl.edu.

flight chess player. This all-consuming experience involved, among other things: introducing his son to chess, teaching him to play, selecting study materials, being a study companion, hiring coaches, monitoring lessons, convincing school personnel to count chess as a credit-bearing subject, financing lessons and tournaments, teaching school chess clubs, organizing and managing a summer camp, writing a weekly chess column, seeking sponsorship and donations, directing a chess foundation, arranging for and traveling to weekly tournaments and events, boosting motivation, and maintaining emotional health. Based on this experience, we sought to determine if other chess parents serve such a prominent and widespread role.

THREE CLASSIC CHESS STORIES

To set the stage for our study, we first examine the talent roots for three historic and iconic chess figures—Bobby Fischer, Susan Polgar, and Josh Waitzkin.

Bobby Fischer: Happenstance and a Child Obsessed

Many consider Fischer the greatest chess player of all time. He is the only American world champion, a title he earned in 1972 by beating then world champion Boris Spassky, from the USSR, in a match widely publicized as a Cold War confrontation. Fischer was considered a chess prodigy. He won his first of eight U.S. championships at age 14 and became the world's youngest grandmaster up until that time at age 15.

Fischer was born in Chicago, IL in 1943 to Gerald and Regina Fischer. Bobby's parents were well educated—Gerald was a biophysicist and Regina was a nurse and teacher—but neither played chess. The parents divorced when Bobby was two. His mother raised Bobby and his older sister in a desert region in Arizona before moving the family to New York (when Bobby was 6) where Regina could attain a master's degree in nursing education. The move to New York was a stroke of good fortune for Bobby's eventual chess career. Biographer Frank Brady (1973) speculated that Bobby Fischer might have never played chess had he not moved to New York City, which was home to about 80% of the country's top players at the time. Brady wrote:

> In America, great players just don't seem to develop outside the New York City area, and if they do, they quickly leave their hometowns (for New York City). As painters and sculptors flocked to Florence during the Renaissance, and writers learned their craft in Paris during the last two centuries, most young American chess players eager to test their skills against the foremost masters, and possibly make a reputation, eventually find their way to (New York City). (p. 3)

Another stroke of good fortune occurred soon after the move to New York. The family lived in an apartment in Brooklyn above a candy store. Bobby's older sister routinely brought games like Monopoly and Parcheesi home from the store to entertain him. One day she purchased a plastic chess set and the two children figured out the complicated moves from the instructions. That summer, Bobby came across an old chess book and "poured over it so intently that he would not reply when spoken to" (Brady, 1973, p. 5). From that point on,

Bobby took full advantage of New York's City's fabulous chess resources. He practiced relentlessly with top players in their homes and at the Brooklyn and Manhattan Chess Clubs, the latter one of the strongest in the world. He played outdoors too in Central Park and Washington Square Park. And, he studied chess books and magazines relentlessly, even those written in Russian.

Early on, Regina was not supportive and was actually worried about her son's chess obsession. She had trouble controlling Bobby's chess mania and felt that he should be pursuing other interests. There were times, for example, when Bobby refused to quit playing a game outdoors in a driving rainstorm, or when Regina would have to take the subway from Brooklyn to Manhattan and literally drag Bobby out of the Manhattan Chess Club after midnight. Regina even enlisted the help of a psychiatrist and asked how she could curb Bobby's chess obsession. The doctor, a chess-playing fanatic himself, said, "I can think of a lot worse things than chess that a person can devote himself to" and recommended that she let him find his own way. Regina said, "For four years I tried everything I knew to discourage him, but it was hopeless" (Brady, 1973, p. 9).

In summary, Bobby's path was one of happenstance. The incidental move to New York and the chance introduction of chess by his sister were critical to his chess introduction and development. Meanwhile, Bobby received little or no support from his mother who actually tried to block Bobby's chess progress. Instead, it was Bobby's chess obsession that drove him to take full advantage of New York's abundant chess resources and master the game he loved.

Susan Polgar: Raised to Play Chess

The path for Susan Polgar and her sisters was anything but happenstance. Their eventual parents, Laszlo Polgar and Klara Alberger, actually made marriage plans as part of a personal experiment to see if they could raise chess champions. The idea was that of Laszlo who was an educational psychologist and the author of the book *Bring Up A Genius* (as cited in Polgar and Shutzman, 1997). Laszlo believed that a child's achievement is due to educational methods rather than heredity. He chose chess, in part, because he was a recreational player, but largely because chess skill is objectively measured using a precise rating system based on results against other rated players. Moreover, there are recognizable titles attained such as master, international master, and grandmaster. The Polgar experiment was especially put to the test because the couple raised three daughters: Susan (1969), Sofia (1974), and Judit (1976) and women, to that point, had not fared well in what was considered a thinking man's game. At the time, no woman had ever earned the grandmaster title or was ranked among the world's top 100 players.

The Polgar experiment began in earnest when Susan was four years old. It was then that Laszlo began specialized chess training. He taught Susan to play, hired an expert trainer to work with her, and took her to a chess club to practice. To teach her, he relied on his modest experience, his library of about 5,000 chess books, and his collection of about 200,000 games clipped from newspapers and categorized for effective study. Susan was home-schooled by her parents from the start, through high school, and even in college (where she majored in chess) because Laszlo believed that schools are an unhealthy and dangerous place for talented children. He said, "School has a leveling out, uniforming effect (that) happens at a low standard" (as cited in Polgar and Shutzman, 1997, p. 17). During the first five years of home schooling, Susan spent about 10% of time studying school subjects and 90% of time studying chess. Eight to 10 hours a day were devoted to chess study. Despite this heavy focus on chess, Susan still excelled on school examinations, learned multiple languages, cared for more than two-dozen pets, and participated in physical sports. Susan's younger sisters, in turn, became curious about chess as they watched her study and play. In time, sisters Sofia and Judit began specialized chess training by age four and progressed through the same chess-studying regime.

The Polgar experiment was an unequivocal chess success. Intensive and long-term chess specialization produced remarkable chess results. For example, all three sisters earned international master titles, and Susan and Judit also earned grandmaster (GM) titles. Susan was the first woman to ever earn the GM title through tournament play, and Judit surpassed Bobby Fischer's world record for the youngest ever to attain the GM title. Although none of the sisters became world champion, Judit broke into the exclusively male Top 100 List and rose to number eight in the world, the highest ranking by any woman ever.

In summary, the Polgar sisters' path to chess supremacy was well calculated, and the parents, especially Laszlo, led the daughters every move. Fischer, on the other hand, stumbled onto chess and got little help from family. In the end, though, both Fischer and the Polgars took full advantage of available resources to master the game they loved.

Josh Waitzkin: Bobby Fischer More Developed than Found

Bobby Fischer's world championship match in 1972 created a chess mania. The nearly two-month, 21-game match was televised live from Iceland, and radio news reports updated the latest moves as a nation desperately followed a foreign game that suddenly became its own. Fischer was on the cover of *Sports Illustrated, Life, Time*, and *Newsweek* and starred on popular late-night shows. Chess sets and books flew from store shelves, and chess became the in thing. "Mothers pulled their sons out of Little League and ferried them to chess lessons, (and) shy, introverted chess players basked in national glory along with running backs and rock stars" (Waitzkin, 1988, p. 14).

Then in 1977, something happened that let the air out of the chess balloon: The enigmatic Fischer disappeared from chess, became a recluse, and never played a meaningful chess game again. For years after, America hoped and searched for the next young chess star, the next Bobby Fischer to fill the chess wasteland. That search uncovered a wave of talented young American players who had been influenced by Fischer, but perhaps none more talented than Josh Waitzkin, the subject of the popular novel (and later film) *Searching for Bobby Fischer*, written by Josh's father, Fred Waitzkin (1988).

Josh's chess storyline falls between that of Fischer and the Polgars. Although Josh's father was a recreational chess player, Josh, like Fischer, stumbled onto the game. It was 1982 and Josh was six years old. While walking past Washington Square Park just a few blocks from his New York City home, he became transfixed by the chess pieces and by the hustlers who moved them about the boards at a feverish pace during games of speed chess. The next day, Josh asked a teacher at an after-school playgroup to show him how the pieces moved. Several weeks later, while passing the park, Josh broke away from his mother and asked a man seated at a chessboard if they could play a game. After the game, the man told Josh's mom that Josh had used pieces in combination to launch attacks, a sign of chess talent. He wrote Josh's name down on a newspaper and said, "I'll look for your name someday" (Waitzkin, 1988, p. 19).

From that time on, Josh was a regular at the park after school and on weekends where he played against and was "coached" by the hustlers who cleaned up their acts when Josh was around. Josh showed rapid progress and some of the old-timers referred to him as "Young Fisher" as they recalled the games that Bobby once played there as a child. Josh not only discovered chess at Washington Square Park, he was discovered there by a top national player and chess teacher named Bruce Pandolfini who had become famous years before while providing television commentary during Fischer's world championship match. Pandolfini offered to provide Josh with formal instruction, and the Waitzkin's accepted his offer. Soon Josh became the top scholastic player in the country and one of the best worldwide. During his scholastic career, Josh won 21 national titles and several world titles (Waitzkin, 1988).

Josh's success can certainly be traced to the Fischer phenomenon and to his New York City roots where he had access to Washington Square Park, the Marshall Chess Club, top-flight instruction, other top young players to push him, and a wide array of competitive tournaments. In addition, Josh changed schools when he was nine years old and enrolled in Dalton School because of its wildly successful chess program. Among the top 50 players age eight and under in the U.S., nearly 30% attended Dalton, a medium-sized private school.

But unlike Fischer, Josh did not and could not make the chess journey without his parents' support. Fred Waitzkin, in particular, was the wheel steering Josh's chess career. Fred Waitzkin (1988) wrote:

> All the top players have at least one parent behind them, encouraging, assisting, worrying. In a sense, the child is only part of the team. Regardless of his gift for the game, he can't compete at the highest level without a good teacher and a supportive parent. (p. 123)

He also wrote:

> I am the coach and Bruce is the teacher. He drills Josh on the openings, hones his tactics, and trains him in endgame technique. I decide which tournaments we'll play and how much practice he should have the week before. I log his weaknesses and strengths and point them out to Pandolfini. I remind Bruce to give him homework, and I pester Josh to do it. I make sure he is asleep early on Tuesday night so that he won't be tired for his Wednesday lesson. (p. 123)
>
> And, when it is time for Joshua's chess lesson, I pray that my neighbor won't sing the blues and that the super's kid won't jump on the trampoline upstairs. It is a special time. We take the baby to the sitter so she won't pull the pieces off the board. Bonnie (Josh's mother) can't run the dishwasher or washing machine. She tries to prepare dinner quietly because a dropped pot might cause Josh to lose his train of thought. (p. 104)

Fred Waitzkin also became preoccupied with Josh's chess and with managing his chess career. He wrote:

> His precocious ability for this board game has seized control of my imagination. I used to worry about my career, my health, my marriage, my friends, my mother. Now I

mostly worry about Josh's chess. I worry about his rating and whether he's done his chess homework. There are tournaments to be concerned about. Has he practiced enough, too much? In years past, while I sat at my desk struggling to write, I often daydreamed about the Knicks or about going fishing. Now in my mind I play over my son's chess games; his sedentary activity has displaced many priorities in my life. (p. 4)

In summary, Josh, like Fischer, stumbled upon chess and reaped the benefits of living in New York City's enriched chess culture. Unlike Fischer, but much like the Polgar sisters, Josh benefited immeasurably from the supportive role his father played. Fischer's heir apparent was not as much found as developed.

PREVIOUS RESEARCH ON THE ROLE OF CHESS PARENTS

We tell these stories because they provide the backdrop for investigating the role that parents play in the development of chess talent. Another backdrop comes from a study that investigated how young chess masters, under age 16, got to be so good so fast (Kiewra, O'Connor, McCrudden, and Liu, 2006). Unsurprisingly, Kiewra and colleagues found that players began studying chess at a young age, practiced arduously and for many years, worked with top coaches, and were committed to chess above all else. But, the researchers also found that parents played a major role. Parents assumed the roles of manager, financier, and counselor. Parents were busy managers spending many hours arranging lessons, planning travel arrangements, and accessing materials. Some organized chess clubs and arranged matches to widen chess opportunities. One parent summed up the managerial role parents play, "My son calls me his agent. That's kind of what I feel like. I do all the planning and everything else and he gets on the plane or in the car and we go" (p. 103). The chess parents also paid a heavy financial price to develop their children's chess talents. Most were spending between $5,000-20,000 annually on lessons, tournament registrations, travel, and materials. Parents also played a counselor role offering motivation and emotional support when needed. Although players were generally highly motivated, parents pushed when necessary and reminded players that parental commitment would only go as far as player commitment. Regarding emotional support, one parent remarked, "I don't advise on chess. There's no advice I can give him really…I guide him emotionally" (p. 103). Another parent said:

> I don't understand the game very well…but I understand the psyche of winning and losing and pressure. I just try to keep him upbeat (at tournaments) and let him know I am there for him. They are just young kids and they need a lot of support. (Kiewra et al., 2006, pp. 103-104)

THE PRESENT STUDY METHODS

The present study extends the work of Kiewra and colleagues (Kiewra et al., 2006) by focusing exclusively on the roles chess parents play. To do so, we collected information from extensive parent interviews and a book written by a chess parent.

In order to further explore previously uncovered elements of parents' roles in chess talent development, while developing a clear understanding of individual families' experiences, a multiple qualitative case study approach was chosen (Stake, 2010). The following subsections describe the participants, data sources, and data analysis.

Participants

The parents of five young chess players who achieved top national standing were purposefully selected for participation using criterion sampling. All five players were the highest rated players nationally for their age group and all had won national or world championships for their age group. The authors contacted the identified players' parents, provided a brief description of the study, and invited them to participate. Table 1 shows the five players; their parents' names; and the players' birth years, FIDE ratings, and highest titles earned. FIDE stands for the World Chess Federation (from its French acronym), the international governing body of chess. FIDE authorizes three chess titles based on performance in top-flight tournaments and rating.

**Table 1. Summary information for the 5 modern
chess players as of September 2012**

Player's Name	Parent's Name	Birth Year	FIDE Rating	Highest Title
Kayden Troff	Kim	1998	2312	FM
Daniel Naroditsky	Vladimir	1995	2483	IM
Ray Robson	Gary	1994	2598	GM
Marc Arnold	Renee	1992	2538	IM
Robert Hess	Carl	1991	2595	GM

From lowest to highest, respectively, they are FM (FIDE master, minimal rating 2300), IM (international master, minimal rating 2400), and GM (grandmaster, minimal rating 2500). Presently, only about a thousand players worldwide hold the GM title.

Data Sources

The authors conducted and audio-recorded interviews (approximately 75 minutes each) by telephone with one parent of each child. The participants first described their experiences with little direction from the interviewer (Creswell, 2007) by answering this open-ended question: "Describe the role(s) you have played in the development of your child's chess talent." Understanding that the existing literature (Kiewra et al., 2006) identified home environment, coaching, practice, and psychological preparation as key components in talent development, follow up questions probed parents' involvement more deeply with respect to those areas. The father of one outstanding chess player declined to be interviewed and instead referred us to the memoir he had written on this topic (Robson, 2010). Because this memoir was written from the father's personal perspective and answered the primary interview question and additional probes, it was treated as an interview for data analysis.

Data Analysis

The data analysis followed the procedures of multiple case study design where the data are analyzed case by case through thematic analysis and later by cross-case analysis (Stake, 2010). Following interview transcription, data analysis began with both authors reading through the transcripts of the interviews for overall understanding and coding each for themes. Following the case-by-case analysis, all themes were used to conduct the cross-case analysis. Themes salient across all cases were kept as well as those that were extremely different. Through this analysis process, we uncovered five different paths to chess greatness, one for each player: Robert Hess: The Perfect Storm; Marc Arnold: Right Place, Right Mom; Daniel Naroditsky: A Good Chess Home, A Good Chess Match; Kayden Troff: Sacrifice to Win; and Ray Robson: A Father Obsessed. Although each story is unique, we were able to construct four major cross case themes: Building the foundation, fostering chess development, parents as managers, and psychological preparation. These themes are highlighted in each case description and in the chapter's conclusion.

FIVE MODERN CHESS STORIES

Here we tell the stories of our five selected chess players, particularly the roles their parents played.

Robert Hess: The Perfect Storm

Robert Hess seemingly had all the makings for becoming a chess champion. First, Robert was raised in New York City—a Mecca for chess—where both Bobby Fischer and Josh Waitzkin began their chess careers. Second, his father, Carl, played chess and one day taught all three of his children how to play when Robert, the middle child, was five. Third, Robert's introduction to chess continued in first grade in his New York City school due to what Carl called "a happy accident." Robert and his classmates were taught chess as part of the school curriculum. Moreover, the chess teacher was no ordinary teacher. He was grandmaster Miron Sher, a world-renowned coach who formerly coached the Russian National Team. GM Sher was employed by New York City's privately funded Chess-in-the-Schools program, which provided free chess instruction to several schools. Carl said:

> One day during first grade I picked Robert up from school and a kind of funny guy with a Russian accent gives me a business card and says, "Your son, he's sort of good at chess, you should call me." I made the call and soon Robert was training twice a week with GM Sher who has been Robert's primary coach ever since.

Robert's family background was also conducive to chess success. In the Hess household, Robert and his siblings are raised in a culture where high achievement is the norm and is expected. Carl said, "There is a strong emphasis on achievement at home that dates back generations. Failure's not an option. It's an expectation that my wife's family had and my family had so it's a given that you're going to succeed." Carl added that the children also feed off of each other's successes in the classroom, where all are top students, and on the athletic fields, where all flourish as well. Robert played on the high school football team.

Developing a champion chess player is expensive. Carl reported that the yearly cost for Robert's private lessons, tournaments, travel, and materials is about $20,000. The family, though, can cover these expenses. Carl is the global director for an investment firm and Carol, his wife, "used to run money (as a Wall Street broker) before running the family's three teenagers." In another stroke of good fortune, Robert's strong play and great potential earned him a rare chess fellowship that pays $40,000 a year for two years. Because of the fellowship, Robert postponed his entry into Yale University to study chess full time.

Robert's parents also take on the role of manager. Carol schedules lessons, makes sure Robert completes chess homework in preparation for those lessons, and makes travel arrangements for the many national and international tournaments Robert plays. Carl, because of his flexible work schedule, travels with Robert to tournaments lasting a few days to two weeks.

In terms of psychological preparation, the Hess parents must sometimes direct Robert's focus and motivate him to study. Carl said that Robert's work ethic is not always sufficient given the family's commitment to Robert's chess success. They tell Robert that if they are going to pay for lessons, he must be prepared for them. They tell him to bring the same rigor to chess and academics because both deserve the same commitment. And, they expect him to be self-motivating because soon he will be on his own without a support network. In terms of emotional strength, Carl said that Robert needed little assistance. He said, "There were only a few times that he needed an arm around his shoulder (after a difficult loss). We modeled and taught him how to roll with the punches."

In summary, Robert's chess success resulted from a perfect storm of chess blessings: a chess-playing father, the enriched New York City chess culture, a Chess-in-the-Schools program, early and consistent grandmaster training, a family culture of success and high expectations, vast financial resources, and parents willing and able to manage his chess career.

Marc Arnold: Right Place, Right Mom

Like Robert Hess, Bobby Fischer, and Josh Waitzkin, Marc Arnold is a product of the New York City chess culture brimming with chess clubs, competitive tournaments, and top players and coaches. Growing up in New York City jumpstarted Marc's chess career. Although neither of his parents played chess, Marc's school offered chess instruction as part of the curriculum (in the same way Robert Hess's school did). Marc was introduced to chess in kindergarten and within months of that introduction began attending the school's after-school chess club too. Also like Robert Hess, Marc was soon singled out as someone with potential. The chess program director said to Marc's Mom, "Marc has a very good demeanor at the board." His Mom asked how she knew that a five-year old has good demeanor at the board, and the director replied, "I know. I've seen enough. I know who has the capability and Marc does." After that, Marc started playing in local tournaments and doing well, including a fifth place finish for his age group at the highly competitive New York City Scholastic Tournament. There, a chess coach named John asked Marc's mother if Marc had a coach. "What do you mean a coach," she said, "I've heard of tennis coaches, but a chess coach?"

"How do you think those other kids who finished ahead of Marc did so well?" John asked. She answered, "I guess they are just really good at chess." "No, they have coaches," John declared. Soon John became Marc's first coach.

What distinguishes Marc's chess development from that point on is the prominent role that his mother, Renee, played in that development. Top chess players, by the way, are typically male and usually it is the child's father who manages the son's chess career (Kiewra et al., 2006). Dr. Renee Arnold is a Doctor of Pharmacy who runs a medical consulting practice. This chosen position allows her flexibility to travel with Marc, the couple's only child, to national and international tournaments. Marc's father, Michael, works for a television network and cannot do much chess travel because of a heavy travel schedule for his job. Renee said, "I have not taken a full time job beyond my consultancy because I wanted to be free to take Marc to tournaments." Renee is one of the few chess moms at tournaments. She said:

> It's usually me and the chess dads at tournaments, but I don't think I threaten any moms by being one of the few women in this. For me, it was wonderful because it made Marc and me really close because I was there with him all the time.

Renee also works as a consultant in order to fund Marc's chess development. Sometimes mother and father clash about Marc competing in chess tournaments that interfere with school or cost the family a lot of money. On each occasion, Renee argues for chess. On one occasion, when Marc's father did not want Marc going overseas to play because of the trip's high cost, Renee said, "Look, one of the reasons I work so hard is to be able to pay for Marc's chess." Marc played. Overall, Renee is the driving force in Marc's chess development. She joked:

> There have been times (when my husband and I have argued about Marc's chess). We've not come to blows; luckily we've been married 23 years and that's gone well. But, I'm definitely—of the two of us—more of the chess proponent.

Renee's commitment to Marc's chess is revealed in other natural ways as she plans lessons and activities, seeks new coaches when necessary, and monitors chess progress. She also keeps Marc grounded. At times when chess became overbearing for Marc, she encouraged him to back off. When a prominent coach, who had once coached Bobby Fischer, suggested that Marc stop playing scholastic tournaments (because the competition is fierce and lowered kids' ratings) and stop participating in sports (because they interfered with chess), Renee parted ways with that coach. She wanted Marc to enjoy those things even if they hindered chess progress.

Renee also provides a dose of motivation when needed. She reported, "Marc's motivation waned during his teenage years because there were other interests and it wasn't so cool at that point to be a good chess player." At that time, she suggested Marc back off until the passion returned. When Marc was closing in on his international master (IM) title, though, she pushed. She said, "Come on, let's go. Let's do this. Hold off on other interests for a while and get this done. If you become an IM, nobody can ever take that away from you." She regularly reminds Marc that his natural ability can only take him so far, that he must not be lackadaisical, and must study more to reach his goal of becoming a grandmaster.

In summary, Marc Arnold's chess success was ignited by New York City's chess environment. It was there that Marc was discovered in a school chess program, was originally coached, and played. It was Marc's mother who navigated him through his chess career, made chess a family priority, and altered her own career to foster Marc's chess development.

Daniel Naroditsky: A Good Chess Home, a Good Chess Match

Daniel was raised outside San Francisco, California—a place with modest chess resources and activities compared to New York City. But, Daniel had an intimate connection to chess through his father, Vladimir, who was raised in Russia where chess is king. Vladimir was a strong player who reached master strength by the time he was in seventh grade. He taught Daniel how to play when Daniel was six years old. But much of the credit for Daniel's early development actually goes to his brother, Allan, who was four years older and was a strong player who had also learned chess from his father. After Vladimir taught Daniel some chess basics, Daniel's skill level increased dramatically from playing a lot of chess with Allan and from Allan's chess instruction. Within just a few months, Daniel was occasionally beating Allan and was surprising his father who had to really think through his moves when playing Daniel.

Daniel also possessed certain organic traits well suited for chess. Daniel has long had a remarkable memory for many topics, and a strong memory is instrumental for learning chess openings and remembering positions from games previously played. His father said that Daniel is a big fan of Jeopardy and because of his strong memory reports about 95% of the answers when he watches the show. When Daniel was five, he had memorized all the capitals of all the countries in the world. Vladimir added this story about Daniel's memory prowess:

> Daniel was interested in classical music and composers. Because of that interest, I gave him a present when he was seven, which was a huge wall poster that contained information for about 900 composers that was laid out in a grid. Daniel would just casually look at the table from time to time, but never actually study it. When Daniel was eight or nine, someone gave him a music encyclopedia for his birthday. Daniel opens the gift with about 20 adults in the room and randomly opens to one of its 2,000 pages and begins reading about one of the composers on that page. No one at the celebration had ever heard of this composer including Daniel's mother who is a professional musician. Daniel suddenly stops reading and remarks, "This is a mistake. He was not born in 1412, he was born in 1411." So, we go to the large grid to check and, sure enough, it turns out that Daniel was right.

Vladimir explains that Daniel's memory is natural. He said:

> Daniel's not learning in a conventional sense. He's not actively memorizing things. It just sticks to him. Everything that has to do with trivia, he reads once and maintains it in some type of orderly fashion. Somehow, he has this wiring inside his brain that allows him to memorize everything that has to do with geography, statistics, numbers, names, and addresses, you name it.

Daniel's father also sensed that Daniel displayed an organic emotional tie to chess. Shortly after Vladimir taught Daniel how to play, he noticed something special about Daniel's connection with chess. Vladimir said:

> Although I was playing against a complete novice, I found it remarkable how he was placing the pieces on the board. It was a tender touch, the way that you would touch a woman that you loved. He moved the pieces with such care and such enjoyment as he placed them on a square. I knew early on that there was something special about this picture.

Daniel's parents are high achievers (Vladimir earned a Ph.D. in math, was a professor, and now runs an investment company; Daniel's mother is a professional musician) who emphasize the joys of reading and learning. The family spends a lot of time together each evening usually reading or studying a topic of interest to the boys. Vladimir said:

> We have a large library of books at home. We as parents read a lot and the kids see that and read a lot too. We watch almost no TV unless it is a special show. We ask Daniel what is happening in school in all his subjects, and we ask him what he wants to learn more about. Perhaps it is Roman History. We then go to the library and get some books on his special topic. And, together we study those topics three to five evenings a week.

One of the intellectual topics Daniel pursued was writing a chess book that was published when he was just 14 years old, making him the youngest chess author in history. Daniel's father said:

> Since Daniel was four years old, he wrote in his notebook. He wrote notes on topics like world history and, of course, his chess games. When Daniel was having trouble with positional chess play around age 12, he started reviewing his extensive chess notes looking for solutions. It was then that he started asking me a lot of strange questions about the book publishing business because he wanted to publish his notes into a book. I told him to type his ideas into the computer and I would show it to some professional chess players.

The players found the book remarkable and so too did a leading publisher who also questioned its authenticity. The publisher wondered how someone so young could have such insight. Vladimir sent the publisher Daniel's original handwritten notes and he was convinced. The publisher not only published the book but contracted with Daniel to write two more.

Vladimir has been instrumental in Daniel's chess training. Vladimir's early chess training produced quick success for Daniel who, in his first tournament at age seven, won all his games in the first through third grade section of the California State Championship. Although Vladimir knew chess, he initially knew nothing about the scholastic chess scene. He said, "I didn't know anything about ratings, registering for tournaments, or hiring coaches. I didn't know anything at all." But, he learned. He began by taking Daniel to a local chess club and talking to people there. He soon hired an "old Russian guy" who was an expert player. He worked with Daniel twice a week. As Daniel progressed, the coach recommended that

Vladimir find Daniel a stronger coach. Daniel next worked with an international master level coach until that relationship broke off. It was then that Vladimir coached Daniel for a time.

He said:

> I had a collection of Russian chess books and started buying more and more books for Daniel. We had regular lessons three or four times a week for a couple hours. We would read the books together and go over the published games.

After that, Vladimir found grandmaster coaches for Daniel who had "an insatiable appetite for chess." One was from Kentucky and another from Israel. Vladimir would arrange for Daniel to take regular lessons via the Internet. In addition, Vladimir arranged for the Kentucky coach to visit their home for a few days several times a year and to work with Daniel there. On these visits, coach and student studied chess all day long. Vladimir also arranged for Daniel to travel to New York to work with former world champion Garry Kasparov.

Vladimir Naroditsky manages Daniel's chess career and said that doing so "is a second job." He equates managing Daniel's chess activities with running his company. He keeps a chess calendar showing tournaments, lessons, and payments. He talks to coaches about lesson goals and plans, and he often sits in on lessons and takes notes that he and Daniel review while studying chess together two or three times a week. Vladimir's secretary makes the travel arrangements for tournaments, and father or mother always accompany Daniel. About 95% of the time, Daniel's mom accompanies him because she teaches piano and has a flexible schedule. When Vladimir attends tournaments, which can span a few days to two weeks, he tries to get work done but has trouble concentrating on things outside of chess. He said, "I always take a book to the tournaments to read, thinking I'll read a lot. But, if I can read two pages during the game, that's great. And, then I don't remember what I read."

Daniel's parents also spend time working with personnel at Daniel's private school and handling school arrangements so Daniel can travel to national and international tournaments during the academic year. Before a big chess trip, Vladimir often gets weeks worth of assignments from teachers and copies hundreds of textbook pages. Daniel's parents also decided to have Daniel take a year off from school (ninth grade) in order to focus on chess development and to travel internationally for chess.

The Naroditsky's pay a large financial price for Daniel's success—about $50,000 per year. Vladimir breaks down some of the costs this way:

> Professional coaches charge $80-$100 per hour and that's for four hours per week. Tournament fees in the United States are $200-$400, plus there are hotels and airline tickets, and Daniel does not travel alone. So, when Daniel goes to, say, Philadelphia for the World Open—do the calculation—six days in the hotel, six days of food, the $400 entrance fee, and you're talking about $2,500, give or take. If it's an international tournament, more than double the cost. Now do the multiplication, three to four international tournaments, two or three national tournaments, and perhaps four local tournaments where we still need a hotel. Add to all this, his coach, entry fees, memberships, and books and I would guesstimate yearly costs north of $50,000. And, so far, all of this has come from our own pocket. This is a huge burden. It's very, very

difficult, but fortunately we can afford it. It's not overstating that our life is entirely structured around (his chess training) and chess tournaments.

Vladimir has little to do when it comes to motivating Daniel. He said:

I don't need to motivate him at all. If anything, it's the other way around. I help him organize his studies so that he is not just focusing on chess development. Otherwise, he can easily study chess 12 hours a day on his own.

Vladimir does take a more active role in guarding Daniel emotionally. He said:

First of all, Daniel's a very emotional child in general. Second, he takes losses very badly. And when he loses a game that he thought he was winning, it's even worse. So, I try to protect him after a game by making sure that he gets the space he needs... It is very important to protect his psychological environment from so-called well wishers... Even when he wins, chess can be very draining and he needs time and space. Most importantly, we tell him that we love him, and not because he is a world champion. He knows he is loved at home (and that chess results don't change that).

In summary, Daniel Naroditsky's chess success was the product of organic abilities well suited for chess and a chess-playing father who guided all aspects of Daniel's chess development, as if it were a second job, from providing instruction, to hiring coaches, to managing Daniel's busy chess calendar. To do all this, Daniel's father mastered the inner workings of chess development himself and covered the annual $50,000 chess price tag. He and his wife provided an enriched home environment that supported learning, traveled extensively to tournaments, and arranged for Daniel to have a year off from school to pursue chess full time.

Kayden Troff: Sacrifice to Win

Kayden Troff was raised in Utah, just outside Salt Lake City, a place with minimal chess resources. Kayden Troff's introduction to chess mirrored Naroditsky's. Kayden's father was a recreational chess player who wanted someone to play chess with so he taught Kayden's older brothers how to play. Kayden sat silently on his Dad's lap and watched his Dad and brothers play. When Kayden barely turned three years old, he announced to his Dad that he was ready to play. Dad thought that he would be a good sport and humor "the baby" so he set up the board and had Kayden try to play. The family was amazed when they saw that Kayden knew how all the pieces moved and how to attack with them without being taught directly. From that moment on, Kayden was a regular player in the Troff household. Kayden's father soon realized that family chess was not enough to contain the boys' interest and skill levels. But, he knew nothing about chess activities outside his home, especially "the scholastic chess world" that awaited them. But, he learned about available resources and scholastic chess and began taking the boys to local tournaments and to a community chess club in the Salt Lake City area where they—including five-year old Kayden—would dominate other kids and even adults.

Kayden's intellectual gifts seem well suited to chess. Kim Troff, Kayden's mother, reported that Kayden was born with an ability to see patterns, a skill that is crucial for chess success. She also reported that Kayden was obsessed early on with following patterns or routines. She said, "He loved to see patterns. He loved following routines. Everything had to be done exactly the same way every day." Kim Troff, however, believes that Kayden's innate gifts account for just about 10% of his chess ability. She said, "I think the rest comes from his willingness to take something that he loves and just put a lot of work into it."

Kayden is the fifth youngest of six children, all of whom are home-schooled by Kim who is also the family homemaker. Husband Dan is a banker. In the Troff home, hard work and high achievement are stressed. Kim Troff said:

> We believe very strongly in hard work. It is a big foundation of ours so we have taught our kids from the time they were very little that they can accomplish anything they want to if they are willing to put the work into it. One way we foster that belief is through family projects. We built a lot of things as a family like patios and walkways made of bricks. We show and teach the kids that hard work is okay (and with it) there is no limit to what can be accomplished.

The family also stresses togetherness and mutual support in the pursuit of excellence. Kim said:

> We tell our kids that if they work hard for something, we will make sure that you have the family's full support. You need not do it alone. We'll be there for you. We are very invested in each other, and we celebrate each other's successes.

In terms of chess instruction, Dan was Kayden's first teacher and he continued to work with Kayden even after Kayden began training with professional coaches. In order to teach Kayden, Dan studied chess on his own 10-15 hours per week during his lunch hour and at night after the kids went to bed. He read books, watched videos, and studied grandmaster games that allowed him to create a chess book with specialized lessons that he and Kayden used to study. During one period when Dan was Kayden's primary teacher, Kayden's chess rating rose an astounding 300 points. Kim Troff is involved in chess instruction as well. When Kayden takes lessons via computer, Kim listens in on all lessons, takes notes, and compiles those notes in a folder that Dan later uses to review lesson material with Kayden.

Because Dan eventually reached his chess instruction ceiling, the Troffs hired a number of professional coaches over the years to work with Kayden. In some cases coaching changes were made because Kayden's ability was exceeding that of his coach. In other cases, coaches were replaced because Kayden's parents were dissatisfied with Kayden's progress or because coach and player were not a good fit. The Troffs, for example, dismissed Kayden's first grandmaster coach because Kayden was not progressing sufficiently relative to the expense for grandmaster lessons. Moreover, the coach was not available to Kayden throughout an entire summer. Kim Troff said, "At that point, we just said, this isn't working. Kayden wasn't progressing at all and was stuck at (a rating of) 1700 for that whole year. And, we were paying $300 a month." The family later hired a new grandmaster coach who lived overseas, and Kayden took three lessons per week. Eventually, though, this coach did not work out either because the Troffs wanted a coach who Kayden could call anytime there was a question and who could be with Kayden at tournaments. Moreover, the Troffs felt that the overseas coach was not up to date with current chess theory. The Troffs eventually found two new GM coaches for Kayden—one who focused exclusively on game openings and another who worked on other aspects of Kayden's game.

Managing and financing Kayden's chess career has been a supreme sacrifice for the Troff family. But just like in chess where players sacrifice material now for long-term gains, the Troff's recognize that their sacrifices are sound and rewarding. Kim said, "The personal sacrifice has been huge, and the money sacrifice has been huge, but the payoff has been well worth it." Kim estimates that they spend about $20,000 per year to cover the costs of Kayden's lessons, tournament fees, materials, and travel to national and international tournaments. Kim said:

> A lot of people say to us, well, of course, Kayden's good because he can take grandmaster lessons. Well that grandmaster requires a price, and it is a very high price. And, we've done some unbelievably crazy things to make chess work.

First, the family lives in a home that is too small for eight people, but they cannot afford to move. Second, the family does extra work trying to raise money for Kayden's chess. The parents worked second jobs as janitors for years at nearby office buildings. Each summer, the family organizes and runs a weeklong chess camp.

Dan spends about 400 hours planning and supervising the camp. And, they have sold things on E-bay. Not just personal items. Kim said, "We purchased truckloads of things and sold them."

Kayden has done work too. He was hired to write a weekly Blog for a chess website in exchange for lesson time with a grandmaster. Of course, because of Kayden's young age, this time consuming task became Kim's as well. She said:

> All the people who read the Blog say that Kayden is the most incredible writer ever. Well, I just want to laugh. He's 12. Yes, they're his ideas and words, but it only works because I'm there saying, "Okay, what do you want to say; what ideas are you trying to get across; or that doesn't sound quite right, can you say it another way?" So, every time he writes, it takes him hours to do it and it takes the same amount of time for me because I can't simply tell him to go write his Blog.

Third, the family developed an elaborate website to chronicle Kayden's chess career and to raise money through advertisements and donations. The website also serves to protect the family's time from the many chess writers and followers who want to know more about Kayden. Finally, the family cuts back whenever possible. Regarding chess, they substitute long drives for flights, stay in modest hotels, and pack suitcases full of food to offset restaurant costs. Kim said this about the family's sacrifices for chess: "You have to understand that (chess success) doesn't just happen. It doesn't. None of it just happens. You have to be willing to sacrifice to make it happen."

Kayden loves chess and practices about six hours per day. Still, his mom provides additional motivation and said that, "My biggest role is being his emotional support."

She once told Kayden this in the midst of an unsuccessful tournament:

> Kayden, you know that Mom's main job is to be your cheerleader, to cheer you on, tell you that you can do it, keep you going. Sometimes my job is to be the listening ear so you can talk and work things out. And, sometimes my job is to give you a kick in the pants, and that's what you are getting right now.

Kim recognizes that chess is not always fun for Kayden and in those times she reminds him of his chess dreams, what it takes to reach them, and that others have invested heavily in his chess development. She said:

> If Kayden's dream ever changes, if he ever gets to the point that he doesn't want to do this anymore, then we pull out. I will never force him to do it. But so long as he is pursuing the dream, when he is lazy, I will sit him down and say, "We've all invested way too much for you not to give your full effort. This isn't just about you. This isn't just your dream. There are a lot of people supporting you."

In summary, Kayden was raised outside an established chess culture. His parents, though, created a chess culture in the home where Kayden learned to play chess with his father and brothers. His parents also made many sacrifices to further Kayden's chess development. His father, for example, studied chess so that he could coach Kayden. And, both parents took on extra jobs as janitors or chess camp directors to fund Kayden's chess. Kayden's mom also pushed Kayden when necessary, reminding him that he represented the many other people who worked hard and supported him behind the scenes.

Ray Robson: A Father Obsessed

> During any given round, I stand as if on a perch, hawk-like in various positions about the room eyeing my chess child. I cannot read or write while the game is on. Even if I remained outside the playing hall, my thoughts would be too locked on the battle inside to allow me to concentrate on anything else... I shut down bodily functions and remain standing motionless and expressionless watching my child's game for hours... I become unaware of the passage of time... I do not eat, I do not drink, I do not go to the bathroom ... I simply cannot do anything else. (Robson, 2010, p. 41)

Gary Robson, Ray's father, has been obsessed with his son's chess development from the time he first taught Ray how to play. This obsession has paved the way for Ray becoming America's youngest grandmaster ever.

Gary Robson was a novice chess player when he innocently introduced Ray to the game when Ray was three years old. Robson wrote:

> Ray learned on the flat tiled floor of our kitchen in Sarasota, Florida. I'd bought a combination checkers-chess set at a nearby K-mart for a few dollars, thinking that we'd start with checkers and would have chess to graduate to in a few years. However, Ray was drawn to the chess pieces (because there were) horses and castles and teepee-shaped objects. He wanted to know how to play *that* game, so I set up the board and showed him

how the pieces moved…He learned how the pieces moved almost immediately and, when I'd come home from work, I'd find him squatting on the floor, moving the knights and other pieces around the board and playing out games of his own creation. And he'd challenge me. Every single afternoon, I'd walk through the door and my three-year old son would look up from the floor and say, "Baba, do you want to play chess?" Of course I said yes. (p. 15)

According to Gary, he and Ray share strong biological traits. Gary reported that both are shy, perfectionists, and fascinated by numbers. When Ray's kindergarten teacher was concerned about Ray doing numerical calculations during non-math lessons, Gary was not worried because he is a counter too, who counts steps and the letters on signs. Both possess a strong memory. Gary is the keeper of the family history, and Ray can read the verbal move notations in chess books and "play out" the long strings of moves on a chessboard in his mind. And, both share the qualities of focus and perseverance. Gary said that when he became interested in something, he "pursued it with passion" because "that's just how I am" (p. 52). Gary tells the story of how he connected with Thoreau's *Walden* and became consumed with it. He read and reread the book and transformed his life to mirror the book's elements. He said, "I joined the Peace Corps, built a bamboo hut, planted a garden, lived a life of simplicity, meditated by a river, … and even made a pilgrimage to Walden pond to swim in the sacred waters and walk in the footsteps of my mentor" (p. 52). Gary admits that this sort of focus is "crazy" but that such intensity and purpose are what make life rewarding. So, when Ray displayed this same intensity and purpose for chess, Gary remarked, "What else could Ray do? It was in his blood" (p. 52).

Ray Robson was born in the U.S. territory of Guam but mostly raised in Sarasota, Florida. Ray is Gary and Yee-chen's only child. Both parents are educators. Gary is presently a professor of education; Yee-chen quit her teaching job to be home with Ray. Their home is completely child centered. Gary silently repeats this mantra at the start of each day: "Enjoy your time with Ray while you are here now and while he is here now, for this is the only time that you have" (p, 132). To live this mantra, Gary has altered or changed jobs several times always with the goal of spending more time with Ray and furthering his chess development. For example, Gary once decided he would attend Ray's upcoming national and international chess events even if it meant losing his job. He reasoned, "As much as I love my students, the job was less important to me than my son and his development" (p. 125). Another time, Gary offered to give up his professorship and become a part-time instructor in order to free up more time to manage Ray's chess career. He wrote, "Chess was on my brain, and I found myself wishing I could be Ray's manager full time" (p. 224).

The child-centered approach was also evident with respect to Ray's education. Gary was frustrated with Ray's schooling. Although Ray was in the gifted program, Gary thought that school wasted Ray's time with "useless homework" and "boring worksheets" and did not afford enough time to study chess. Ray's parents decided to home-school Ray using Gary's vision of a truly intellectual education that included classic literature, fun reads, current science lectures, math lessons from a virtual school, and a lot of chess. Gary said, "I'll be honest, with the new arrangement, Ray spent the bulk of his time studying chess" (p. 161).

Overall, Gary immersed himself in Ray's life as a labor of love. He delighted in spending time with Ray and setting the groundwork for a successful future.

He wrote:

> I realize today how important my actions were. Instead of playing the spelling game
> over and over, I could have shut him down by saying "why don't you watch TV for a
> while?" Instead of encouraging him, I could have stifled his creativity and his fascination
> for manipulating numbers by giving him a pill… All that I needed to do was to show
> interest in what my child was doing, to try and solve puzzles that he created for me, and
> to talk with him about that which he loved. How easy such things were for someone who
> already enjoyed spending time with his son more than anything else. (p. 27)

Gary Robson controlled Ray's chess coaching. In fact, he was Ray's primary chess coach
throughout much of Ray's development even though he was a novice player himself when the
two began playing chess. At the start, they played hundreds of games and Gary would use
these games to point out things Ray missed and where he could improve his moves. When
Ray was just four years old, he beat his father for the first time. When one loss became two,
and then three, and then too many to count, Gary purchased a chess book to improve his chess
game so that Ray would improve his. Gary said:

> We used the book in this way: I read it first, practiced what I learned on the board
> against Ray, and, after I'd won, explained to him the concepts presented in the book that
> I'd applied in my win. Ray would then apply those same concepts in his games against
> me. (After the games), we'd analyze as best we could, and then I'd read more and start
> the cycle all over again. (p. 20)

From that point on, Gary purchased many chess books for Ray and him to study. And
father and son studied chess for hours every day. Intermittently, Gary would hire a
professional coach to work with Ray. But, even during those times, Gary continued to coach
Ray too. For example, Gary remarked:

> I hired a tutor, but, of course, I never gave up (my role as coach) entirely. I continued
> to work on improving myself. I sat in on every lesson, studied (chess books), and put
> more energy into this game that my son loved so much, so that even though I would no
> longer be his only teacher, I would still be an integral part of the process. (p. 35)

Gary managed all aspects of Ray's chess career with painstaking detail. Here he recounts
a routine that he and Ray followed for weekend tournaments:

> I would wake up an hour before Ray and (get ready). I'd quietly walk into Ray's
> room and pull out his clothes for the day—shorts, socks, T-shirt, sweatshirt (in case the
> air conditioning was too cold), and usually a red cap that he liked to wear. Then I'd make
> sandwiches and put them in a bag with some apples for lunch. I'd add other food to the
> bag for an on-the-road breakfast. Next, I'd pack his chess bag, clock, score pad, and
> pens… At the tournament hall, we'd register and then play catch with a football (to keep
> Ray relaxed) before the start of round one. On our walk to the tournament room, I'd
> begin my pep talk (and remind him to) take his time and make good moves. At the table I
> would help Ray set up the board and the clock—not because he needed help, but because
> it was … a way of being part of the process. I'd then whisper into his ear my final

words—the mantra that had evolved to fit Ray's changing needs over the years: "Take your time but watch the clock. Focus. Make good moves." And then I'd stand nearby as the game got underway. (pp. 77-78)

Another aspect of managing Ray's chess career was covering the $25,000 annual cost, an amount that sometimes ballooned because of an overseas trip that might cost an additional $10,000. Because Yee-chen did not work outside the home and because Gary often took lower paying jobs or unpaid leaves to travel with Ray, Gary did all he could to cut chess travel costs.

To save money, Gary and Ray took the cheapest flights even if they had many stops and long layovers, used public transportation or walked, and used a home-stay network that allowed them to bunk on strangers' couches or floors, which was not always comfortable. Gary wrote, "We slept on a hard floor in an unkempt room where cats wrestled over us and chewed our hair each night and where cat dander was so heavy that Ray had mump-like bumps on his face" (p. 149). The family also cut costs at home to finance chess. Gary said:

> Our home in sunny Florida had been without a working air conditioning unit for the past two years, and we endured the summers with windows and doors open, fans running in each room, and shorts and T-shirts as our daily attire. (p. 199)

On the plus side, Gary was instrumental in securing outside funding for some of Ray's international travel (after writing dozens of letters to prospective donors) and in Ray earning a prestigious chess fellowship (the same one that Robert Hess received) that paid about $80,000 over two years for chess training. Moreover, Ray's first place finish in a national tournament earned him an eventual free-ride college scholarship.

In terms of psychological preparation, Gary is also instrumental in boosting Ray's motivation and emotional strength. To bolster motivation, Gary helped Ray set challenging chess goals and emphasized that hard work is the means for reaching those goals. He then periodically reminded Ray of his goals and his progress toward them. Gary called himself, "Ray's supportive coach and emotional manager" (p. 216). To strengthen emotion, Gary encouraged Ray every day telling him he was getting smarter and better at chess. Gary also led Ray through a pre-game meditation to get him emotionally ready. This involved playing catch to relieve tension and reciting a mantra that reminded Ray of his strengths and his winning approach.

Although we might conclude that it is impossible to separate Ray's success from Gary's efforts, Gary has a much different take on his role and Ray's success. He wrote,

> I was a supportive coach and his emotional manager, yes, but Ray was the one doing all the work. One relative frequently said to me—and also to Ray—that we were a great team, always overemphasizing my own role and making it seem as if Ray's successes would have been impossible without me. Nothing could make me feel angrier, short of a direct insult to Ray. I later told Ray that he was the one who was spending four to six hours every day in concentrated study and that he was the one sitting at the board playing out the moves for every game... Ray's success is due to Ray, and he should fully own all the things he has earned himself. (p.166)

And, in the end, Gary stands firm about his deep involvement. He said,

> I have no regrets because every single thing that I did in the past has brought Ray into my life. Everything that seemed to be a mistake or a hardship or a sacrifice was the right thing done at the right time… I felt lucky to share this with my son. (p. 249)

In summary, Gary Robson has been intricately linked to all aspects of Ray's development: teaching him how to play, coaching him, taking him out of school so he could focus more on chess, and being his ardent manager and supporter.

CONCLUSION

These five modern stories and the three classic ones told earlier, offer insights into the unique roles that parents play in chess development. Fischer's parents, for example, played a minor role and actually tried to diminish Bobby's chess involvement. On the other end of the involvement spectrum, Lazlo Polgar engineered the perfect chess development environment for his three daughters, while Gary Robson was intertwined in all aspects of Ray's chess growth. These stories now told, we conclude by pointing out the parenting generalities that emerged from these chess stories.

First, the chess parents, based on their recollections, bore children with intellectual capabilities seemingly well suited to chess such as keen memories, strong pattern recognition, perseverance, and a penchant for order and routine. Although such traits might help, research shows that biological advantages are not sufficient for attaining talent; certain environmental factors that stem from the parent-child relationship must be in play (Hunt, 2006).

In most cases, chess was introduced in the home by a parent with previous chess knowledge. In some cases, chess-playing siblings supplemented that introduction. For some, school chess programs played a critical role by introducing chess, discovering talent, or fostering development. In other cases, parents perceived school as a chess barrier. They removed children from school over long periods for chess competitions, chose to home school them, or had them take a year off from school to concentrate on chess completely.

Some children were raised in an environment perfectly suited for chess development (like New York City), whereas others were raised well outside such centers of excellence. In either case, parents made sure that the child had access to all the materials, teachers, and tournaments necessary for success. The Internet, by the way, has recently made chess progress possible for almost anyone. Lessons with a grandmaster are possible via Skype, recent grandmaster games are available for analysis, tutorials are commonplace, and playing sites are just a click away. The families stressed hard work, success, and other positive values. With the exception of Fischer, all were raised in child centered two-parent homes where one parent stayed at home or chose a career with a flexible schedule intended to foster chess development.

Although only one parent was a serious chess player in his own right, several fathers fulfilled the primary coaching role from time to time. This meant studying the game on their own, developing lessons, and conducting frequent training sessions with their children. When not fulfilling this role, parents were still heavily involved in coach selection and lesson monitoring. They also played a significant role in arranging other high-level training opportunities.

Managing their child's chess career was like a second job, and parents ranged from consumed to obsess with fulfilling the manager role. First, chess careers were expensive, between $20,000 to 50,000 annually, so parents made many personal and financial sacrifices. For example, they studied chess and wrote chess Blogs during their free time, chose less prestigious and lower-paying jobs that freed up time for chess, took on extra work as janitors to pay the chess bills, lived in homes that were too small or without air conditioning because they chose chess over comfort, and saved money at distant tournaments by sleeping on strangers' floors littered with cat dander. They handled all aspects of their child's chess careers including teaching, hiring and communicating with coaches, monitoring progress, purchasing materials, scheduling tournaments, making travel plans, and traveling extensively to national and international events where they do all they can to have their young champion psychologically ready for battle.

From a psychological standpoint, parents sometimes looked to foster motivation and emotional strength. This was not always necessary, of course, because their young players were passionate about chess and were fierce competitors. In terms of motivation, parents occasionally directed the child's focus away from leisure and other activities back to chess and reminded him that parent commitment only goes as far as the child's. Much like the parents that Kiewra and colleagues (Kiewra et al., 2006) studied, these parents took the stance that the choice (once made) to excel in chess requires complete commitment. On the other hand, parents allowed for the natural waning of motivation from time to time and rolled with it such as when Josh Waitzkin spent a summer fishing and recharging his chess battery. In terms of emotion, the parents naturally strived to sooth the pain children experienced from losing and helped them roll with the punches. Moreover, these parents safeguarded their children's psychological environment from the many adults who entered their world as competitors, coaches, well-wishers, and critics.

Having completed this study, first author Kenneth Kiewra can now see that his own supreme efforts to nurture a chess champion were not unique but common among parents raising elite chess children. Chess is a game where every move counts and every move is painstakingly calculated. This chapter revealed that the same is true for the parents of elite young players. Their moves are well calculated and strong and, at times, daring. In the final analysis, parents' moves are instrumental, if not critical, to their child's chess success. Chess champions are not born, but made.

ACKNOWLEDGMENTS

We would like to acknowledge Sarah Rogers and Kyle Perry for their contributions to this study.

REFERENCES

Bloom, B. (1985). *Developing Talent in Young People*. New York, NY: Ballantine Books.
Brady, F. (1973). *Bobby Fischer: Profile of a Prodigy*. New York, NY: Dover.
Colvin, G. (2008). *Talent is Overrated*. New York, NY: Penguin Group.

Creswell, J. W. (2007). *Qualitative Inquiry and Research Design: Choosing Among Five Approaches*. Thousand Oaks, CA: Sage.

Ericsson, K. A. (2002). Attaining excellence through deliberate practice: Insights from the study of expert performance. In M. Ferrari (Ed.), *The pursuit of excellence in education* (pp. 21-55). Hillsdale, NJ: Erlbaum.

Gardner, H. (1997). *Extraordinary Minds*. New York, NY: Basic Books.

Gladwell, M. (2008). *Outliers*. New York, NY: Little, Brown and Company.

Gobet, F., and Charness, N. (2006). Expertise in chess. In K. A. Ericsson, N. Charness, P. J. Feltovich, and R. R. Hoffman (Eds.), *The Cambridge handbook of experts and expert performance* (pp. 523-538). New York, NY: Cambridge University Press.

Hunt, E. (2006). Expertise, talent, and social encouragement. In K. A. Ericsson, N. Charness, P. J. Feltovich, and R. R. Hoffman (Eds.), *The Cambridge handbook of experts and expert performance* (pp. 31-38). New York, NY: Cambridge University Press.

Kiewra, K. A., O'Connor, T., McCrudden, M., and Liu, X. (2006). Developing young chess masters: A collective case study. In T. Redman (Ed.), *Chess in education: Essays from the Koltanowski conference* (pp. 98–108). Richardson, TX: Chess Program at The University of Dallas.

Polgar, S., and Shutzman, J. (1997). *Queen of the Kings Game*. New York, NY: CompChess.

Robson, G. (2010). *Chess Child: The Story of Ray Robson, America's Youngest Grandmaster*. Seminole, FL: Nipa Hut.

Stake, R. E. (2010). *Qualitative Research: Studying How Things Work*. New York, NY: Guildford.

Waitzkin, F. (1988). *Searching for Bobby Fischer*. New York, NY: Penguin.

Winner, E. (2000). Giftedness: Current theory and research. *Current Directions in Psychological Science, 9*, 153-156. Doi: 10.1111/1467-8721.00082.

In: The Nurturing of Talent, Skills and Abilities
Editor: Michael F. Shaughnessy

ISBN: 978-1-62618-521-0
© 2013 Nova Science Publishers, Inc.

Chapter 13

THE ROLE OF DELIBERATE PRACTICE IN THE DEVELOPMENT OF GRADUATE RESEARCHERS

Gwen C. Marchand, Gregory Schraw* and Lori Olafson
Educational Psychology and Higher Education,
University of Nevada, Las Vegas, Las Vegas, Nevada, US

The need for improving research competencies in social science and educational research is important for at least two reasons (Henson, Hull and Williams, 2010; Shulman, Golde, Conklin and Garabedian, 2006). One is that individuals do not begin to master their craft until beginning graduate school, often 15 to 20 years later than other disciplines. Research suggests that new skills are more easily transferred to new domains when acquired early in life and those intellectual skills may peak between the ages of 20 to 35 (Ericsson, Nandagopal and Roring, 2009). A second reason is that researchers must master a variety of competencies which we describe in detail below, including theories of knowledge, content expertise, methodological knowledge, statistics and data-analysis skills, and a high degree of expertise in professional writing in order to disseminate their research findings.

This chapter considers the multiple challenges of training researchers in the social sciences and how training programs may better prepare students to become expert researchers. We do so by using models of skill acquisition (Charness, Krampe, and Mayr,1996), expertise (Glaser and Chi, 1988), and deliberate practice (Ericsson, 2003) to better understand the task demands of teaching research and to consider training strategies that help meet these demands. These models and related instructional practices have produced great success in a variety of settings over the past three decades. We believe that all universities can improve research training by reflecting on a competency model that promotes expertise, sequencing courses in the most efficient manner based on principles of skill acquisition, and including a variety of instructional and research-based experiences throughout graduate training based on the deliberate practice model.

---

* Correspondence should be addressed to Gregory Schraw. E-mail: gschraw@unlv.nevada.edu.

There are three main sections of this chapter. The first provides an overview of five core competencies needed to develop expertise in quantitative research in social sciences. The second section reviews literature related to the development of expertise in all domains. The third section summarizes previous research on teaching research methods in the social sciences and discusses six instructional strategies that may be used to elevate novice students to a state of competency in conducting research.

FIVE ESSENTIAL RESEARCH COMPETENCIES

A competency model refers to the collection of knowledge, skills, attitudes, and self-regulatory capabilities needed for successful job performance. We distilled five core competencies of quantitative research expertise based on a review of relevant literature. Figure 1 shows five core competency strands that we believe represent the minimal core knowledge and skills for professional quantitative researchers in the social sciences. These competencies correspond to explicit beliefs and professional values about knowledge and the research process, content knowledge, methodology, data-analysis, and writing expertise.

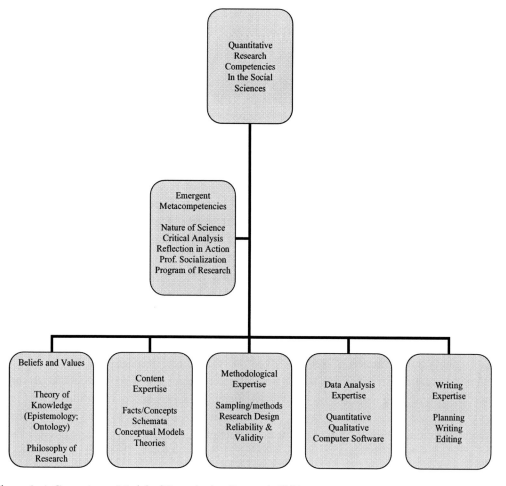

Figure 1. A Competency Model of Quantitative Research Skills.

A sixth strand of emergent competencies representing higher-order skills is included as well with the understanding students may not receive any direct instruction or discussion regarding the development of these skills. It should be noted that the purpose of our model is to further discussion about the improvement of research skills and training for these skills rather than to provide a comprehensive job or task-analysis of the domain.

Beliefs and Values

Professional beliefs guide researchers in decisions related to research topics, methodology, and conclusions drawn from findings, which ultimately promote the shared values that guide professional self-regulation (Steneck, 2007). Epistemology, ontology, and beliefs about the research process itself are central in this regard. We define epistemology as beliefs about the origin and acquisition of knowledge (Hofer and Pintrich, 1997). We define ontology as beliefs about the nature of reality and being (Lincoln and Guba, 2000). Ontology typically treats with questions about the nature of reality and what can be known about reality.

Researchers hold distinct theories of knowledge and theories of knowledge-change, both of which shape the professional values of researchers during the research process (Bedo, 2007; Henson et al., 2010). Theories of knowledge refer to the assumptions one makes about the nature, acquisition, stability, objectivity, and imparting of knowledge that comprise different theoretical positions such as positivism, postpositivism, and postmodern worldviews (Bedo, 2006; Lincoln and Guba, 2000). Theories of knowledge-change have critical implications for the way that scientific knowledge is advanced by research. Philosophers of science have proposed theories of scientific change that draw on different epistemological and ontological underpinnings of the research process (Kuhn, 1962; Lakatos, 1978). The Kuhnian perspective holds that theories change due to periodic cataclysmic rejection of their core tenets, which leads to old theories being replaced outright by new ones. The Lakatosian perspective holds that incremental change of peripheral and core assumptions leads to dynamic evolution of a theory such that an existing theory may undergo dramatic change over time yet remain viable.

Graduate programs rarely offer courses devoted to personal beliefs and values, yet good research training programs include some degree of formal instruction about personal beliefs and values, most commonly through the context of advanced quantitative and qualitative research classes. Students may also gather insight into their beliefs and values through discussion with their peers and faculty when defending particular perspectives or when learning about professional self-regulation. Greater awareness of one's beliefs and values promotes greater professional identity and more ethical practice (Drotar, Palermo and Landis, 2003; Steneck, 2007).

Content Expertise

Researchers at all levels exercise their research skills to address content knowledge questions. Emerging researchers are likely expected to acquire a range of content knowledge spanning facts and concepts to a working knowledge of important theories in interest areas.

We assume that this content expertise is acquired through formal coursework particularly courses focused on deep conceptual understanding of models and theories, which in turn lay the foundation for research questions. Most graduate students would be expected to engage in four to eight courses in their broad content area and at least two in-depth seminars or independent study courses. Of course, students also gain content expertise through practice, such as through participation with student research collaborations or faculty-directed research teams.

Methodological Expertise

Methodological demands of graduate programs tend toward a wide range of both quantitative and qualitative methods. Research indicates that graduate students desire this methodological pluralism (Wagner, Garner and Kawulich, 2011) and the trend toward pluralism is clearly increasing (Llamas and Boza, 2011). Programs vary from institution to institution, but even a basic training program includes an introductory course in both quantitative and qualitative methods, as well as an advanced class in one of these areas. Many programs also include classes in allied areas such as program evaluation, survey methods, interviewing, and writing-oriented seminars.

Students are also expected to develop expertise in professional conduct associated with the research process. Unfortunately, programs may not offer a cohesive array of methodological courses or guidance in professional conduct, which can lead to gaps in both conceptual and procedural knowledge of the research process. Henson et al. (2010) proposed a pedagogical framework they refer to as collective quantitative proficiency (CQP) which focuses on the development of a comprehensive, integrated understanding of quantitative research methods spanning the five competencies shown in Figure 1. Through this explicit understanding, it is expected that researchers will establish quantitative habits of mind, which refers to a theory of practice based on a deep grasp of quantitative methods and the nature of science. In part, Henson and colleagues call for more and better integrated curriculum, as well as research training situated within a student-focused community of practice to improve CQP.

Data-Analysis Expertise

Graduate students and faculty are expected to develop a very wide set of data-analysis competencies in order to keep abreast of developing statistics and statistical software, as well as hybrid research such as mixed-methods. Many of these procedures such as structural equation modeling, hierarchical linear modeling, and item response theory are extremely sophisticated and time-consuming to master. In addition, techniques that once were rarely encountered in education such as logistic regression, log-linear modeling, time series, cluster analysis, discriminant function analysis, and panoply of non-parametric techniques are becoming more common. In current graduate programs, a minimum of three advanced statistics courses would be required (i.e., experimental, correlational, and multivariate) and perhaps an additional two to four course would be recommended depending upon the graduate student's interest and comfort level. The breadth and depth of recent developments is staggering and challenging to keep up with if one hopes to possess enough expertise in all of these areas to competently choose the appropriate method for which to analyze complex data or to provide well-informed, accurate reviews for professional journals.

Writing Expertise

Students rarely receive structured training in technical writing, even though faculty expects students to know how to write and penalize them when writing is insufficient (Kellogg and Whiteford. 2009; Sallee, Hallett and Tierney, 2011). Of the formal writing training that occurs in university settings, the bulk of it occurs while writing a thesis or dissertation. From a practical standpoint, this means that expertise (i.e., literature reviews, research articles, professional reviews) occurs primarily within the context of small research groups that take place outside the bounds of formal course work (Belcher, 2009).

Research suggests that the benefits of writing instruction are invaluable to students (Belcher, 2009; Nolan and Tonette, 2009). Graduate programs that schedule writing courses early in the program, have committed instructors, and expect research writing in multiple courses may have a strong impact on the development of writing proficiency. Further, Sallee et al. (2011) provided five guidelines for increasing the impact of writing instruction, including breaking research and writing into manageable units, encouraging student support, focusing on all aspects of writing, model the writing process, and provide feedback and support.

Summary

The five competencies summarized above reveal the tremendous breadth of expertise that emerging researchers are expected to master. Yet, the real goal of graduate training is to develop emergent competencies, or what we refer to as metacompetence. Successful students will gain metacompetencies that include an understanding of the nature of science (Sadler, Burgin, McKinney and Ponjuan, 2010), a repertoire of critical analysis skills (Ritchhart and Perkins, 2005), reflection-in-action in which individuals possess explicit conceptual understanding of a domain and the ability to reflect upon and change that understanding (Schön, 1987), a high degree of professional socialization (Steneck, 2007), and a sustainable, theoretically-driven program of research that supports subsequent publication, funding, and graduate student development. Although most graduate students do not exit programs at this ambitious level, they should be well on their way toward this goal with the understanding that an additional five to 10 years of professional development will bestow upon them true expertise.

UNDERSTANDING EXPERT PERFORMANCE

This section focuses on three components of highly skilled performance in any domain, including skill acquisition, characteristics of experts, and the role of deliberate practice in expertise.

Skill Acquisition

Skill acquisition refers to stages in the development of a specific skill or set of related skills. A skill is a particular behavior routine used to accomplish a goal and may range from simple to complex. Researchers have identified three stages referred to as knowledge accumulation, knowledge integration, and automation and tuning (Alexander, 2003; Wilkins and Rawson, 2010). A fourth stage, the knowledge transfer stage, was proposed by Ericsson (1996) as characterized by novel transfer of skills and skill-related heuristics to new domains.

Characteristics of the four stages are listed in Table 1. The knowledge acquisition stage consists of accumulating declarative knowledge needed to understand and perform a skill (Ericsson, 2003). The knowledge integration stage marks the transition from accumulating isolated segments of knowledge to integrating that knowledge into larger conceptual chunks such as schemata and scripts, or still larger chunks such as explicit conceptual models of a complex process that support procedural competence. Complex skills may require years to integrate. For example, many graduate students and university professors never fully master the process of writing scholarly research reports.

Table 1. Four Stages of Skill Acquisition

Stage	Activities	Level of Expertise	Example: Conducting a research experiment
Knowledge Accumulation	Acquire facts and concepts related to content, methods and data analysis.	1. Non-automated apprentice.	Acquire knowledge about educational research, including content knowledge, research methods, data analysis, and drawing valid conclusions.
Knowledge Integration	Organize information into schemata, procedural routines, and theories.	2. Automated apprentice.	Integrate knowledge into schemata and script. Use to plan, execute, and evaluate research. Construct hypothesis to test theory. Select appropriate methods and statistics.
Knowledge automation and tuning	Practice routines until they are fully automated and self-regulated. Plan, test, and revise theory of knowledge. Extend knowledge.	3. Automated expert.	Integrate findings into evidence-based conclusions. Generate theoretical and practical implications from findings. Revise and clarify guiding theory.
Knowledge transfer	Apply knowledge to new domains or novel problems. Create and generalize new knowledge.	4. Transfer of expertise to novel problems and settings.	Apply or generalize knowledge and findings to new domains or problems. Use old knowledge to identify and solve problems in unrelated domains. Explicit theory of one's expertise.

As a skill is practiced over an extended period of time, skill development enters the automation and tuning stage during which skills are performed more quickly and efficiently (Zhukov, 2009). Not all skills become fully automated due to their level of complexity and contextual variability under which many skills are performed (Ericsson, 2003), and even highly automated skills are tuned frequently in an effort to optimize performance in local conditions. The fourth stage, the knowledge transfer stage, requires experts to apply existing knowledge to new domains or novel problems. Experts engaged with this level of skill development often find themselves fully absorbed in the application of existing knowledge to a new problem, a process which generates new knowledge and high levels of creativity (Ericsson, 1996). Individuals also are more likely at this stage to possess an explicit theory of their own expertise and expertise of others that can be used to regulate their own performance as well as help others improve performance (Côté and Gilbert, 2009; Glaser and Chi, 1988).

Researchers have identified a common developmental trajectory in expertise. First, at least five years is needed to reach any level of expertise, although the norm is typically 10-20 years (Ericsson et al., 2009). Next, developing expertise is associated with increasing automaticity and accuracy of skill performance. Third, advanced skill development is characterized by strategy generalization and skill transfer within and between old and new problem-types. Finally, individuals become more adept at using metacognitive and self-regulatory strategies as they progress toward expertise.

Characteristics of Experts

Expertise may be thought of as the end-point or highest level of skill acquisition (Wilkins and Rawson, 2010). Regardless of the domain, experts appear to share many core characteristics. Glaser and Chi (1988) summarized the seven characteristics of experts, which include: excelling in a single domain; possession of an enormous amount of well-organized information; faster and more automatized skill deployment; efficient use of memory and limited cognitive resources; representation of problems at a deep level; greater time spent identifying and analyzing problems, but less time spent problem-solving; and strong monitoring and self-regulation practices.

Research on expertise supports the conclusion that experts are faster, more planful and efficient, and more reflective because of the depth and breadth of their knowledge (Alexander, 2004; Ericsson et al., 2009). Nevertheless, knowledge in the absence of a large repertoire of well-coordinated problem-solving strategies does not yield expertise. Rather, it is through accruing up to 50,000 hours of practice that individuals develop the characteristics associated with expertise (Ericsson, 2003). This level of commitment and type of work in the service of skill development is referred to by researchers as deliberate practice.

Deliberate Practice

Deliberate practice may be defined as concentrated, purposeful practice activities designed to increase knowledge and performance of a particular skill (Ericsson et al., 2009; McGaghie, 2008). Deliberate practice shares a unique, positive relation with skilled performance and research indicates that it is the most important cognitive-developmental mechanism on the path to high-level expertise, surpassing even initial ability and talent (Charness, Tuffiash, Krampe, Reingold and Vasyukova, 2005; Ericsson, 2003; Ward et al., 2007).

Eight domain-general principles of deliberate practice have been identified in the research literature (McGaghie, 2008). Deliberate practice is goal-driven, typically focused on a specific skill or knowledge gap, and highly structured, often utilizing physical and mental rehearsal (Nordin, Cumming, Vincent and McGrory, 2006). Second, practice usually occurs early in the morning or as the first major activity of the day, lasts two to four hours, and is geared toward incremental progress. Third, practice is motivated by both activity-specific intrinsic motivation and general achievement motivation, though of the two, research suggests that activity-specific motivation is a stronger predictor of performance.

Table 2. Seven Microstructure Components of Deliberate Practice Activities

Component	Purpose	Benefits	Example
1. Planned individual practice	2 to 4 hours of intentional practice beyond current performance limits.	1. Reveals deficiencies in current skill level. 2. Increases speed and fluency.	Typing. Musical scales or a performance piece using Suzuki method. Mental rehearsal and imagery of sport drills.
2. Focus on a specific practice goal	Practice with the intent to improve a specific skill of perceived knowledge gap.	1. Identify and correct weaknesses. 2. Fill knowledge or skill gap.	Rehearsal of a specific skill such as a musical passage or sport skill (e.g., exiting starting blocks in a sprint race).
3. Planned individual or group study	Increase knowledge via study of theory and expert performance.	1. Acquisition of knowledge and theories. 2. Identify and coordinate strategies.	Studying chess manuals or tournament games. Studying musical scores. Watching videos.
4. Peer/team practice	Practice or review performance with peers.	1. Feedback embedded within practice. 2. Observational learning. 3. Peer motivation	Intentional and covert modeling of peers.
5. Supervised, tailored training from coach.	Modify goals and performance routines and standard under expert tutelage.	1. Learn to set practice and performance goals. 2. Improvement of technique. 3. Theory, tactics, and strategy. 4. Motivation	In vivo practice feedback with coach. Reviewing game plans and video tapes.
6. Self-generated feedback and analysis	Evaluate performance strengths and weaknesses during practice	Formative and summative analysis of performance, strategies, theory and resource management.	Notebooks, logs and performance journals. Rehearsal with self-talk.
7. Feedback and analysis from expert or mentor.	Evaluate performance strengths and weaknesses during practice and competition.	Formative and summative analysis of performance, strategies, game theory, and resource management.	Drills with feedback. Video analysis. Demonstrations and modeling by coach. Mentor's critical analysis.

This motivation allows individuals to remain engaged with practice even through boredom and tedium. Fourth, practice occurs at the high point of an individual's current skill level, or what has been referred to as in the social-cognitive learning literature as the zone of proximal development (Werstch, 2008). Fifth, practice often begins at a very early age, which is linked to stronger later skill development (Ford, Ward, Hodges and Williams, 2009). Sixth, practice is supervised by a coach, peers, self or parent. Seventh, both formative and summative feedback related to performance, strategy use, and resource management is used to improve and streamline practice. Finally, once proximal goals are met, new goals and higher level conceptual understanding commensurate with Table 1 are pursued using a set of updated goals.

Research indicates that the eight principles of deliberate practice may be supported through seven microstructure components of practice (see Table 2). Individuals who engage in these activities derive a variety of advantages, including three overarching performance benefits. First, there is a direct relationship between practice amount and performance, with early and frequent practice associated with greater psychological and physical benefits than less practice (Ericsson et al., 2009; Ward et al., 2009; Zhukov, 2009). Second, study that includes books, videos, and activity-relevant theoretical exercises, as well as high level discussion with experts, leads to greater performance compared to little or no study of such materials. Third, supervised, tailored mentoring from an advanced expert greatly facilitates the development of expertise and conceptual understanding of one's own expertise. Coaches or mentors influence motivation and have a direct impact on the development of technical, strategic, and tactical skills to the extent that Charness et al. (2005) reported that presence of high-level coaches explains as much or more variance in expertise than any other factor except concentrated study.

The most vital causal factor in the development of expertise is daily structured practice (Ericsson et al., 2009). Some disciplines, such as music, have clear expectations for technical skills that must be practiced (Charness et al., 2005; Zhukov, 2009), whereas other disciplines such as quantitative research are less clear about what to practice, although reasonably much practice could be devoted to methodology, data analysis, or writing (Kellogg and Whiteford, 2009). Research suggests four hours of practice per day for 10 years is necessary to become a true expert, with true experts committing between 20-40 hours of practice (excluding performance and study) per week. This practice often occurs at the beginning of the work day, with experts engaged in deliberate practice first thing, and followed by study, rehearsal, and peer-oriented practice activities before moving to play (Ericsson et al., 2009). However, informal practice, rehearsal, or casual play does not impart the same benefits as goal-focused deliberate practice. Yet, elite experts typically participate in a greater amount of both formal and informal practice compared to less-skilled peers. From the standpoint of quality, the ideal scenario for practice is to set specific goals, utilize feedback, use repetition to identify and correct errors, comparison of one's performance with a peer or coach, and to incorporate mental rehearsal as well.

Summary

This section reviewed research on the development of expertise. Models of skill acquisition describe how knowledge becomes increasingly sophisticated. The study of expertise demonstrates important characteristics that emerge as individuals move from novice to expert levels of skill. Finally, the theory of deliberate practice provides specific principles and components for training experts.

ISSUES IN THE TRAINING OF NOVICE-TO-EXPERT RESEARCHERS

Training graduate students to become expert researchers requires careful program planning and ongoing deliberate practice. Yet students in the social sciences face a broad array of possible methodological areas in which to pursue expertise. For this reason, students usually choose one or two pathways and drill deep within them using learning experiences consistent with deliberate practice.

Table 3. Six Instructional Activities that Promote Research Competence

Instructional Activity	Purposes	Examples
Formal Instruction		
Other-directed	Codified skill and knowledge acquisition from expert.	Required courses. Seminars. Field-based practica.
Self-directed	Intensive study of specific skills and performance of experts. Simulated practice of experts.	Individual study. Goal-directed daily practice. Analysis of experts' performance.
Peer Learning		
Peers (Dyads)	Learning and reflection within current zone of proximal development. Modeling and feedback. Motivational support. Practice partner.	Practice, feedback, and reflection with classmates. Peer assisted tutoring. Participation in clubs.
Team-learning	Community of practice. Practice in real-world, often competitive settings. Context-specific (e.g., multivariate statistics) analysis of skills and strategies.	Simulated play. Tournaments. Collaborative research projects. Team drills with feedback.
Expert Guidance		
Coaches	Expert modeling and feedback, usually with detailed cognitive and performance process feedback. Analysis of tactical, physical and psychological abilities. Instructional scaffolding.	Private lessons. Master classes. Real or virtual expert tutors.
Apprenticeship (with mentor)	Sustained cognitive apprenticeship. Theory of practice. Explicit awareness of emergent skills and skill monitoring. Professional self-regulation.	Doctoral advisor. Research assistant. Independent study. Directed internship.

Graduate programs provide the opportunities for students to develop these skills through a variety of instructional approaches and strategies (Lei, 2009; Llamas and Boza, 2011; Wagner et al., 2011). These include course offerings that represent methodological pluralism, explicit theoretical and applied linkages between courses, collaboration among teachers, discussion of recent primary professional research literature, and use of real-world examples in an inquiry-based setting.

Recent illustrations of instructional approaches suggest that programs including a variety of pedagogical opportunities to learn from peers and experts are particularly effective (Drotar et al., 2003; Shostak eta l., 2010). We suspect that these approaches were successful because they incorporated important aspects of deliberate practice such as seminars that facilitate knowledge and skill development, peers that support inquiry and reflection, and coaches and mentors that model expert problem solving and professional self-regulation. A finer-grained analysis of the research training literature revealed six instructional practices (see Table 3) characteristic of three pedagogical strategies we describe as formal instruction, peer learning opportunities, and expert guidance that illustrate in greater detail the generic approaches described by Drotar et al. (2003) and Shostak et al. (2010).

Formal instruction. Two different types of formal instruction are described in the training literature, which we refer to as other-directed and self-directed instruction. Other-directed instruction is characterized by a structured learning environment that is directed by a content or procedural expert and is designed to disseminate a large body of knowledge and skills quickly. Much of this instruction is based on direct transmission of information rather than constructive learning (Brew, 2003). In contrast, self-directed instruction provides opportunities for deep study of expert strategies through engagement with study guides, vignettes, analyses of expert performances, or simulated games (Charness et al., 1996). This type of learning tends to be more constructivist than other-directed instruction, and requires the learner to organize and apply the knowledge in a personalized manner (Brew, 2003).

Recent literature reviews and meta-analyses suggest that formal instruction may be an especially effective way to help novices establish an integrated knowledge base and procedural skills during the early stages of skill acquisition (Magliaro, Lockee and Burton, 2005) and that explicit instruction outperformed other types of learning (Alfieri, Brooks, Aldrich and Tenenbaum, 2011Spada and Tomita, 2011). When training novices, explicit formal instruction may be the most efficient method to transmit technical knowledge about research methodology, analytic skills, and domain content. Alfieiri et al. (2011) identified four specific aspects of explicit instruction that enhanced learning, including feedback, worked examples, scaffolding, and explicit explanation of the process or conceptual structure of information. Overall, research suggests that both other-directed and self-directed learning play extremely important roles in the development of expertise. Moreover, formal instruction appears to provide the instructional bedrock for subsequent deliberate practice activities with peers, coaches, and mentors.

Peer learning. One hallmark of graduate training is participation in a variety of peer-learning activities such as small group sessions, collaborative projects, and brain-storming teams in which peer dynamics are characterized by dialectical constructivism in line with the tenets of sociocultural learning (Werstch, 2008). These peer-assisted activities are associated with higher levels of confidence, self-regulation, skill level, explicit understanding of the task, aspirations and motivation, self-concept, and sustained engagement (Ginsburg-Block, Rohrbeck and Fantuzzo, 2006; Resta and Laferrière, 2007; Terrion and Leonard, 2007). These types of benefits have been documented in the context of graduate research methods and research oriented writing courses (Sallee et al., 2011) courses. Peer learning fosters these outcomes through a variety of social-emotional developmental mechanisms, including: similarity in age and experience, mutual empathy, trustworthiness, and perceived supportiveness, as well as cognitive mechanisms such as discussion, conceptual scaffolding, scripted problem solving, competitive partnering, and feedback (Resta and Laferrière, 2007). Further, engagement in structured peer learning elevates skill development through high-level competition and increased awareness of higher-level skills, decision-making ability, and creativity in individual play (Ward et al., 2007).

Studies show that the cognitive and motivational benefits of teamwork support the development of expertise (DeChurch and Mesmer-Magnus, 2010; Mesmer-Magnus and DeChurch, 2009). Team work enhances performance because it is goal-focused, uses high performance standards, focuses on the use of tactics and group-regulated behavior, and promotes decision-making and adaptive anticipation (Côté, J., Baker, J., and Abernethy, 2007; Ford et al., 2009). Specifically, when working in teams, students must acquire declarative and procedural expertise, generate plausible problem solutions, share information, and participate in socially distributed cognition during which complex problems are broken down and solved in sequence by different work teams. Teams that maximize breadth of knowledge and group openness (Mesmer-Magnus and. DeChurch, 2009) have particularly strong influences on student outcomes.

In terms of advancing novices to experts in the context of graduate training, one crucial component of teams and peer collaborations is that they satisfy a need for close contact for intensive periods of time in a manner that is impossible for teachers and mentors who must divide their time among multiple students. Further, teams and collaborate peer learning can act as support systems for student motivation and perseverance by promoting the development of situated learning within a community of learners, which is often lacking at the level of formal instruction. Finally, there is evidence that a community of practice substantially increases learning and performance due to shared knowledge and the construction of a group mental model which may be used to identify and solve problems (Andres and Shipps, 2010).

Expert guidance. Expert guidance in the form of coaches, mentors and extended apprenticeships helps to focus and guide emerging experts to a deeper understanding of a domain. It is important to note that coaches and mentors are not necessarily the same. Coaches frequently work with large groups whereas mentors frequently work with individuals or small groups. Coaches usually focus on the development of specific skills or aspects of team play, whereas mentors focus on the "total package" of skills with a single mentee. Although coaches may be mentors and mentors may be coaches, they usually assume well-defined roles that differ in important ways (Ford et al., 2009; Zellers, Zellers, Howard and Barcic, 2008).

Overall, the coaching literature suggests that expert coaches have explicit knowledge of their coaching skills and use them to diagnosis, remediate, teach, and promote development in those they coach. Coaches also tend to remain mindful of the desired outcomes of their trainees and recognize contextual constraints on coaching practices (Côté and Gilbert 2009). Students may change coaches frequently as their expertise develops to maintain a sound match in expertise, but there is consensus that students who retain coaches develop much faster with expert coaches, plateau quickly without a coach, and rarely outgrow the need for coaching.

Unlike coaches, mentors provide sustained one-on-one guidance to a mentee through long-term relationships (Lumpkin, 2011). Graduate students who experience a high quality mentoring relationship with faculty have access to tutoring and modeling of expert behavior via dialectal interactions. Faculty mentors serve a variety of roles, including instructor, advisor, agent of socialization, modeler of skills, and professional advocate (Lechuga, 2011).

Universities with formal mentoring programs help surmount barriers associated with mismatches in gender, culture, intellectual interests, or confidence in establishing mentor-mentee relationships. These formal programs initiate relationships that benefit students and beginning faculty in terms of cultural adaptation, emotional support, networking, and increased job performance (Zellers et al., 2008). However, relationships that evolve naturally are more likely to develop into what we refer to as cognitive apprenticeships, by which we mean sustained practice-based relationships in an authentic setting (Werstch, 2008). Cognitive apprenticeships strengthen as mentees develop expertise and apprenticeships appear to offer a variety of benefits to both mentors and mentees. A recent meta-analysis of scientific research apprenticeship studies found that both mentors and mentees enjoyed the experience, graduate student retention and interest increased, learning and expertise improved, self-efficacy and confidence grew stronger, and professional socialization and networking were enhanced, yet it was unclear as to whether apprenticeships contributed to a better understanding of the nature of science (Sadler et al., 2010).

Guidelines for incorporating cognitive apprenticeships in graduate training have been proposed by a number of researchers (Backus, Keegan, Gluck and Gulick, 2010), and include immersion in authentic situated practice, cultivating high expectations, making explicit the skills of scholarship within the domain, providing extensive guided practice and feedback, and creating or participating in a community of scholars characterized by explicit reflection on practice with other experts.

Summary

Pedagogical pluralism is as important to the development of expertise as methodological pluralism. We expanded on the key arguments of Henson et al. (2010) by describing how programs that address each of the five competencies in Figure 1 using the six core instructional strategies in Table 3 have the best chance of instilling collective quantitative proficiency in graduate students and faculty. Striving to integrate these competencies into metacompetencies and a deep understanding of the nature of science, likewise, is perhaps the best way to establish the quantitative habits of mind needed to produce accurate, credible, and noteworthy research.

CONCLUSION

Our goals for this chapter were first to identify and present core competencies we feel are necessary to develop expertise in quantitative research methods. Then, we reviewed theories and models that broadly contributed to our understanding of how skills develop over time and factors that contribute to attaining expertise in any field. Finally, we integrated the two sections on competencies and expertise to highlight instructional strategies we believe can help graduate programs grow novice researchers into expert practitioners of quantitative methods. We believe that the application of principles of deliberate practice outlined in this chapter generalize to training programs regardless of discipline. We hope that the material presented in this chapter encourages both successful and developing graduate programs to reflect upon how to best support students in becoming thoughtful, prepared researchers through cohesive and varied instructional programming.

REFERENCES

Alexander, P. A. (2004). A model of domain learning: Reinterpreting expertise as a multidimensional, multistage process. In D. Y. Dai and R. J. Sternberg (Eds.), Motivation, emotion, and cognition: Integrative perspectives on intellectual functioning and development (pp.273-298). Mahwah, N.J.: Lawrence Erlbaum Associates.

Alfieri, L., Brooks, P. J., Aldrich, N. J., and Tenenbaum, H. R. (2011). Does discovery-based instruction enhance learning? *Journal of Educational Psychology*, 103, 1-18.

Andres, H. P., and Shipps, B. P. (2010). Team learning in technology-mediated distributed teams. *Journal of Information Systems Education*, 21, 213-21.

Backus, C., Keegan, K., Gluck, C., and Gulick, L. M. (2010). Accelerating leadership development via immersive learning and cognitive apprenticeship. *International Journal of Training and Development*, 14, 144-149.

Bedo, E. (2007). Philosophies of educational research. In J. Grenn, G, Camilli and P. B. Elmore (Eds)., *Handbook of complementary methods in education research* (pp. 3-32). Mahwah, NJ: Erlbaum.

Belcher, W. L. (2009). Reflections on ten years of teaching writing for publication to graduate students and junior faculty. *Journal of Scholarly Publishing*, 40, 184-200.

Brew, A. 2003. Teaching and research: New relationships and their implications for inquiry-based teaching and learning in higher education. *Higher Education Research and Development*, 22, 3–18.

Charness, N., Krampe, R., and Mayr, U. (1996). The role of practice and coaching in entrepreneurial skill domains: an international comparison of life-span chess skill acquisition. In K. A. Ericsson (Ed.), The road to excellence: The acquisition of expert performance in the Arts and Sciences, Sports and Games (pp. 51–80). Mahwah, NJ: Erlbaum.

Charness, N., Tuffiash, M., Krampe, R., Reingold, E., and Vasyukova, E. (2005). The role of deliberate practice in chess expertise. *Applied Cognitive Psychology*, 19, 151–165.

Côté, J., and Gilbert, W. (2009). An integrative definition of coaching effectiveness and expertise. *International Journal of Sports Science and Coaching*, 4, 307-323.

Côté, J., Baker, J., and Abernethy, B. (2007). Practice and play in the development of sport expertise. In G. Tenenbaum and R.C. Eklund (Eds.), *Handbook of sport psychology* (pp. 184–202). Princeton, New Jersey: John Wiley and Sons.

Crooks, V. A., Castleden, H., and Meerveld, I. T. (2010). Teaching research methods courses in human geography: Critical reflections. *Journal of Geography in Higher Education*, 34, 155–171.

DeChurch, L. A., and Mesmer-Magnus, J. R. (2010). The cognitive underpinnings of effective teamwork: A meta-analysis. *Journal of Applied Psychology*, 95, 32–53.

Drotar, D., Palermo, T, and Landis, C. E. (2003). Training graduate-level pediatric psychology researchers at Case Western Reserve University: Meeting the challenges of the new millennium. *Journal of Pediatric Psychology*, 28, 123-133.

Ericsson, K. A. (1996). The acquisition of expert performance: An introduction to some of the issues. In K. A. Ericsson (Ed.), The road to excellence: The acquisition of expert performance in the arts and sciences, sports, and games (pp. 1–50). Mahwah, NJ: Lawrence Erlbaum Associates.

Ericsson, K. A. (2003). The acquisition of expert performance as problem solving: Construction and modification of mediating mechanisms through deliberate practice. In J. E. Davidson and R. J. Sternberg (Eds.), *The psychology of problem solving* (pp. 31–83). Cambridge, England: Cambridge University Press.

Ericsson, K. A., and Ward, P. (2007). Capturing the naturally occurring superior performance of experts in the laboratory: Toward a science of expert and exceptional performance. *Current Directions in Psychological Science*, 16, 346-350.

Ericsson, K. A., Nandagopal, K., and Roring, R. W. (2009). Toward a science of exceptional achievement: Attaining superior performance through deliberate practice. Annals of the New York Academy of Science, 1172, 199–217.

Ford, P. A., Ward, P., Hodges, N, J., and Williams, M. (2009). The role of deliberate practice and play in career progression in sport: the early engagement hypothesis. *High Ability Studies*, 20, 65–75.

Ford, P., Coughlan, E., and Williams, M. (2009). The expert-performance approach as a framework for understanding and enhancing coaching performance, expertise and learning. *International Journal of Sports Science and Coaching*, 4, 451-463.

Ginsburg-Block, M. D., Rohrbeck, C. A., and Fantuzzo, J. W. (2006). A meta-analytic review of social, self-concept, and behavioral outcomes of peer-assisted learning. *Journal of Educational Psychology*, 98, 732–749.

Glaser, R., and Chi, M. T. (1988). Overview. In M. Chi, R. Glaser, and M Farr (Eds.), The nature of expertise (pp. 15-28). Mahwah, NJ: Erlbaum.

Henson, R. K., Hull, D. M., and Williams, C. S. (2010). Methodology in our education research culture: Toward a stronger collective quantitative proficiency. *Educational Researcher*, 39, 229-240.

Hofer, B. K., and Pintrich, P. R. (1997). The development of epistemological theories: beliefs about knowledge and knowing and their relation to learning. *Review of Educational Research*, 67, 88-140.

Kellogg, R. T., and Whiteford, A. P. (2009). Training advanced writing skills: The case for deliberate practice. *Educational Psychologist*, 44, 250-266.

Kuhn, T. S. (1962). The structure of scientific revolutions. Chicago, IL: University of Chicago Press.

Lakatos, I. (1978). The methodology of scientific research programmes. Cambridge, England: Cambridge University Press.

Lechuga, V. M. (2011). Faculty-graduate student mentoring relationships: Mentors' perceived roles and responsibilities. *Higher Education*, 62, 757–771.

Lei, S. (2009. Factors changing attitudes of graduate schools students toward an introductory research methodology course. *Education*, 128, 667-685.

Lincoln, Y. S., and Guba, E. G. (2000). Paradigmatic controversies, contradictions, and emerging confluences. In N. K. Denzin and Y. S. Lincoln (Eds.), *Handbook of qualitative research* (2nd edition, pp. 163-188). Thousand Oaks, CA: Sage Publications.

Llamas, J. M. C., and Boza, A. (2011). Teaching research methods for doctoral students in education: Learning to enquire in the university. *International Journal of Social Research Methodology*. 14, 77–90.

Lumpkin, A. (2011). A model for mentoring university faculty. *The Educational Forum*, 75, 357–368.

Magliaro, S. G., Lockee, B. B., and Burton, J. K. (2005). Direct instruction revisited: A key model for instructional technology. *Educational Technology Research and Development*, 53, 41-55.

McGaghie, W. C. (2008). Research opportunities in simulation-based medical education using deliberate practice. *Academic Emergency Medicine*, 15, 995–1001.

Mesmer-Magnus, J. R., and. DeChurch, L. A. (2009). Information sharing and team performance: A meta-analysis. *Journal of Applied Psychology*, 94, 535-546.

Nolan, R., and Tonette, R. (2009). Teaching graduate students in the social sciences writing for publication. *International Journal of Teaching and Learning in Higher Education*, 20, 267-273.

Nordin, S. M., Cumming, J., Vincent, J., and McGrory, S. (2006). Mental practice or spontaneous play? Examining which types of imagery constitute deliberate practice in sport. *Journal of Applied Sport Psychology*, 18, 345–362.

Resta, P., and Laferrière, T. (2007). Technology in support of collaborative learning. *Educational Psychology Review*, 19, 65-83.

Ritchhart, R., and Perkins, D. N. (2005). Learning to think: The challenges of teaching thinking. In K. J. Holyoak and R. G. Morrison (Eds.), *The Cambridge handbook of thinking and reasoning* (pp. 775–802). Cambridge: Cambridge University Press.

Sadler, T. D., Burgin, S., McKinney, L., and Ponjuan, L. (2010). Learning science through research apprenticeships: A critical review of the literature. *Journal of Research in Science Teaching*, 47, 235–256.

Sallee, M., Hallett, R., and Tierney, W. (2011). Teaching writing in graduate school. *College Teaching*, 59, 66–72.

Schmidt, H. G., van der Molen, H. T., te Winkel W. W. R., and Wijnen, W. H. F. W. (2009). Constructivist, problem-based learning does work: A meta-analysis of curricular comparisons involving a single medical school. *Educational Psychologist*, 44, 227–249.

Schön, D.A. (1987). Educating the reflective practitioner. San Francisco, CA: Jossey-Bass.

Shadish, W. R., Cook, T. D., and Campbell, D. T. (2002). Experimental and quasi-experimental designs for generalized causal inference. Boston, MA: Houghton Mifflin Co.

Shostak, S., Girouard, J., Cunningham, D., and Cadge, W. (2010). Teaching graduate and undergraduate research methods: A multipronged departmental initiative. *Teaching Sociology*, 38, 93–105.

Shulman, L., Golde, C., Conklin, A., and Garabedian, K. (2006). Reclaiming education's doctorates: A critique and a proposal. *Educational Researcher*, 35, 25–32.

Spada, N., and Tomita, Y. (2011). Interactions between type of instruction and type of language feature: A meta-analysis. *Language Learning*, 60, 263- 308.

Steneck, N. H. (2007). ORI introduction to the responsible conduct of research. Washington, DC: Office of Research Integrity, Department of Health and Human Services.

Terrion, J. L., and Leonard, D. (2007). A taxonomy of the characteristics of student peer mentors in higher education: Findings from a literature review. *Mentoring and Tutoring*, 15, 149–164.

Wagner, C., Garner, M., and Kawulich, B. (2011). The state of the art of teaching research methods in the social sciences: towards a pedagogical culture. *Studies in Higher Education*, 36, 75–88.

Ward, P., Hodges, N. J., Starkes, N. J., and Williams, M. (2007). The road to excellence: Deliberate practice and the development of expertise. *High Ability Studies*, 18, 119–153.

Werstch, J. V. (2008). From social interaction to higher psychological processes: A clarification and application of Vygotsky's theory. *Human Development*, 51, 66-79.

Wilkins, N. J. and Rawson, K. A. (2010). Loss of cognitive skill across delays: Constraints for theories of cognitive skill acquisition. *Journal of Experimental Psychology: Learning, Memory, and Cognition*, 36, 1134–1149.

Zellers, D. F., Howard, V. M., and Barcic, M. A. (2008). Faculty mentoring programs: Reenvisioning rather than reinventing the wheel. *Review of Educational Research*, 78, 552–588.

Zhukov, K. (2009). Effective practising: A research perspective. *Australian Journal of Music Education*, 11, 3-12.

In: The Nurturing of Talent, Skills and Abilities
Editor: Michael F. Shaughnessy
ISBN: 978-1-62618-521-0
© 2013 Nova Science Publishers, Inc.

Chapter 14

WHAT COUNSELORS NEED TO LEARN: SKILLS, TALENTS AND ABILITIES

Adam Blatner[*]

Senior University Georgetown, TX, US

Counselors are people-helpers, relative experts in the art of drawing people into their higher potentials. To be helpful or therapeutic, they need to learn skills for being appropriately supportive or nurturing while also helping their clients learn a variety of skills related to emotional or interpersonal problem-solving, improved communications, and insight.

My background is as a psychiatrist back from the olden days when my profession was more oriented to using psychological approaches to help people learn about these skills. (A psychiatrist is a physician, an M.D., specializing in the diagnosis and treatment of disorders of the mind.) We talked and listened and only occasionally used the prescription pad. I was eclectic—not overly beholden to any particular school of thought, and willing to use the best of many. (Now most counselors are more like this, but back then there was more pressure to choose one approach and stick with it.)

So, in the following chapter I am summarizing some of the high points I've learned about the art of bringing people forth—because that's what therapy is.

DEVELOP A WORKING ALLIANCE

Relationship is the foundation. This is tricky—it can't be described fully by any manual. It has to do with your cultivation of yourself as a nice person. It's not that hard to become so caught up in technique or knowing stuff that you forget that it all counts for little compared to your capacity to build a good working alliance, develop some genuine rapport with your client. If you can't really develop what Carl Rogers called "unconditional positive regard," then refer your client to someone who may be a better fit.

---

[*] E-mail: adam@blatner.com. www.blatner.com/adam/bio1.html.

As you listen with your imagination, your "third ear," as it has been called, imagine that what is being described were true for you, and what, in consequence, you might think and feel. This is basically what empathy is about. Remember, though, that you might be mistaken, so allow your clients to correct you as you seek to help them to find the words to express themselves more fully. Listen for illusions that follow the rules of non-rational rhetoric—this is part of listening critically—; and listen also for what isn't being said but yet felt.

Part of your skill involves finding what you can agree with, validate. This is the art of tact. Patients will allow you to question or probe if they feel that you're really with them. Try to make eye contact on occasion, or at times, to sustain eye contact. There's no rule book here—you've got to use your intuition as to when it works. The point is that an optimal connection requires the artful interposition of these glances—understanding, liking, appreciating, sympathizing.

As you approach closure of the session, or nearing the end of therapy, open to the real question that generally remains unasked: "So, doc, am I crazy? Was I wrong for feeling what I felt, or did it make sense? Even if I misinterpreted and was foolish and over-reactive, etc., can you see that I'm really trying? I'm not a bad person, am I?" If you can offer some reassurance on these, your presence and manner—more than your words—will go with the client into the future.

PROMOTING PSYCHOLOGICAL MINDEDNESS

The first skill I think counselors need to learn and impart in turn to their clients is psychological mindedness. Basically, this skill involves learning how to be curious about and how to find out about the workings of one's own mind. This is the basis of psychological growth, development, and self-actualization. Let's also add learning that this activity can be fun!

Psychological mindedness is not obviously fun. Just as some kids experience learning about basic anatomy as a bit "yucky," so, too, most people aren't really comfortable with the idea that they often fool themselves. Part of this involves the fear that others will look down on them for not being in full self-control, but the art of shifting this involves the counselor's being confident in just admitting that we all do it, it's part of human nature, and to approach this as a matter-of-fact function, like urinating or defecating. It's helpful if counselors can admit that they have learned to do this from the beginning of their career training, and that counselors also have many items that they can work on in their own lives. Of course dysfunctional dynamics will be discovered, but don't be discouraged. It's like learning to floss one's teeth. It can be made into a lifelong fun project—and believe me, it never ends! (I'm seventy-five and still discover quirks!) Selling this attitude is a primary skill.

TAKE THE HISTORY AGAIN

It's effective to express a bit of humility and be open to not thinking you've gotten the whole story right off. It shows you're really interested. Your clients know intuitively they haven't told you everything; they sense they haven't even told *themselves* everything! So going back and going over this or that point delivers a willingness to show that you're really thinking about what happened and what happens—you're not just hearing some clues and jumping to conclusions.

The word "diagnosis" should not be taken as just slapping on a label. It's related to the word roots for "through-knowing," and it really suggests genuine understanding. Really, the diagnostic process should never end! Even when a treatment process is decided upon, one fit for the diagnosis, fine tuning is needed. More diagnosis is needed to ensure that this approach can be appropriately modified to fit the client's temperament or other unique needs.

Counseling is one of those roles in which the skills can deepen and be refined for a lifetime. If you remain open to new discoveries in the field, you will be better after 40 years of practice than you were after 20 years. So again, make a game of it. To paraphrase Hippocrates, sometimes called "the father of medicine," learning the true art of healing involves a process that is far greater than any single lifetime. One spin-off of this idea is that you may discover some refinements in diagnosis or therapy that in the long run may help others, so dare to write a paper about it!

ENCOURAGE THE CLIENT

Alfred Adler was asked by a naive and therefore mildly impudent reporter to summarize what he had learned in his many years as a psychotherapist. Adler rose to the occasion: "Encourage the child!" The art of encouragement deserves to be pondered: It involves helping your client to enter the edge where things are a bit scarey: "Perhaps I was foolish. Perhaps I made a mistake. Perhaps I suffered from an illusion." How can you gradually build a context of support and friendliness so the client can feel, "Oh, well, that was then. It doesn't have to prove anything about me. I can learn to do it differently." This series of thoughts should not be taken for granted! Encouragement involves the active unlearning of habitual unconscious thoughts that suggest the opposite: "I messed up and that proves that I'm hopeless! I'll never learn to get it right! I have no idea what doing it right involves!" The counselor can offer a mixture of reassurance and support as old beliefs are released and new approaches cultivated and practiced. (It seems to me to be a bit like what good camp counselors do in teaching kids to swim.)

MULTIPLE FACETS

If only it were simple so that all you had to do was to learn just one thing! But then it would be a craft, like learning to make teacups. Becoming a professional means learning many, many bits of knowledge and skills for balancing and applying them. The skills, especially, and the deeper understanding of the facts are learned by *doing*. Helping clients learn assertiveness cannot be achieved only by talking about it—they need to practice. Extending this, effectiveness often involves the cross-learning of many different elements at the same time—just as in dancing one learns balance and a sense of coordination along with the flow of rhythm and the full range of motion and effort of certain muscle groups. It helps to explain that it's a bit tricky but you're confident that the client can learn it. (You might have gotten the idea—correctly—that I was never a therapist who sat there silently and allowed my clients to thrash around in their own desperate confusion. They have enough motivation without having to add that artificial element of ambiguity.)

MANY LEVELS OF INTERVENTION

Counseling, psychotherapy, people-helping, involves all levels of human functioning. We are not merely physical beings who have spiritual experiences; it is equally valid to say that we are spiritual beings who have physical experiences. In between we may look at ourselves again from many perspectives:

We are individuals with many conflicting inner roles, such as the part that wants to think as a child and enjoy the entitlements of being little; and that complex also is in natural conflict with other parts that want to be grown up, enjoy being competent, successfully independent, useful to others, and so forth. There are many such inner conflicts—many of them innate to healthy development. Some of them, alas, reflect little byways that end up bringing clients into therapy.

We are family members and members of various clubs and small groups, and we have tendencies to fall into certain roles. We may become aware of those tendencies and modify their expression; there's no rule that we have to be dominated by our tendencies.

We are members of a variety of larger demographic categories—gender, sexual orientation, race, vocation, status in the extended family, ethnic sub-group, socio-economic class, religion and sub-denomination, nation, supporter of this or that type of art or recreation or interest, and so forth. Especially nowadays, many of these roles break out of the ways that people in the past defined them, so our activity in re-defining these roles for ourselves and others in our group is in a way co-creating the ongoing evolution of our larger culture.

I mentioned both body and spirit, and again both these domains are being expanded greatly by research into neuro-psychology and other aspects of the body-mind connection, on one hand; and in the broadest, philosophical context, how we imagine ourselves in the greater scheme of the cosmos. The point is that we exist, live, "are" on all these levels simultaneously.

Equally important is the reality that at different times people identify more strongly with one or a few facets and/or levels of the aforementioned elements than others. In turn, helping clients to open to and enjoy the fullness of their being is an honor and a challenge. Because we continue to find out more about all these dimensions, the broader field of helping people come forth continues to open to and incorporate new insights. This is another reason you can get better over the next many decades. For example, some folks strongly identify not with their age group so much as their profession or socio-economic class. Others more with their

religion or their sexual orientation. You might think of someone according to her ethnicity, but she doesn't think of herself particularly as typical of or even that loyal to this category. So what's important is not what other people might think about when the learn about any aspects of a person's identity so much as what the clients themselves are noticing or valuing. What we feel is important about us may be not be what many others think about our status. (I have this problem when people find out I used to be a psychiatrist and that calls up all sorts of stereotypes that were never true about me! Something similar may have happened in your life, too.)

Let's not forget that we live in an era of accelerating change, so what was true for our parents and teachers may not be true for us. Fashions in clothes, grooming, language, relations to modern technology, expectations, and so forth—all are in transition. (It's kind of funny, if you let it be; occasionally it makes for misunderstanding and trouble.) As culture speeds up, sub-generation gaps open up! Nevertheless, sometimes these larger loyalties account more for behavior than a family background, and often people are relatively unconscious of the assumptions that go with a generational or cultural worldview. Many really don't get that others really think or believe in quite different ways—and they aren't thereby stupid or evil.

COMPLEXITY

A useful skill for counselors is the development of a capacity to entertain a sense of the innate complexity of life! This effort goes counter to a more innate and childish unconscious tendency to seek—and believe in—things being simple such as the idea that "There is one psychotherapy that really works and all the others are folly. There is one technique that is the key." Alas, no. A great philosopher, Alfred North Whitehead, said, "We should try to make things as simple as possible, but not simpler." I'm all for clarity and simplification when that is possible.

This chapter was edited a number of times to that end. But the truth of this field of psychotherapy is that it really, truly is incredibly, almost inconceivably complex! It helps to open to ignorance (which is morally neutral—you can always learn more), and resist the temptation to give in to the illusion that what you do know is sufficient—a trap I call "stupidity." This doesn't mean that you should give up and crawl away; rather, it means that it's a game with no clear upper limit, one that invites a balance of intellectual humility and courage to keep learning and giving. You don't have to know everything in order to be helpful to people. Many are so desperate and lonely that mere kindness is a fair beginning. (Indeed, great expertise without kindness may work for some surgical specialties, but for therapy mere knowledge without kindness won't suffice. It's a delicate process, bringing people forth into their greater potential won't work. (This resonates with the New Testament book of Corinthians 13:1, where St. Paul says, "If I speak with the tongues of men and of angels, but do not have love [charity], I have become a noisy gong or a clanging cymbal.")

In other words, keep developing professionally, learn more, don't worry about ever getting it all, and develop your art. Base it first on kindness, presence, stuff like that— cleverness will come if you stay open to developing.

TREAT THE PERSON, NOT THE DISEASE

I'm sorry that it really is so complicated, but deeply accepting this and knowing that you won't be able to come up with adequate treatment plans based on diagnoses or age or culture or any single criterion is part of your maturation as a clinician. People rarely have diseases that can be treated irrespective of a score of other variables. It happens, but in general, most people's problems are really combinations that reflect their individuality in many ways. People differ in a variety of ways—temperament, strengths, weaknesses, background, historical era, interests, preferences, and so forth, and each of these are really just categories with many more specific examples for each person in each category. Everyone has a unique blend of several areas of natural talent and either under-developed potentials or natural no-talent, and of course gradients in-between. Interestingly, many people adopt at a superficial level beliefs about what they think they prefer and value, but given some time to get away from what others think they should value, many find that what they do value deep down in fact differs with what they have learned to comply with what others valued. In other words, coming out of the brain-washing of parents, peer pressure, religion, politics, and other social norms is one of the continuing role transitions in life. "I liked x because I thought I should like x, but I've come to realize that I really don't care, or even—now that you mention it—prefer y!" (This subtle type of consciousness raising doesn't get addressed enough!)

KEY VARIABLES IN TRUE DIAGNOSIS

With diagnosis referring not just to what's wrong, but also what's going on, several other variables are most relevant to how well the therapy progresses—i.e., the "prognosis." These include the following:

Voluntariness: How much does the person want to even show up, or work with this particular therapist, or put in the time and effort to do the work? Lots of folks are half-hearted this way and it makes a big difference.

Psychological Mindedness: How much can the person show any degree of ability to be curious about and critical of the way s/he thinks? Many people want relief from the symptoms of distress they feel when they are abandoned by a spouse or lover, fired from a job, but it hardly occurs to them that these misfortunes have anything to do with their own behavior!

Just getting people to develop a treatment alliance about these two sets of variables is part of the art and in truth it is only somewhat the responsibility of the therapist to generate these attitudes. The best therapists in the world can't succeed with a good many clients who aren't ready to get down to business.

"Ego Strength": These elements of achievement or character are major skill gradients that underlie but don't closely correlate with what symptoms are chosen. They have to do with how much the client has been able to establish herself as a mature adult, and more. Some people are overall pretty healthy but have recently been subject to an unusual stress. Other people have much fewer personal resources and succumb to milder stress. The symptoms may be similar, but the former, given a bit of help, bounces back with greater resilience than the latter.

Psychosocial Resources: Some people truly lack the family support, the financial savings, the access to transportation, etc., that others have. In the mid-20th century the only ones who could afford therapy were people who were relatively well off, had some free time, and good transportation. They could shift their schedules to fit the therapist! But in fact, many have a great deal of trouble getting any family support, finding financial resources to pay the clinic bill, arranging for a ride in and back, babysitting, and don't forget the cost of those doggone medicines! Believe me, a whole therapy can rise or fall depending on the management of these kinds of variables—and again, I don't expect that a "good" therapist can adequately compensate for a severe lack in any of these respects.

These four categories, I have found—voluntariness, psychological mindedness, ego strength, and socioeconomic resources—correlate more with outcome than anything the diagnostic manual can describe!

So, the point is that no generalizations are absolutely valid, and often the exception applies. Thus, what's needed is a careful diagnostic process—by which I do not mean slapping a label on the patient. Diagnosis means seeing through, really developing a formulation. I have several webpages that go into many of these themes in greater detail, mentioned in the references at the end of this chapter.

MISLEADING EXPECTATIONS

Because your teachers wanted you to not give up hope—and neither do I—they tried to protect you from the immensity of your challenge. But it's like medicine in a way: Everyone will die. Our job as physicians—a quote from a great master, William Osler—is to cure rarely, ameliorate occasionally, and comfort always. You can certainly lend some comfort and then get on with seeing what can be done beyond that.

What needs to be diagnosed at a systems level for counselors are the many pressures and attitudes that lead to unrealistic expectations—often of oneself—and consequent "burn-out." One of these is the pretensions in our profession that this is a science, as if that were something good. First of all, it's a culturally fashionable role—scientist. In truth, when you get up close, the ignorance in the mainstream sciences is a thousand times greater than what we have learned in the last century. It just seems like we are knowledgeable because compared to a century ago, we are! But not compared to what there is yet to learn. The point here is to get more real about our work, and why I call it more of an art than a science.

Occasionally some elements of true science may shed some light on this or that dynamic, and I appreciate this. But for the most part what is involved in this process is keeping up the therapeutic alliance: That means getting the client to want to work with you, to be willing to face some self-criticism, to feel supported and valued, encouraged and willing therefore to tolerate some frustration, to work, to pay the bills and show up, to participate in the questioning of acting-out behaviors regarding the previously-mentioned situations, etc. All these require artfulness.

Freudians think this is transference, but there's a broader theme also operating here: It is a transference in a larger sense: Entitlement. "Why should I have to pay anyone? I didn't have to pay my mother. If you really cared you'd work free. Aren't I interesting enough to get you to want to do that? Why don't you want to give me that? You're so mean and withholding! It isn't fair. No, I don't want to look at this whole attitude or whatever you call it."

Some people have this complex more strongly than others, but it's pretty common. A few will recognize and own the temptations to give into this spoiled complex, but since the general community isn't talking about it—though really they should—it can seem as if it didn't exist.

To put it another way, many people don't really want to get better. They don't really want to shift their deeper attitudes about what to aim for. (Alfred Adler is the only one who stated this clearly: The only thing that will work as a mature person is to want to be useful to the social network, and the joy of belonging. He called this a feeling for the community, "Gemeinschaeft-gefuehl.") So I heard that Fritz Perls noted something similar: People want to learn how to be better at being neurotic—meaning how can I keep manipulating without shame and yet get away with it instead of having my wife or employer get disgusted with me?

These are the most common complexes. Happily, most people only have a mild dose of this subtle malignant narcissism, but it still complicates the work—and again, that variable—close to the treatment alliance—sometimes doesn't show up on tests, because clients are "being good." That's before they start to become aware that their deeper attitudes are on the line.

Major Mental Illness

Shifting the focus. On occasion you'll find yourself confronted with clients who are in four very complex categories:

1. These are sliding into a major mental breakdown, escalating. It's not always easy to diagnose these, but you've got to at least consider this possibility—and document what you do, because if that's what's happening, things get messy. Such clients, if they don't hurt themselves or someone else, end up in jail or hospital.
2. These clients have a history of major trauma, which is more common now with veterans. These can cook silently and blow. They're not actively psychotic, but rather painfully sensitive to various triggers. There are many variables at play here.
3. Substance abuse can operate alone or compound any of the other problems. Alcohol, cocaine or methamphetamine are especially problematical. But always the variables that matter relate to the person, not the "disease." Other types of addiction are also to be considered.
4. Neurological and medical causes of illness are not uncommon! Some symptoms arise in people with brain tumors, viral encephalitis, mid-life senility, untreated syphilis and other neurological conditions, hormonal (endocrine) disorders—these medical conditions can seem at first like just anxiety, depression, minor personality changes. If you don't think of them you certainly won't pick them up. The good news is that evidence accumulates.

A corollary of this: Back to getting a good diagnosis. In many cases, take a history also from close others, especially spouse, parent, adult child, best friend, and so forth. Often clients will welcome some validation. If they "want to keep it private," my index of suspicion shoots up that there are several things they're not likely to tell you, even if you ask: Sex or internet porn addiction, gambling or secret investments, an affair on the side, erectile dysfunction (impotence), homosexual impulses, and the list goes on.

THE RANGE OF SKILLS

I wish it could be simplified, but the list of topics to master is no less than what a physician is faced with. For psychotherapists, it includes such general skill areas as questioning, probing, exploring, interpreting, validating, clarifying, and all these need to be done with empathy, genuineness, congruence, professionalism, and so forth. All these can be developed, and then as you get pretty good, you'll discover still other ways to develop them further.

Being Creative

Open to the possibility that what you will learn will come together in a unique way, intersect with your own blends of talents, interests, and temperament. You may have other elements in your background that are woven in, and so the way you do therapy will be affected by a variety of themes:

- the wounded healer. In certain ways, it's possible—not always present, but often— that you yourself were consciously wounded, or felt your inferiority, or suffered through certain stresses or traumas. You may have an inclination to go into a sub-specialty interest treating what you were able to overcome. This is compensation, and when it's done consciously, it's a good thing! The problem, though, is that you may get caught up in some of the counter-transference games, overly sympathizing, overly rescuing, avoiding asking about, or in other ways undercutting your effectiveness because of residuals to your own neurotic wounds. It's okay if you know this is likely and you make use of supervision, consultation, even go back in to some short term therapy when certain patients really push your buttons. If you wrestle with this, forgive yourself and know this kind of thing is part of the game, it'll make you a better therapist in the long run.
- your background: You used to be a dancer, or an artist, or you still are. You were the leader of a boy- or girl-scout troop or some other youth group. You have this talent or that one, and in time you may or may not find that you may be able to integrate what you've learned in other realms and it makes you a better therapist. You don't have to do this, of course—sometimes it's better to keep these roles separate; but maybe.
- your cultural, ethnic, or language background: As with other themes, this may not be of interest for you, but on the other hand, it might turn out to be a real aid in working with others who have experienced similar kinds of problems.

Here's some advice I heard early in my career and it really worked for me: Find out what you don't do well... and don't do it! Let others who are naturally good at it do it! I am very good at a number of facets in my field, but also fairly weak in others. I was a bit of an outsider with a mild inferiority complex and I feel bad if people get cross with me. I don't work well with fairly manipulative people, but I know others who are more thick-skinned and they love this work! I get bored with play therapy but I have friends who have a marvelous talent for being present, and they like to do that sort of thing.

I used to think—right out of training—that I should be an all-A student, good at all components of my profession. I had the impression that mere effort could overcome my shortcomings. Wrong. I gradually learned to back away from roles where I not only didn't do well, but I also didn't like doing it at all. So watch for that dynamic as you evolve.

ABOUT "DIAGNOSIS"

Some foolish professionals deny the need for diagnosis, in the sense of believing in the validity of labels, and to some degree I agree, about some clients. But what may be difficult is to realize that for other situations, diagnosis is a very powerful element in treatment. People want to know what's going on, why it happened, what's going to happen, and for some conditions, these are fair questions. The problem is confused because there are multiple sub-categories and for one of the more commonly encountered types the issue of "labeling" is hardly valid: For many, anxiety and depression, in varying combinations and permutations, is the result or reflection of a life that is messy.

One of the techniques I use for diagnosis is what I call the daytime talk show technique: If this story would be shown in detail to an audience for a daytime talk show (as an imagined event), I find two categories of response: In some cases, the "audience" would say, "Oh, wow, if that stuff had been happening in my life, I'd be twice as upset!" In a few cases, they might say, "What? That sort of thing happens! What's the big deal?" If in imagining this scene I tend towards the "What a mess!" reaction—the first option—then I dig into what *else* might be adding to the stress. It usually makes sense when you get the whole story. If I tend towards feeling some discrepancy between the reaction and the stress, I look more into there being another type of cause:

- some people are really sensitive and react far more strongly than you'd expect. This in turn could be because of past trauma, neurological hypersensitivity, temperamental sensitivity, incipient psychotic processes, and so forth.
- some people are hiding another co-morbid condition they haven't told you about, an addiction, a related trauma
- sometimes it's physical: there are medical or psychiatric conditions that lead people to really over-react. So I again dig deeper checking out other symptoms and signs.

You don't need to be able to make the final diagnosis in every case. I don't ask this of my specialist colleagues. What I do expect, though, is that if you suspect something that doesn't fit, some "atypical" presentation or feature, please don't hesitate to get consultation! This is not a reflection on your competence! Actively opening to intellectual humility is a sign of true professionalism!

DEVELOPING THE EXECUTIVE FUNCTION

Finally, perhaps the main thing counselors can do is to help their clients learn how to develop their own inner counselor role. We all have those ego functions, which involve (among other components) self-observation, will, choice, modulation of impulses and mediation of inner conflicts. Most people do this a bit, and often slip into over-identification with one or another of their own roles. The counselor is able to maintain more distance, and operates as an outside ideal ego, asking such questions as "how can we check out that belief?" I think that therapy should include a side agenda of the clients' learning to take on that role, consolidate it into a sort of inner manager, avoid allowing it to be swallowed into another role during the passions of the moment. This "choosing self" or "meta-role" can be far more skillful and even serve as a bridge to a transpersonal identity or spiritual values.

The key here is simply to talk about this function, as if you expect the client to learn this—it's a skill. It's as if you graduate from reading to your child to having your child read to you, and then to herself. You say, "Okay, we've sort of approached this kind of problem before. Whatever you remember that I would say as a strategy—now you say it: What's the first step?" This kind of approach can fit easily with, say, cognitive-behavior therapy, but there's that extra sense of self- respect that is gained as the client exercises her competence in becoming a more skilled "self-therapist."

A USER-FRIENDLY LANGUAGE

One of the challenges to therapy is that much of psychology has been buried under a blanket of obscure abstraction, some taken from psychoanalysis, some from other sources. Attention should be given to people using terms that feel more meaningful. I've found that the role concept serves this purpose well—people can address the vast majority of intrapsychic and interpersonal issues by imagining that we're all interacting on a virtual stage, rehearsing, as it were. "How else might this scene be played? What else can your inner coach say to you? Let's play that scene out and see where it goes."

NO DISEASES, ONLY REAL PEOPLE WITH DIS-EASE

In general, disease presents not because the key "cause," say, an infectious agent, is present, but more, because for many and as yet still rather mysterious reasons, the person becomes susceptible to that agent. And now there are many more types of illnesses that have no identifiable single cause. More, it's quite ambiguous of the number of causes that can be identified as operating in any dis-ease process which one finally was the proverbial "straw that broke the camel's back."

Treatment involves several themes: (1) Reducing the symptoms, which involves more countering the body's own over-reaction to whatever is causing the problem. (2) Stopping or countering the actual causes or triggers. This has been over-emphasized in an era of antibiotics and surgery and for many conditions cannot be easily identified, much less treated. (3) Another theme is reducing the various kinds of stresses that might be adding to the vital imbalance. Along with this, and something noted from the time of the ancient Greek legendary father of medicine, Hippocrates, is (4) doing what's needed to promote the body's own resistance, resilience, healing, vibrancy. It should be noted that this last category is often not all that specific, and more importantly, no one else can do it for the patient. The patient must exercise sometimes a great deal of effort countering an unhealthy habit or many habits and building new patterns. This is true for many general life-style diseases such as sugar and junk-food addiction (obesity, diabetes), smoking (bronchitis, emphysema, asthma), and so forth.

More subtle but deeply true and not widely identified are psycho-social patterns that also overlap with psycho-physical patterns. One is the idea that doctors or therapists can "help," and help overlaps with the traditional medical model of "do me something." In truth, many situations involve the person NOT looking to spouse, family, or therapist, but rather taking up the task of doing the work herself. A therapist theoretically can be a guide, but might have to talk for a few sessions and then refuse to see the client again until the client has clearly done something for herself! This is not a great way to earn a comfortable and secure living, but regular sessions regardless of whether a client has done her homework actually subtly rewards the unconscious passivity. "The therapist really could help me if she only would," is not adequately countered. "Because why does she keep having me come back if I haven't done my homework?"

However, a fair percentage of our clients feel empty and behave in a passive-dependent fashion, at least in part. Not understanding the dynamics, they're often unwilling to truly do what a thousand self-help books say in generating a spiritual connection. It's the psycho-spiritual equivalent to beginning a more healthful diet, stopping smoking, exercising, etc. Excuses why one doesn't do these fairly elementary activities should not be rewarded by being listened to.

Calling it dealing with resistance might also be a rationalization by the therapist for being co-dependent, preying on the money paid. The visit with the hoped-for rewarder of goodies is the reinforcement, and if the visits happen even though the homework isn't done, then the client is rewarded for being helpless. I might be wrong here, but I suspect that this is not an uncommon pattern.

The mental matrix that must be identified includes not only "dis-ease," but the larger field that includes not only weaknesses, but also potential strengths, intelligence, achievements, talents, positive introjects (people's positive responses) and such. Building on these is not easy for many, because we have been living in a world that focuses on the negative. Psychopharmacology is a fine tool, but it can be used in a counter-productive fashion. If the sales message is that this will make you feel better, it's a fraud, because the person is still embedded in a situation (in many but not all cases) that would bring down anyone.

So better the message should be that at best this will take the edge off of the most disabling symptoms, but then the hard work of cleaning up the mess, dealing with the decisions, working on the relationships, shifting attitudes, changing habits, etc.—if this isn't done, many patients would be crazy if they weren't anxious or depressed, because those are perfectly plausible reactions to responses to their own negative behaviors!

THE PLACE OF CATHARSIS

It's not all a matter of straightening out clients' thinking—that is, treating only the thought patterns that lead to problematic reactions. It is good to interrupt the cycle in which over-generalizations lead to catastrophic images and affects. But first it's important to help the client recognize the underlying feelings that feed the mistaken thoughts in a positive feedback cycle. Otherwise, negative feelings based on negative thoughts seem to prove that the negative thoughts were valid.

Catharsis brings into consciousness feelings that were hardly conscious. Often anxiety itself, or underlying shame, guilt, fear, and anger pile up along with other thoughts and feelings and the client is mystified and congested. All they can say is "I feel bad." Maybe they can be led to say that they feel angry or guilty, but this second level is also an over-simplified sum of a number of other, deeper feelings that are themselves the products of negative thoughts. The "peeling down" process must proceed in order and all brought to light. We should not assume that people know why they're angry. They also are angry at themselves for mysterious feelings, so bringing such feelings into consciousness may involve some time, and helping them to own that they in fact do indeed harbor all these feelings, it's understandable that they do, and they are fed by the various thought patterns that must be addressed—all is part of the process. It's like a surgeon needing to go through several levels of different kinds of tissue or bone, often taking the steps needed to manage the bleeding or other problems associated with that level, before getting to the actual source of the core surgical problem. But managing these preliminary layers correctly is essential to the over-all result.

CONCLUSION

These are some of the perspectives I've developed during the 45 years I've been doing psychotherapy. I hope they will stimulate the readers' thoughts and deepen their journey.

REFERENCES

I have many papers on psychology and psychotherapy that I think would be quite useful to counselors-in-training, and recommend your browsing among these. Know that the internet—via email—allows you to challenge me, correct me, and know that I'll be open to discussing and possibly, with your help, modifying this or that point. Just type my name into any web-search engine such as Google.

In: The Nurturing of Talent, Skills and Abilities
Editor: Michael F. Shaughnessy

ISBN: 978-1-62618-521-0
© 2013 Nova Science Publishers, Inc.

Chapter 15

THE CURSE OF COLLEGE ENGLISH: FRESHMAN COMPOSITION

Antony Oldknow[*]
Eastern New Mexico University, New Mexico, US

Abolish it! Abolish Freshman Composition! I've heard this cry increasingly frequently in many parts of the country—probably teachers in other countries suffer similar curses. Obviously, there is a big problem; equally obviously, there are no panaceas for it—there are no panaceas for anything, but that doesn't stop the public, politicians, and some college administrators expecting cures for what they may imagine to be a relatively simple problem.

We are talking about the perennial observation made by some English professors that incoming Freshmen, armed with high-school diplomas apparently guaranteeing literacy for their holders, are in far too many cases instead held by illiterates. Many college professors think sadly that these students should never have received such diplomas. If those diplomas actually did guarantee student literacy sufficient to tackle college-level courses effectively, then, indeed, we might be able to abolish Freshman Composition Courses—along with beginning non-credit courses for students whose literacy levels were well below the chart. However, such conditions are not likely to occur in the near future. So, like it or not, we are stuck with the problem.

Student literacy problems (and numeracy ones) cannot be solved simply, if at all. In spite of nostalgic dreams about balmy past conditions, such problems are not new. In the past, in Britain, for example, before 1944, probably, few bothered much about plebeian literacy, though some self-taught were surprisingly literate. Then, very few institutions of higher education existed; today, by comparison, their numbers are legion and, in spite of world fiscal problems, they seem to be growing.

We might well ask a question, which many of us who have made a living from higher education campuses might not wish to ask: aren't there too many places called perhaps euphemistically colleges and universities, institutions that are very expensive to run, even when professors' salaries are abysmally low? And wouldn't it be a good idea to close most of

---

[*] E-mail: Antony.Oldknow@enmu.edu.

them and only educate in special exclusive colleges truly near-genius students wherever they can be found? And would many countries not be better off, or at least no worse, were most contemporary institutions of higher learning to disappear? After all, what are many of them today other than glorified high schools?—and not so very glorified ones at that?

Very nasty, Tony! What a traitor you are for saying this! Are you not in fact biting the hand that fed you for almost fifty years? Of course, and definitely for other reasons than narrow self-interest, I am not suggesting that all these institutions should close down, thus putting faculty, administrators, and other staff out of work, while and in consequence simultaneously flooding the job market with vast numbers of former students who, instantly unemployed and unemployable, will bring an immense burden on the whole population. No, but, such practical problems aside, I would very much like to find means to improve higher education and what it does, and thus provide clear-cut defensible reasons for their continued (and, of course, substantially enhanced) existence.

DEVELOPING THE WRITING SKILLS OF FRESHMEN

First-year student literacy problems are characterized by a vast matrix of variables that are fairly easy to understand, but nevertheless demand people of goodwill with deep-seated interest in the situation to consider the problem fully, objectively, and realistically. First of all, for all sorts of linguistically explicable reasons, most people seem to not really believe—even if they say and/or write otherwise—that their own communicational skills contain abundant flaws. They think their talking, reading, and writing methods are fine as they are. To improve their communicational competence, therefore, they have to be successfully persuaded that such competence really needs amelioration. Thus, it follows that many if not most incoming college freshmen think that because their high-school diplomas suggest they are satisfactorily literate, they really are as literate as they need to be. Therefore they do not think they should to be in Freshmen English classes, and this probably holds equally true for those relegated to non-credit remedial basic-writing classes since their literacy levels have been deemed totally unacceptable.

Consequently, many Freshman Composition students are initially disgruntled. And, guess what? English professors, who have to spur these students into an understanding of their true literacy needs and make necessary ameliorative moves, are in many cases, especially if they are newly-minted tenure-track scholars fresh from graduate schools, all too often consider themselves much too well-qualified to descend to working with Freshmen illiterates. One can certainly understand their viewpoint: having developed to where they can successfully juggle complex thoughts and communicate them with confident accuracy, really look forward to the constant company of like-minded and similarly trained colleagues as they engage in the delightful tasks of teaching properly motivated students. It comes therefore as a terrible shock for many new professors to have to encounter freshmen and be forced to figure out how to get through to them. In many such situations there is a good deal of hatred between students, teachers, and composition directors, who in a variety of different ways have to advise and even sometimes have to order instructors how to do their jobs. Many such directors consider tasks impossible and they wish they could do something else. I think they should be able to do so. I truly believe from experience being directed by such people and even sometimes acting as a composition director myself, that the position of composition director should be considered redundant or even counterproductive and thus abolished. The people who actually have to teach Freshmen Composition, should, instead of being directed, in many cases imperiously so, be able to work together as committees solving composition-teaching problems often through the adoption of innovational methods. As a corollary to this, I really believe the professional ethos prevalent in higher education should become characterized by maximal faculty governance.

After all, who best knows what should be done in the various disciplines than those people specifically trained in them? This notion certainly applies to those who teach English, though there are, alas many who think that since we all speak English, we can all teach it effectively.

DEVELOPING WRITTEN LANGUAGE

Unsurprisingly perhaps, in view of what has just been written, many politicians, members of the general public, and college administrators really do seem to think they know all about language and ought to be able to pontificate and give orders about these things that make sense and are bound to bring about immediate improvements in them. The result is all too often the imposition of totally stupid ideas counterproductive to effective education. That very sexy complex of notions "no child left behind" is a very good example of the sort of nonsense I have in mind: that all students can be with strict adherence to democratic principles be taught the same way in the same place and at the same time, because they are all equals.

I do believe they are of equal worth, of course, and I would like to treat them accordingly, but treated in all respects identically, as alike as two peas in a pod—no, no way! In fact, anyone who has like me worked in a pea-canning factory, knows that a careful look at an open peapod reveals every pea is clearly different in many respects— and so it is with children, much more so, indeed. We must be very careful about "no child left behind"—its overall intention may have been good—but it would be all too easy for the project to end up teaching to the lowest common denominator with the result that no child is ever advanced.

The negative Freshman Composition situation is also currently exacerbated by contemporary educational climates that are increasingly marred by what is called the general college-campus bullying culture (often considered, perhaps unfairly, to have mainly emanated from Arizona), a culture redolent of the "do-the-boys" methods of Gradgrind and Squeers, negative educational conditions characterized by parts of Hard Times and Nicholas Nickleby that should surely find no place in a humane approach to education for a kinder gentler America. However, in my experience and that of many others, the educational climate in America today is one increasingly dominated by bullying, harshness, punitive attitudes, and mental cruelty—educationally counterproductive elements. In the present pervasive fiscal austerity, this brutal bullying culture might well be thought of as having arisen as naturally as English nineteenth-century workhouse attitudes from the situations of many professionals cursed by truncated dreams. Their students are all too often lost, unmotivated, surly, uncertain, disillusioned, and their condition is not helped by teachers continuously bullied by fiscally harassed supervisors, all too often ignorant of the skills their subordinates are attempting to impart. And then, the bullied faculty, harassed daily, increasingly under army-like orders often from supervisors with little practical idea of education essentials, themselves resort to bullying methods with their students charges. With little prestige, and mostly powerless, teachers visit their frustrations on students, in the case of English Composition classes all too often prone to relish resort to things like "turnitin" and delight in drastic punishment just one act of plagiarism. Such behavior is hardly consonant with the glowing masthead declarations some schools have, ones filled with positive suggestion like one excellent southwestern University proclaims: "Student Success, that is what it's all about!"

Another typically negative example occurs when teachers grace their syllabi with notices like "One unexplained absence entails class failure." How stupid! Whether we like it or not, we need to treat the students holistically—try to find out as much as possible about them as individuals, then proceed with kindness and an encouraging spirit—and as many second chances as possible. Draconian judgments perhaps solace some frustrated intellectuals, who can, however, do immense harm to individuals judged delinquent, punished—and sometimes even tossed out.

All bullying cultures must be abandoned, hostile work places replaced by friendly ones, friendly to all. Students must truly be in focus in a university, as too should faculty, both accorded maximum respect. As I told a candidate for governor some years ago, we teachers are humans and have to deal with students humanely, not as cans of peas—neither they nor we, must be treated like cans of peas. Teachers treated with kindness and professional respect usually treat their students in a similar manner to the general good. In some institutions of higher learning there is increased faculty autonomy, governance, and zero tolerance for people who get their rocks off by bullying others. top-heavy with administrators at several levels in many cases, ones serving as dictators. I think we should let the teachers increasingly govern themselves by democratic means. This is no panacea, remember!

But getting all levels of government increasingly off the backs of teaching and research personnel would seem to favor a situation in which teaching-learning matrices are gradually ameliorated in regard to their respective missions.

As things are, in composition and other environments, the relatively ignorant are all-too often giving stupid counterproductive commands to subordinates who have learned their disciplines and found ways to teach effectively, and thus continuously reducing their academic freedom. The result is that increasingly subordinated instructors have themselves have been becoming increasingly disillusioned and dejected and all too to prone visit on their students the bullying they have been receiving themselves. And, though there are nationally instituted legal methods of bringing to general light reprehensible and corrupt methods that make schools, colleges, and universities hostile work environments, the victims have to beware of trying to make use of such remedies as whistle-blowers at all levels are likely to find themselves hobbled by the very authority figures who need to be disciplined: corrupt supervisory staff commonly find ways of dismissing such whistle-blowers from their jobs before any chance of redress can come about.

This is not a good situation. Harassed teachers, including composition teachers with nowhere to turn for redress do not teach effectively. They are in dire need of Scandinavian-style independent ombudsmen, persons appointed to look with the fullest possible objectivity at corruptions and abuses. Despite views emanating from in Wisconsin, teachers, the majority of whom are state employees, are in urgent need of collective bargaining. Some politicians up for election declare themselves in favor of it, then once elected conveniently forget their promises. There must be truly effective systems of redress for grievances, if we are to have contented teachers actually able and willing to do the best job they can.

THE BASICS OF COMPOSITION

Very simply, however, coming back to the nitty-gritty of composition, we have to remember the current unending cycle of cause and effect in the area. This is not, alas, a reading age, a factor that is crucial to the problems of student illiteracy, for in spite of what some writers have proclaimed to the contrary, a clear-cut strong connection for most people between the functions of writing and reading: thus, if students read a great deal for pleasure, then for them learning to write will in many cases prove relatively easy—but for success in this area emphasis has to be at least at first upon reading for enjoyment. When I was a child, I used to slip away in the summers, climb onto the top of my father's shed, and read there under the shelter of a large elder tree, though I knew my father discouraged this since he said he was afraid of my getting what he called a "brain storm," some nasty undefined and almost certainly mortal disease that would kill me if I kept on reading so much--so much being too much. Since I was adjured not to read, as Bertrand Russell for one rightly said of children, forbid me things, and I'll somehow manage to disobey!

I myself wasn't at first taught to get pleasure from reading. My earliest years found me under the tutelage of my step-grandmother, a woman enthusiastic for German-style strict-discipline educational methods, who also couldn't avoid long stretches as my babysitter, and made sure from my second birthday on that I began reading immediately and became increasingly effective in doing so under constant threat of corporal punishment, if I didn't. I was born August 15, 1939, nineteen days before Britain's World War II action began. By them, my father was already serving in the British army, and went to serve successively in France, Belgium, Algeria, Tunisia, and Italy, being demobilized in late 1945.

Meanwhile, my mother was doing secret munitions-factory work in my home town, Peterborough, while I was subjected to Prussian-style elementary education by my stern grandmother, who taught me to read and write long before I started infants' school on February 15, 1944, when I was four and a half! The focal text of my early punishing instruction was a small-print King James Bible, which I had to read aloud to her as we sat in her front-bedroom window before a sea of steam-engines marshaling freight trains and behind them war planes preparing for take-off. That small-print book made me learn to read the hard way, and also gave me sight problems. But I did learn, and was quite soon finding ways to read for pleasure.

Constant repetitions of sessions reading for pleasure leads many students to, in the main, unconsciously learn to distinguish socially acceptable texts from flawed ones, and eventually recognize and eliminate flaws occurring in their own writing. However, today, there are many more delightful distractions for growing children than there had been seventy years ago when I grew up. Television and the movies are just some powerful distractions militating against childhood pleasure reading, and currently there are many more ways to contact our fellow humans than simply by writing to them—though, paradoxically, the contemporary habit of texting may be to some extent reversing this trend. In this computer age all kinds of quick-fix methods of direct and indirect communication are availed of rather than setting thoughts down on paper and mailing them. Some students, when asked, have told me that never up to then had they actually cracked a book--and they appeared very proud that such was the case.

Another impediment to student literacy is the continuous peer pressure that prevailed, even when I was a pupil in English schools between 1944 and 1958, a cultural pressure among students doing homework or any other adult-sponsored intellectual task was seen as "totally uncool".

Such group resistance undoubtedly still assails teachers today, and adds to their frustration which is further reinforced by the generally low esteem in which their profession tends to be held—if you can't do, teach!—some recall with some fondness the discipline to which students in the recent past had had to succumb, but I doubt their nostalgia is justified. In any case, we can't live in the past. As teachers we have to adapt to the new conditions we find ourselves in, and as changes in these conditions accelerate at an ever-increasing rate. We need to be constantly questing to be ever more resourceful and wary of what is going on around us.

BACK TO BASICS

The last thing we can afford for ourselves is the idea that we can go back to old basic values and force them willy-nilly on our students. Of course, some of the disciplines and skills found valuable in the past, a degree of rote-learning, for example, can be used effectively now, but, instead imagining that we can reproduce a scenario in which we are like non-commissioned officers in some rigid military, in which one obeyed without question and drilled and drilled and drilled because one was told to do so, nobody with the increased feelings of autonomy young people these days have is going to obey orders with blind faithfulness. At the very least, explanations that make clear sense must be repeatedly injected into the student brain with some kind of fierce drive that is immediately compelling. We must meet students where they are at, both individually and as group members. If literacy really is an essential component of the mature and satisfied adult, we shall have to make full use of all our creativity and available resources to persuade them that such is truly the case.

Perhaps the most effective best kind of teaching is ultimately one-on-one--I don't know--but no doubt but that many students do learn as many one-on-one contacts with their teachers as is possible, especially when they are able to feel that their teachers and their aides really care what happens to them. The personal touch, these days, with classes that are in many cases too big and at the same time increasingly imbued with very strong pressure, is all too often missing—and, in fact, the distance between education givers and their charges has become and is progressively becoming more and more distant. Some good things can no doubt come about through distance-education ventures, and they are very attractive from a fiscal viewpoint, but the teacher/apprentice situation is really of paramount importance, especially, I think, in the teaching of composition. Perhaps distance-education techniques can be developed in time so that they can truly substitute effectively for the advantages of hands-on approaches, but, for the foreseeable future I really believe for really effective composition teaching, especially in its earliest stages, much more of the one-on-one and small-groups kinds of approach needs to continue, and the use of the various other kinds of approach needs to be very carefully researched and scrutinized for maximal educational effectiveness.

All composition teachers, as they are trained, have to be conditioned, and educated to keep on considering most carefully and enthusiastically, all new methodologies as they arrive to complement new technologies.

However, obviously not all things at all times can be dealt with equally effectively, and rather than forced along with innovations in a kind of army-type lockstep, though teachers must be encouraged to aim at agreed standards, they must be able to do so in their own individual ways, because when they develop enthusiasm for some approaches, they will likely make their students become enthusiastic learners too, and, in many cases, eventually become enthusiastic and effective teachers in their turn. I should hate to see evolve for the United States the quite mistaken approach to education once characteristic for France, one that became fixed in my horrified eye as an image of Ministers of Education for the French Community being able to open their office files and at a glance the precise lockstep details of instruction that are going on in all every classroom over which the minister has authority.

Under the goads of what I have heard of as Arizonization, such approaches are more and more being pushed to flourish all over the United States, until eventually teachers evolve to become their classrooms merely watchers while their students imbibe from TV Screens and Computer monitors what is given to them by some great educational vozhd, in Arizona, perhaps, or a specially chosen ivy-league set of schools, while the local teachers have the undignified mind-numbing grading duties commanded by remote authority as they and their students respond without question to behests from distant ghoul-like purveyors of regimented excellence.

I am all for some kinds of widely accepted standardizations in writing and the teaching of writing. But standardization can obviously go too far, and I understand now that in some states may be set to decree that schools and universities in their jurisdiction will no longer be able to duplicate subjects and subject groups, but there will instead be only one authority per discipline area in the state, and all universities and colleges will teach only what is not already being taught by one or other of the similar institutions in the same state. Thus, for example, if one university were allotted to teach Shakespeare tragedies, none of the other schools in the system would be allowed to do so, and if students wished to know about the tragedies concerned, then they would have to tune into a central wisdom inculcated exclusively by experts in the institution designated to specialize in that area.

WRITING AND THE REALM OF EMOTION

I find that sort of thing demoralizing in prospect; many others feel the same way. Nevertheless, centralizing economically based imperatives are tending to govern new plans, ones, for example, that shape the evolution of teaching in the visual arts. There, for example, since paints and papers, canvases, and so on produce mess and involve relatively great material expenditures, art departments may well come to find themselves abandoning everything in the field of painting and drawing but electronic methods with "clean" dependence on computerization.

Such limiting authoritarianism may also increasingly occur in all fields of English, even in literature, with deleterious effects. I saw the kind of thing I detest developing one evening when I was for some years functioning as methods instructor. A student once invited a head

English teacher from a nearby town to address my students. At one point, she said, with a voice of competent authority, that all of us knew of course precisely what Hamlet means. For her, the work clearly meant one thing and one only. She clearly exemplified a tendency to simplify for convenience the meanings of literature, even though writers and readers with any degree of sophistication know that one of the great joys of literature and its humanizing tendencies is that, all words having more than one meaning, all texts are multiply ambiguous and to some extent intended to be so by their authors. The richness, usefulness, and enjoyment of the texts concerned would likely be totally lost if there were big-brother-like authorities allowed to insist that each and every text has only one meaning and that her subordinate teachers' charges, to receive passing grades, would have to be able to provide on demand, a Gradgrind-like knee-jerk approved account of the one true meaning of each text.

Indeed, I suspect that the powers that be, for the cause of maximum convenience and fiscal efficiency, are more and more wishing to enforce a situation where, in all disciplines, including English, teachers will be forced to teach so-called single right answers to a very small set of exam questions and then decide degrees of student literacy on the basis of such lockstep Orwellian and Gradgrind stimuli. Would citizens taught in this way inevitably become the best kinds of citizens? Well, if what government authorities and their delegates are all after is the evolution of a new feudalism or institutional slavery in which new droit de seigneur desires are instantly in play and the vast majority of citizens become new serfs, then, yes, I suppose that is what we should all aim for. But I for one, want no part of it.

Throughout my career in Education in four countries, but mainly for the past forty-six years in the United States, I have been collecting ideas that seem to me to have been effective in helping in develop good citizens, and by "good," though I mean much else, I consider fluent literacy to be a major criterion.

I would like now to mention some of these ideas now, though in no particular order, and contrast them with materials I think need replacing because they are totally counterproductive to the good things of education. I set my standards by what I thought to be good things, ones I first started to notice while a pupil at my grammar school, King's, Peterborough, in the period 1950-1958. These matters neither singularly nor collectively constitute panaceas; they are simply individual items that, developed by myself and/or collected from several places, have proved to be capable of moving a fair number of students from apathy and passivity in regard to their literacy into having a clear sense of needing to improve their control of both written and spoken language and been moved to make at least the first steps in the process.

A POTPOURRI OF USEFUL APPROACHES TO ENHANCED FRESHMAN COMPOSITION COMPETENCE AND PERFORMANCE

First of all, we King's pupils didn't see that our school as particularly good when we were attending it—its virtues can be seen only in retrospect.

The education system the school belonged to did not think all students should be taught exactly the same way, no matter what their individual potential educational profiles suggested. Perhaps there was a degree of snobbery still present in the selection procedures, which did not turn out to be as sophisticated as their original architects had intended. But, that flaw aside, the students in the school had been preselected as having the maximum of qualities in common. The 1944 Education Act, the so-called Butler Act, which was pretty well thought out by a wartime coalition government with minimal class bias, determined that though absolute year-by-year identically for all of curricula was not a good idea, and, one-on-one instruction was obviously so labor-intensive, however good, to be economically feasible, but the substituted idea was to gradually arrive at a set of curricula items and levels that would be optimal for a preselected set of student types. Two of these were at once identified and described: one was for high-intellectual or grammar-school instruction, the other for students identified as likely to do best in a technologically-based education environment. After Britain's war end near bankruptcy, the democratization inherent in the Butler Act fell for what was intended at first to be only a short period. I believe while about 10% of the population was selected for high-intellectual training, aimed ultimately at university education, and a few technical schools were built and developed, the remaining 80% or so, went into what was called secondary-modern education, schools that as time went on and Britain's fiscal situation continued abominable, tended to become ages eleven through fifteen babysitting entities that looked after the inmates in enforced tranquility until they were released upon the world of mainly industrial labor work when they reached fifteen.

The 11+ exams, which had been originally intended to preselect with some flexibility students to be able to be trained in special ways fitted to their desires and abilities, came to be exams that students passed or failed, and the 10% selected from all classes combined got sent to elite schools that would develop them into a kind of leadership cadre, and at the same time provided safety valves for avoiding the possibility that highly intelligent and competent plebeans, disillusioned by their low status in society, might set about to become social revolutionaries. Of course, the good things of the grammar schools, the really good things, should have ultimately been, as to some extent they now have, shared by all.

However, working-class people like myself who attended the grammar schools and didn't exactly understand why, were treated extremely well, right up by being sent ultimately with all-fees-prepaid and generous living stipends, extremely generous ones, through the universities for two successive degrees, a specialty bachelor's degree, like mine in English, for example, and then further, so as to be useful to society mainly as teachers to an education degree, also received, in my case from the University of Leeds.

We received a very thorough education that not only prepared us for a variety of professional careers, but also made us fully aware, and in some detail, of the broad culture of Britain that had evolved for us to fit in. Thus, for example, when we came to understand literature and language, we learned about history and geography in the broadest sense and in intense detail, what our studies fitted into.

At high school, we studied so as for the most part to have achieved a great deal that occurs in North American undergraduate degrees, and in some respects, what we studied for our first degrees was more or less at the level of United States masters' degrees.

By the time we left school we had, in our first national qualification, the General Certificate of Education Ordinary Level, assimilated a great deal of important general knowledge that all too many United States freshmen students have failed to assimilate. I believe that since we cannot write effectively in a vacuum, some attempts should be made in student's freshman years to get them to assimilate such materials that would enable them to know a great deal about the country and the wider universe in which they live, and thus enable them to greatly enrich their imaginations and inform them with richness their written texts.

At age fifteen, I took the GCE exams in ten subjects and passed them all. The school I went to prepared us for these, but they and the Advanced final college entrance level exams that were typically taken two and/or three years later were graded in total anonymity by examiners in other areas of the country who had no ways of knowing the candidates' identities, examiners who were selected by branches of the universities, in our case Oxford University. The teachers told us that our passing was in no case in their hands; there was no way that they could fudge the results. If we wanted to pass, we would have to know our materials thoroughly and be able to satisfy experts appointed by Oxford who would be totally objective in their assessments. No one I ever heard of tried to do what all too many American students do at all levels, try to negotiate with their professors for good grades, something that they all too often have success in doing. I was thoroughly astonished by this phenomenon when in 1966 I first encountered this, in a United States university—there is no doubt that this vice still continues widespread to the obvious detriment of the whole education system.

And it was not just students who tried, and probably still try, by various means to negotiate grades; such corruption tends to be a life-long habit, right up to the goings-on in Congress. There was an amazing amount of corruption in this area, though the corruption wasn't and isn't totally ubiquitous, but there is certainly still too much of it. External examiners at university level in Britain are universally used and designed to make sure that corruption is so far as is possible obviated and grade standards kept up. There are certainly some flaws in the system, but on the whole it works very well. I think the US should do something about beginning thorough systems of external examiners if it wishes to maintain and improve grade honesty in general and at all levels.

My first introduction to the US composition grading-problem situation occurred when the head football coach at a university I was working in called me up one day to inform me, in case I didn't know, that three of his starting team members, including the quarterback, were in my class, and were, as he assured me, going to pass my class. I replied that they would pass if they passed, and he replied that he was sure I must have misunderstood him, and repeated that they were certainly going to pass--he was, after all, the football coach. No, I said, you don't understand me, I am an assistant professor of English, and they will pass if they truly deserve to do so. We had several acrimonious interchanges during that call with regard to his insistence that I would pass his players in their Freshman English activities, no matter what, and my insistence that they would only pass if they met the required standards.

Finally, obviously exasperated, indeed clearly extremely angry, the coach slammed down the phone. The next day, those student players in question had been withdrawn from my class, and I expect one of my colleagues succumbed to the coach's pressure and fixed things so that they eventually passed. That coach had a perennially winning team, and later worked as a coach in the NFL. When eighteen years later, I worked at the University of Kansas for three years, 1984-1987, the school's head coach did not have a winning team--quite the reverse. He phoned me at the start of my first term at Kansas. Amazingly enough, it turned out I had his starting quarterback and two of his linebackers in my class. This head coach told me that none of these players were to be given special favors. If they passed my class, which all three finally did—they were good students— then they passed. Otherwise, they were not to do so. I liked that, but as one might guess, his team remained a losing team. No one ever offered to bribe me for grades, and I'm glad about that, but I know such thing often happened to others.

In fact, in my opinion, the Freshman English system at the University of Kansas was so good that even if I had wanted to do so I could not have passed those students if they had not met the grade. The UK English Composition system obviated that possibility. Indeed, it was so good that later when I was in the middle of my eight-year term as department head at one University, I tried to have the University of Kansas Freshman Composition system adopted in my department for the Freshman Composition program. I failed.

My colleagues, after long debate to my deep sadness, vetoed my initiative at a special faculty meeting. I will briefly indicate what the system involved—it is quite a commonsense policy and in a way substituted well for the external examiners system in Britain.

UNIVERSITY OF KANSAS FRESHMAN COMPOSITION PROGRAM ADVANTAGES

KU Freshman Composition students were exposed at the end of the term to compulsory exit-exercise activities—as I recall them, they were ones in which students each wrote an essay in exam conditions, a choice from a limited number of topics they had previously been introduced to, but couldn't write up beforehand to take to the test. The student efforts were kept numbered but otherwise anonymous, and so arranged that the teacher of record for each student were unable to grade their students' essays The weekend after the test all the composition teachers assembled together and each read papers and test quizzes and awarded grades. Each student paper and quiz was read by two different examiners. If both examiners awarded a passing grade to a student, then he or she was eligible to pass out of Freshman Composition at that level.

On the other hand, if both graders agreed that the student concerned failed, then that student was failed for the class and had to retake the class. If a given paper was awarded a pass by one examiner and a fail by the other, then a third examiner was called in, and asked to assess the material; after that, if the material received two fails out of three, the student failed the class; if, on the other hand, the result was two passes out of three, then as with students already passed by the system, the student concerned was eligible to pass the class. Finally, it would be up to the teacher of record to decide whether or not, based on all the information about the student and his or her work, the student otherwise eligible to pass, ultimately failed the class based on other considerations. I liked that method of assuring grade honesty. It had the great advantage that I could tell my students with total honesty that their success or failure was largely out of my hands, and that there was no way whatever that they could negotiate a pass if they didn't deserve one.

What I failed to recognize when I tried to have the system applied at another university was that the only people who actually taught Freshman Composition at Kansas were people like me on three-year limited-term contracts, along with other kinds of non-tenure-track personnel, people who had no choice but to do the bidding of the composition director. They couldn't refuse, even if they were not paid extra to engage in the compulsory end-of-term grading marathon already described. The majority of my tenured and tenure-track colleagues at Eastern simply could not agree to the extra work involved in adopting the Kansas grading method.

Not really well paid and saddled with quite large classes, these instructors were certainly colleagues whose reluctance I could understand, but I was sad about it, because the system could have worked, and was certainly not illegal, as some of the colleagues concluded.

However, I hadn't done my homework as thoroughly as I should have. The failure concerned was the only serious one I suffered in my eight-year term as chair. Of course, as has been stated already, teachers of Freshman Composition are faced with abundant difficulties, one of the most difficult arising out of the fact that though all their students do have high-school diplomas suggesting they are fully literate, their relative degrees of literacy are all over the map. This is crucial to understand!

Nevertheless, composition instructors face the demand that in two successive classes they get their students to achieve what they have not already achieved in in twelve years' pre-college education. Of course, a fair number of schools that do a reasonably good job in trying situations and many graduates turn up well-equipped to tackle college-level instruction, but far too many schools where such is not the case, and obviously if Freshman Composition, is to be improved then something has to be done to radically improve English-teaching in all pre-college school systems—but, obviously, while we wait for this to happen, we can't simply throw-in the towel, pass the buck. A vicious circle operates here, and all elements in that circle have to be improved, not just one. In a worst-case scenario which does possess elements of unpleasant truth, beginning students, inadequately prepared for college, but possessing high-school diplomas certifying literacy, take both Freshman both English courses and manage to finagle passes, though very poor students.

Such students typically do not do well in their majors, merely scrape by, and then choose to prepare to teach, and enter Education Departments. In these, the professors are understandably frustrated, and, as is the case, in other university departments, many of them are for whatever reason, poor pay being an important one, they become over the years reduced to mere place-holders and time-servers, hurrying to just get students through, as their colleagues at all levels in a head-count-finance environment are under pressure to do. The students concerned get what they think they need from the education department, and some of them come through with deservedly high honors. Many others, however, manage to finagle their way through their education courses, including practical-teaching ones, and into the schools they go, to meet with schedules of too many classes, each with too many students, most of whom not really wanting to be where they are, and not much encouraged by social systems and families to buckle down to the hard work which is necessary, or should be necessary, for success.

Those students, not taught well, and not self-starters either, get through the system somehow, arrive at beginning college courses, including Freshman English and Math, and they go through the same set of happenings, and many of them go on to be inadequate teachers, and so on ...

THE CURRENT SITUATION

Currently, there is a great deal of talk about assessment—mostly teacher and course assessment, procedures thought capable of halting the rot and getting more effective, literate graduates. However, faculty dislike and even fear assessment, especially if it gets applied to hiring, firing, tenure, and promotions, and it is easy to see why. What has in the past all too often resulted from the pressure for assessment is that the faculty and administrators, all human, and most wanting the best for themselves and their colleagues, contrive to produce self-assessments in one way or another, even though such assessments are usually useless—because, who is going to be truly objective about his or her own performances and achievements? Nevertheless, objectively fair assessment is vitally necessary if educational matters are to improve. These things should optimally be focally formative, not punitive. A common view, however of all kinds of assessment is that administrators piously declare they are intended to be formative, but mostly ignore them unless they have reasons for wanting to punish subordinates and use assessments for finding evidence to punish employees, even fire them if necessary. As a result of such feelings, assessment initiatives or proposed initiatives all too often result in climates of fear not conducive to good teaching, quite the reverse. Where standards are concerned, achievement depends upon clear good will and assessment methods that are clearly seen as fair and formative, rather than punitive in scope.

We must hope that in the not-too-distant future, improvements in pre-college school systems will make substantial progress. Until that day comes, those of us charged with teaching Freshmen Composition must do our best to rectify as best we can the shortcomings of our situation, not throw in the towel and become mere place-holders and time-servers waiting on a generous pension and social-security and medicare packages.

One southwestern university has always prided itself in continuously enhancing fundamental approaches to teaching and learning to radically improve its total mission, the Freshman Composition mission included. Early in my career, one university made a quite serious attempt to enhance its mission by adopting the precepts and practices of "Re:Learning" approaches pioneered by Rhode Island's Ted Sizer. To my way of thinking this attempt failed in the long-run through the near impossibility of converting assessments of the enterprise concerned so that they could be used as effective credits for students wishing to transfer to other institutions.

This was too bad, because, though there is nothing particularly profound about Sizer's initiatives, they do entail salutary effects, and as a member of it's task force, I wish we had been able to make an effective pioneer Re: Learning university. Instead, however, in spite of some lasting good effects—in art, for example—the experiment passed into the unconscious of the institution as merely one more fugitive VPAA fad, which not unexpectedly bit the dust.

However, even if the entire matrix of Re: Learning desiderata cannot now be adopted, some of its salient components are so good that their application to Freshman Composition for example, could well prove very salutary indeed. I liked Re: Learning right from the start, a feeling in great part triggered by the fact that I had previously registered some composition successes through using some of the attitudes and methods characteristic of Re: Learning, successes admittedly initiated through fortuitous accident that occurred in Grand Forks, ND in the mid 1970s when I was at the University of North Dakota, as graduate teaching assistant in English who frequently taught Freshman Composition courses. One afternoon, one of my students, a rather pushy individual, knocked on my part-open door, walked in, and seemed about too to make some jocular vaguely impolite greeting when his eye caught the title of a book sprawled among many all over my desk. The title was The American Way of Death by Jessica Mitford.

"What's this, then?" the student said rather rudely. "What are you doing with this?"—and then suddenly, "Can I borrow it?"

I was astounded. Mostly, freshmen students didn't try borrowing books; many of them, as now, seemed to be trying to avoid any contact at all with such things. I said he might borrow it. He didn't wait to ask any further details, but hurried off without bothering to let me know whatever he had in mind when he came in. I thought that was probably the last I'd ever see of that book, but early the next morning, he came in with it, clearly enthused, and asked eagerly, "Can I discuss this with the class today, tell them about it?"

I responded immediately and in the affirmative, though I was puzzled, and not overly sure where all this would lead, but I'm usually willing for a challenge and it was hard to see what harm his initiative could do. In class later that morning, I could see that he must be a quick and efficient reader, because even though for many this was a scandalous book , the usual run of Freshmen, in my experience, would have taken several days to read it, if they finished it at all. This man was fired up, though. He'd been shocked, and remembered very vividly the passages that shocked him, summarized them succinctly, and quoted some verbatim. The students listened to him for about twenty minutes, then, a debate started. The majority got fired up, eager to find out about morticians and undertakers and their activities in North Dakota, and what the state's people's attitude was to all this.

Obviously, I didn't know. I had read Mitford's book out of curiosity, finding it interesting as a kind of sequel to Evelyn Waugh's provocative satire, The Loved One, a novel focused on American funeral habits as they applied to both human and animal corpses. I had not personally fired these students up. The student who had borrowed the book had managed to do that. However, I thought I saw a vital pedagogical opportunity emerging, and, even if a tad apprehensive, followed up on the start that had been made. I was flexible enough as a teacher to go with any opportunity I thought might result in the students becoming increasingly creative free thinkers and improved readers and writers. Re:Learning encourages teachers that way, and our brand of the project, my initiative resulted in a general exhortation that its instructors act, so far as possible, as co-workers and co-research workers with their students, operating for the most part as typical Re:Learning enthusiasts, recognizing that sometimes students have valuable things to teach their instructors. I learned a great from this particular enterprise and its initial instigator.

In any case, I began to realize as a practical truth that when a teacher is simultaneously him- or herself engaged with tasks complementary to the tasks the students are performing, the bonhomie developed between really enthused co-workers especially when publication is a goal, spurs students to strive to make sure that what they write will be such that it enhances their general reputation and prevents them looking like fools. In this case, the students began to organize themselves under the direction of my original interlocutor aided discreetly by myself. They undertook to write letters to members of the local funeral industry asking to inspect their premises and find out about their methods. In the course of the correspondence concerned, one particular establishment began by being very amenable to students' desires, and agreements were well underway for the necessary visitations and interviews, when, out of the blue, the firm concerned wrote the students a harsh letter indicating unwillingness to entertain subversives on their premises.

The mostly conservative students were both astonished and resentful, and from that point, on dedicated themselves to approaching all sorts of political and business people, and, indeed, anyone at all who might conceivably be interested in their situation. The students gradually organized themselves into a working party to analyze and evaluate all local elements of the funeral situation, and eventually found ways of discovering what they wanted to know by doing so, in a remarkably polite, diplomatic, manner. To pursue their investigation, they were, of course, forced to read and write a good many texts of all kinds, and find ways of meeting many different people and learning their feelings about this very complicated and sensitive matter. They had engaged in a very practical learning approach to research and conclusions based on them, and clear-cut written accounts of what they had done. Of course, they all learned to vet their ongoing texts for all kinds of inconsistencies, typos, and inaccuracies, and they learned to how to work as a semi-autonomous team doing this.

I, myself, learned a great deal from the project, and set about (with the aid of the composition director and some of my fellow instructors) figuring out how to objectively assess the progress of each individual in the team, a process that proved very valuable for ongoing enterprises of the kind we had spontaneously initiated.

After this, there were some at UND who imagined that such semi-autonomous group student research endeavors focusing on local history and its ramifications constituted something of a panacea, and several people at the time started experiments of a similar nature to The American Way of Death one.

Unsurprisingly, such projects usually proved to be, very enjoyable, and certainly helped students and faculty investigate or reinvestigate research methods that could be used for starting students on the path to research work generally. However, obviously, such local history projects wouldn't always spontaneously erupt in a way analogous to the first one. We teachers found many kinds of research that could be helpful, but needed to find ways to spark interest, irrespective of the availability of text entrepreneurs like my student.

All attempts of this kind, in addition, have to pay attention to serious restrictions: in local history projects, one cannot reasonably expect to keep on mining the same seams, the informants concerned could very soon get tired of being descended upon by avid student investigators. I came, in the end, to feel rather that as English professors we should avail ourselves so far as possible of opportunities to investigate all kinds of works by all kinds of writers, thus not only performing a general service to the institution, that of teaching students how to do research generally, but at the same time by attempting to spur students to an interest in the discipline and enjoyment of our literary riches, confident that research methods once learned effectively, can be readily transferred from one subject specialty to another.

The American Way of Death project demonstrated also very cogently that English is not simply something to bother with just in English classes and be of no consequence outside them; in addition, it was also clear that the full meaning of all texts depended to a very great extent on textual interrelations or meanings in the fullest sense of the universal context of situation.

Subsequently to my Grand Forks funeral-investigation project, I have found that, like the students who had been turned on to the project by the near fanaticism of the original student, many if not most students work really well, even at the beginning Freshman-Composition level, when engaged in pursuits that they come to feel really matter to them. They do so particularly effectively if as the project proceeds their student colleagues gain respect and enthusiasm for the topic being collectively researched, though only if the professors concerned are doing their best to work in complementary fashion alongside, helping students in any way they can. The keystone to the success arch of the enterprise concerned is in the Re: Learning Collegiate Renewal environment typically the ultimate production of an interesting, and generally useful public demonstration of excellence. Really effective Freshman Composition end-products are not simply sets of good exam results (though these are, of course, still potentially very valuable), they are, instead, pieces of writing, clearly not in a vacuum, that can in many cases nowadays be easily, effectively, and very inexpensively transformed into published books, articles, anthologies.

Of course, the fine arts, theater, music, painting, sculpture, and the like find the Re:Learning approach is in many ways what they have been inculcating all along, with the demonstrations of practical excellence occurring in performances of plays, concerts and recitals, exhibitions of graphic art, and so on. Early on in my teaching career, I started my small press in association with creative-writing classes and poetry and prose readings to demonstrate the needs students who write have to get their messages over to the public. The Grand Forks endeavor and those that developed from it, was simply a method of transferring the usual activities in the creative-writing arena to that of those writing generally.

In English-teaching areas now, however, I think we must be very careful about some kinds of zealots who have the idea that students already all know what they are supposed to do when they arrive at the Freshman Composition level, and that all one has to do with them is set them projects, which, when completed, are simply to be graded, and, if unsatisfactory, ultimately result in student failure.

To these zealots—and, alas, they really do exist—any attempt to help the students understand their errors and give them advice on ways they might fix them constitutes academic dishonesty—that is to say they think this when they find out that such help does not in fact, constitute an example of their favorite sin, plagiarism. We need to keep on remembering that vital axiom: student success (not student failure, note!) is what it's all about. We must in all situations attempt to be formative initially, not punitive—indeed, we should be punitive only in the very last resort.

One corollary to punitive-first kinds of nonsense is the notion that the students do not need grammar—I have increasingly come to the conclusion that many teachers who do not wish to teach their students anything to do with grammar—by which really, they really mean language mechanics—work this way because they themselves are almost totally ignorant of such notions and the positive values they have. However, how could teachers help students with their recurrent language- mechanics problems if they refuse to discuss them? Surely, they should, instead of dealing with them in no other way than punitively, explain clearly what these problems are, how they work, and how connected errors can be avoided--working them through, complete with cogent examples, in most expeditious ways until these problems concerned have been solved.

Various solutions to such problems, admittedly for the present attempted only piecemeal, can be attempted successfully. However, another main problem must be rigorously dealt with, and I have found the various institutions for which I have worked, though piously expressing the need for it, have in the long-run for various reasons, done very little about it. It is no use at all for students to leave English Composition classes with the idea that what is taught there applies exclusively to English classes. There is no doubt at all but that all instructors, in all courses, in a given institution must if literacy is to be generally maintained and enhanced, subscribe to the ideals being put forward in the composition classes, indeed, much be able to operate in their only writing to the necessary rigorous standards and make sure that in writing to their specialties, the students keep always to the standards inculcated in the English classes. If the various non-English instructors don't have the standards concerned, then the institution much make sure in the kindest, gentlest sort of way that they learn to do so, and do that as a necessary element for their continued employment. As in total-immersion language-learning situations, if a given complex of language standards is to be maintained, all must subscribe to it, and practice it on all occasions.

Of course, it goes without saying that if in the K-12 situation all students began learning one or, preferably, two foreign languages from Kindergarten on, the need for knowing English language mechanics would be readily apparent to them, and reinforced through inevitable notice of the grammatical (i.e. language-mechanics) differences that exist between languages. Thus, for example, a student learning German would very quickly recognize what a noun is, since all German nouns, not just proper ones, as in English, have in writing to be begin with an upper-case letter "das Buch" ("the book"). For example; students, learning French, would analogously certainly get a strong idea what an adjective is through the need to learn that in most cases in French, it is customary for adjectives to follow the noun they are modifying, not, as in the case of English, preceding it (thus, for example, we find "Moulin Rouge," instead of its English equivalent "Red Mill"), and so on.

It is clear that this kind of optimal language situation does not generally exist in the US at present, and that it would take much more than simply money to introduce it—such a situation does not generally obtain in England, either, even though I personally was very much helped with the English language mechanics because at King's Peterborough, I and my classmates learned French and Latin one period each five days a week for the first five years there, and then for one period each for three days a week in our final three years. Although there are traces of a good system for second and third-language acquisition currently apparent in some, if not most, universities and colleges, it seems, in many cases, that insistence on learning in this way, though obviously good for the students in all kinds of ways including improving their English, is dwindling. I believe the situation for Freshman English would be improved if the trend to eliminate second and third language acquisition from university curricula were reversed.

However, in addition to that, needs for teaching foreign languages like French, German, Latin, Spanish, Russian, Mandarin, etc. should be dealt with in the education of United States students as early in their lives as possible, for obvious reasons, one of the most obvious being that the sooner in life one starts learning second and third languages the more easily competence in these media is acquired, and kept.

In addition, Re:Learning Collegiate Renewal-style approaches should I think, be increased in application, at least substantially. The mission of such initiatives is, of course, always understood to be dominantly formative- instead of punitive. Instructors must be open to the fact that they and any assistants they may be allowed, including volunteer instructors developed from among the students themselves in the classes, each having a set of specialties for helping others in the class with the problems concerned, just as happened place with "The American Way of Death project at Grand Forks. The object is, locate and pinpoint flaws that occur, not behave as if the students concerned should already understand all potential flaws, doing so for the legal reason that their high-school diplomas decree that they have attained literacy already. We must be real, deal with what we have, where the student already is, go for that, and in our teaching use as many hands-on situations as possible. Always, too, teachers must explain, and keep on explaining that the significance of literacy and its need is universal, will not go away, and has important effects on all parts of a person's life, including, by no means insignificantly, yet not exclusively, their professional developments and successes in whatever field they are focused on, not just in two compulsory English Composition classes. It will be very hard at first for the students to believe that such is the case, but, repetition in variation that such really is the case, and practical examples of how this can be so, can certainly help in the long-run.

Total-immersion style four-week workshops as with the Peruvian farmers might be one way of attaining mechanical near perfection.

During my school and university studies and my teaching career, I have kept solidly in mind what sort of things work when attaining skills generally and English competence in particular. Good teachers are always serious-minded, good-humored, well-organized psychologically. Such teachers are modest in demeanor, but well aware of what is important and enthusiastically insistent in getting it across, and keeping patiently at it, in spite of inevitable setbacks.

I had four teachers in high-school, the Latin teacher, Mr. Vigor, the Math teacher, Mr. Oliver, and the English teacher, Mr. Mowat, and Mr. Hackett, the art teacher, who were truly splendid examples: always open to new things, still evidently learning new methods themselves in a vigorous fashion, and imbued with bonhomie, but with strict discipline at base. They knew we had to learn some things by rote. We might have been resistant, but they carefully explained why such learning, a little at a time, but regularly, was important. Mr. Vigor, the Latin teacher had us stand up and with great humor taught us—led us like an orchestral or choral conductor, really--through the rigors of noun, adjective, pronoun declensions, and the conjugations of all verb forms. I still remember those things today and taught them from memory in linguistic classes, and sometimes in English ones. It was easy for me both to know and teach English grammar effectively, because I had had to learn all the English translations of all the forms, and thus all about their English mechanics equivalents.

Mr. Vigor did all this with great amusement, promising that if we got all the goals of Latin for a given term assimilated perfectly before the end of the term, in the remaining class periods, he would read us M.R. James ghost stories. We worked, we laughed, we stood up and chanted, and, as I say, I still know Latin, and have occasionally taught it. Mr Howitt, the French teacher, did not work quite so vigorously, but according essentially to similar methods. The result was that I did my doctoral dissertation in French Literature—he would have been amazed—and I taught successfully for two years in a French University in Quebec. He would have been astonished. All of the teachers mentioned were full of hands-on enthusiasm, and, in truth, in their classrooms, no child was ever left behind. These teachers also made it clear that what was being learned never took place not in a vacuum, but in the continuity of what Firth calls a full context of situation. Thus, Mr. Jennings, a Geography teacher, took all his fifteen specialists--I was one at the time--for ten days on a total-immersion course living and working on the Scottish Island of Arran in the Firth of Clyde. We worked with everything to be found there—including working out through trigonometry learned in math, the height of the largest mountain on the island, doing so on a beach at a distance from the peak and with the crudest possible means, and getting it right—a perfect example of a Re:Learning method public demonstration of learning effectiveness. Math was valuable because it was, amongst many other things, practical. These teachers believed that departmental barriers, should so far as was possible be opened up and the importance and effectiveness for all subjects emphasized by continual cross-disciplinary cooperation.

Later, at a southwestern university at which I worked, we hoped through Re:Learning to make English efficiency and effectiveness enhanced by using as many of the other disciplines practiced in the university informed by what we were doing as we were informed by what they were doing, and without in any way teaching elements in vacuums.

I thought that the methodology of Latin, French, and Math, including practice of essential rote learning, could be made effective in solving one major problem Freshmen Composition students almost habitually and comprehensively exhibit, paucity of vocabulary. Solutions to this problem should, of course, have been continuously enhanced and reinforced as the students read regularly and were encouraged to do so in classes K-12. Obviously, even so, in all too many cases, the vocabulary of many entering Freshman Composition students is quite inadequate, so their reading speed and comprehension are also inadequate. There is no quick fix solution for this. There is no pill or pill-substitute that can give students powerful vocabularies overnight. Naturally, student vocabulary can be gradually expanded, if students can be persuaded to develop regular reading sessions that are both increasing pleasurable and increasing complex the necessary persuasion should be begun as soon as possible, but any radical kind of improvement is bound to take a great deal of time and effort. Nevertheless, at one point I came across a book embodying the findings of a Columbia University research project, which compiled a basic list of words researched from all sorts of disciplines' and students' needs K-Ph.D., a list that would, if thoroughly learned and continuously used, serve to quickly enhance students' reading and writing effectiveness, comprehension, and thought speed. Always positively skeptical, I rather doubted the claims made, but, thought I'd try the list out on my students.

I took the word list, added some words I thought additionally important and divided the product into sixteen groups, thus creating sixteen sublists each of forty items apiece, and then according to the methodologies of Vigor, Oliver, and Howitt, worked parts of each 102 class on a week-by-week cumulative basis, so that the students concerned would learn the words, partly through working complementary exercises seeking to have what had been learned reinforced.

With student help, I gradually extensively modified what was in the list and how it was arranged, rearranging it so as to answer to their expressed needs. The results were over the years quite astonishing. It turned out that there was indeed a great deal of truth in what the Columbia researchers had maintained.

Curiously enough, I myself found when I was working with these lists that I was learning words I really hadn't known before, and my own language functioning in all respects became clearly enhanced as I did so. As for the students, they seemed to relish my evident enjoyment in pronouncing, explaining, and using the words concerned, and, indeed, as some of them succeeded at my suggestion in becoming members of student senate. I was delighted in my role as a faculty advisor in watching and hearing them engage in debates, often in leadership roles as their increased effective literacy impressed their peers and made them more and more confident of their linguistic competence and performance.

PRECISION WRITING

For five years (1980-1984) I was an instructor, counselor, academic coordinator, and assistant director of the University of Wisconsin-Stevens Point Upward Bound Project. I learned there the advantages instructors and, indeed, some administrators have when trying to get students to learn essential skills when the staff members concerned can be seen clearly doing the kinds of things what they are asking their students to do. Once, during a recreation break out at a student camp situation in the forestry reserve, I was minding my own business sitting in a shed for shade and protection against possible rain, doing what I very often do for pleasure and therapy, painting pictures. Some students going by, noticed me, asked what I was, doing, asked if they could do it too, and set about learning to paint. Later, when I was working on a research project in a similar situation, trying to get to grips with the fullest possible interpretational contours for Thomas Hardy's short story "The Three Strangers," at-risk teenage students from six Native American tribes became more than delighted and capable of getting enthused, doing parts of the research involved themselves, coming up with new discoveries and new ideas about these discoveries, then writing up their findings effectively, with my master/apprentice kind of help, of course.

I never enter a situation thinking and certainly not saying that any intellectual activities are impossible for my students. Just as in creative writing classes, when just like my art master at school, I work on my pieces side by side with the students, I find that researching and writing papers along with one or more of the students working on their own similar projects is of great value to both them, and me. I never wish to have students do for class things I am unwilling to do myself and be seen doing them.

I remember very well being for two years a delighted apprentice to the great Shakespearian scholar George Wilson Knight functioning along with seven other students as his tutorial students, who each wrote him once a week a five-page scholarly essay and presenting it to him at the beginning of the appropriate weekly three-hour session in his office. These papers, a total in two years work of sixty essays per student, were always returned to us on time, and, on each occasion returned covered with red ink, suggesting various ways of reworking our research projects and writing them up.

We learned by example. There are, alas, a fair number of contemporary English instructors, whom I have met and worked with at several universities, who would be prone to condemn people working like Wilson Knight in this master/apprentice relationship, suggesting that in doing so, they are encouraging plagiarism and intellectual dishonesty. I have repeatedly wondered what it is that such instructors actually do with their students, not much new probably, and all too often, I imagine are prone to sit back on their cathedral-like thrones censoring without explanation and condemning wherever whim led. Wilson Knight and others of his caliber with whom I have been privileged to work, are among my models for teaching and learning. They too were delighted when their students did brand-new interesting scholarly things and had great pleasure in watching them, as in some cases I myself have, developing into good scholars, writers, and even teachers.

In somewhat analogous fashion to the methods of Knight, I started a small press named Scopcræft, doing so in Fargo, North Dakota, in October, 1966. Students helped me start the press and worked voluntarily as teams publishing first a literary magazine that came out every two months. We started by using the dean's mimeograph machine that operated under a stairwell, then gathered the printed sheets together by walking around a table picking them off piles then taking them to be fitted into premade covers then stapled. Then we sold them at 15 cents a copy for the first six copy volume.

Over the years, I have kept using the press to publish magazines, chapbooks, and books wherever I have gone, and always I have had willing students and teaching colleagues who have worked with me and learned a great deal in the process. Scopcræft (whose title might mean "literature" in Old English) was at first purely concerned with literary publication, but over the years it has expanded (now with over 250 titles under its belt) so that it produces, always with colleague and student help, books including textbooks that have proved very useful to a parts of our profession.

One of these had been a constantly expanding dictionary of literary terms, another, germane indeed to the materials important to this study, is a book I compiled so as to be filled with things important and clearly useful to composition students. The book is called Precision Writing, and had been gradually very much improved over the years. According to many, if not most, of its users, it has proved very effective in helping students enhance their writing abilities.

In it, I started by including my Columbia-based sixteen-week essential vocabulary-building lists, gradually modified as a result of consulting students' needs and making them optimally effective. Some of the students, of course, as I had expected, were initially hostile to my rigorous methods which included rote-learning of important elements like the CCS rule, the vocabulary-building items, and the Oldknow 19-point rubric for expository writing research papers.

Indeed, I had humorously but quite seriously indicated that they would probably all hate me in the course of the class because of my Vigor-like learning and testing activities, and I know that at all times some students, in spite of acknowledging how much they felt they had learned, gave me relatively negative evaluations, declaring that what I was having them learn was too hard.

However, afterwards, a relatively large number of students came back to my office in search of the materials (which eventually became the Precision Writing book), because they had mislaid them and knew how valuable they were. Sometimes, they wanted to get copies of them so that one or more of their fellow students, family members, or friends could get the benefit of the materials concerned. In several cases I know of, students corralled their spouses into learning the materials concerned and sometime later introduced me to the spouses concerned who testified to the treatment and admitted that what they had learned had in fact helped them.

Also included in this volume is an exposition of what I call "Criteria for Clear Statement and Graces of Prose," a much expanded set of criteria set forth in a very valuable book by the poet Robert Graves and his colleague Alan Hodge and entitled The Reader Over Your Shoulder, a text developed during World War II for the use of people who needed to improve their communication skills, particularly as they worked in the war effort. In compiling this book, Graves and Hodge authors worked with wit and humor applying their principles to examples of flawed passages found in the works of deservedly famous authors, who, nevertheless, for all their skills, managed, as we all do from time to time, to construct unfortunate and very amusing passages when their concentration slipped. Some of the principles needed revision, and more principles needed to be added.

Precision Writing was used according to the principle that to deal effectively with all the flaws they are likely to make in their writing, students have first to be fully aware of most of the flaws that regularly occur in written texts, and have the means to recognize and remove the flaws in the texts they make. The Graves and Hodge text identifies two types of flaw, one that is mainly mechanical in basic nature, and called The Principles of Clear Statement," and the other, which deals with mainly esthetic considerations, is entitled "The Graces of Prose." The first section items are identified by Arabic numeral and explicatory title, e.g. #14 Material Omission; the second section items are identified by Roman Upper-Case letters and explicatory titles, e.g. #C Metaphor Confused with Reality. Long experience with these principles eventually led to my considerably expanding the number of "Principles of Clear Statement" and adding one or two further "Graces of Prose." Graves and Hodge used a good deal of delightful humor with the passages they examined to exemplify their criteria. My expanded list embodied in Precision Writing also makes ample use of humor, using materials found mainly as fillers by back numbers of the New Yorker magazine—a methodology suggested to me initially by my friend the Minnesota poet Ronald Gower.

Dr. Gower was my chair the year (1982-3) I worked as a one-year emergency-replacement assistant professor at Mankato State University, and simultaneously completed my Ph.D. dissertation in six weeks.

Through Dr. Gower's suggestions, I was led to effectively complement my expanded Graves and Hodge materials. The New Yorker fillers are short flawed and very amusing passages taken from a wide variety of sources sent in by correspondents to The New Yorker, entertaining readers as they exemplify language flaws found in pieces published in magazines, books, police blotters, and so on. Dr. Gower said that if I collected many of these and used them, they would have the effect of causing students to laugh as they worked, for it is much easier at first to spot the errors and laugh at flawed materials in writers' work other than in one's own. I collected several hundred of these items and used many of them in Precision Writing--and Dr. Gower was right. The students were amused by the materials, learned how to apply the errors outlined in the "Criteria for Clear Statement" and "Graces of Prose" sections of the book to develop an understanding what was wrong in them and needed in future to be avoided in the students' own writing. I went on to find various new examples of such flawed passages, and in the course of their work, students through encouragement found many more. Of course, they learned gradually to apply these principles to analyses of colleague students' work, and finally to their own when they were subjecting texts to successive ameliorative drafts.

Doing this kind of thing with the Graves/Hodge/Oldknow materials and those served up weekly by The New Yorker very effectively caused, with the advantages of humor the students to make better and better written texts. Some contemporary composition directors and teachers seem to feel that instructors should not teach students the kinds of errors they are both likely to find and themselves make. I think this attitude essentially flawed, because how exactly can students be expected to correct flaws in their work whose type whose existence is quite unknown to them. Perhaps many of those who wish to ignore such flaws do so because they can't recognize the flaws concerned themselves.

I have found that analysis of the flaws in the amusing "New Yorker Fillers" and explaining according to the Graves/Hodge/Oldknow rules has led many students to master language and meaning complexity buoyed up in doing so by the extreme fun that occurs through the irony inherent in such texts. I want my writing students to know as much as possible about the things in writing which could potentially make them appear ridiculous if they made them, so that they can at all times avoid making them.

EXAMPLE NEW YORKER FILLER PASSAGE #36

Goldsmith said he "requested" twenty deputy prosecutors get into a marked police car and ride with Indianapolis patrolmen and Marion County Sheriff's deputies a minimum of eight hours. —Indianapolis News.

So they'll be in shape for their court appearance. —New Yorker editorial comment.

AFTER APPLICATION OF CRITERIA FOR CLEAR
STATEMENT RULES

Goldsmith said he "requested" each of twenty deputy prosecutors to get into a marked police car and ride with either Indianapolis patrol officers or Marion County Sheriff's deputies a minimum of eight hours.

Also used in my methodology to complement the Graves/Hodge/Oldknow and New Yorker Filler materials is the well-known basics book Punctuation, Capitalization, and Spelling by Eugene Erhlich, added to the syllabus in order to have students hone their proofreading skills, which being essentially very simple to learn, which once assimilated effectively, should serve to enhance student confidence: good punctuation with no sweat makes students feel much better about themselves. Complementing the Ehrlich elements, I included in the Precision Writing book a set of passages called "Members of My Family," which are filled with errors of all kinds, mainly punctuational, most very obvious, and all for the most part very interesting and sometimes very funny, all original and based on people and happenings closely or loosely associated with members of my family. The object is to have the students increasingly able to look very closely at every letter in the words they read and write, things most people don't do, but most important if specially written texts are to be made nearly perfect.

Use of Precision Writing was at first mainly for students of the first section of the Freshman Composition series, the one in which they were intended to polish up their control of the basics of the writing process before going on to the second section entitled, rather misleadingly I thought, "Composition and Research."

Later, I incorporated into the book's text elements intended to show the students how to structure texts they would write so that they would embody logical explication reports of new research they had been doing. This was a 19-point rubric including model examples of various kinds of research I had been doing myself—once again, never work with students without showing them that I was willing to do things of the same kind myself, just as Wilson Knight did for his students including me to great effect. I for one believe also that if the title of a course is Composition and Research, the resulting Re:Learning Collegiate Renewal exhibition of excellence should embody examples of real research, not be simply exposition of satisfactory reports, even though I recognize that report writing is a very necessary part of the whole composition matrix. I believe that the misleadingly ambiguous word "research" in such titles can cause a great deal of trouble in the minds of students and faculty alike. If a university is to encourage real research in its mission, then in the curricula of "Composition and Research" courses, real research methods should be fully and usefully inculcated, not mere report-writing exercises.

Report writing was, and is for me, something that belongs essentially to the first component of the Freshman Composition sequence, where amongst all the other items in the Precision Writing book, the Graves/Hodge/Oldknow principles and "The New Yorker Fillers" can be used systematically and amusingly wherever possible in honing the students' basic skills before going on to work on literary-criticism basics and/or their equivalents for other subjects used in creating pieces of true scholarly research.

One thing I used the report writing section for with some success was in the creation of what I called The Portales Archives, for which students explored the territory of Roosevelt

County of which, Eastern New Mexico University's home, Portales, is the county seat to account for things and people of interest there and write them up as illustrated publishable reports, which, once completed could be put on display and ultimately archived for reference purposes.

What happened with these items was very much in synch with what had been done, as I reported above, at Grand Forks earlier in my career and starting with the fortuitously student-initiated work on applying The American Way of Death critical criteria to Grand Forks area morticians and undertakers.

The Portales Archive project started in the late 80s, was put on ice in the early 90s after I was elected and appointed department chair, but the materials which the students seem to have very much enjoyed producing, lie in my files still, and I intend to work on them and publish some in the not-too-distant future.

Members of My Family presented students for study and rigorous testing with passages of increasing complexity all initially as they saw them deeply flawed and to some extent amusing based on people in my family and their environments. It was felt that if a given student could by the end of term correct all the passages at sight, so that they were fully proofread and corrected according to standard punctuzational and grammatical methods that would be one very clear sign of their enhanced literacy. I will give one example for this section, so that the reader can see the kind of thing that was presented.

MEMBERS OF MY FAMILY PRACTICE PASSAGE #27

these was the wifes off king henry viii catherine off aragon whom was buryed inn peterborough cathedral the gratest building inn my home town ann boleyn mother off queen elizabeth ii unlike her dauhter the mother was executed they use the soared knot the garret jane seymour henrys favorite since she provided hymn with an mail air later two be cum kind Edward vi an dye young ann off cleves who henry did not like an that he divorced after an month Katherine Howard whom seems two have committed adultery and was throne from the thrown too the axemans block and Katherine Parr whom outlive the imminent king.

These were the wives of King Henry VIII: Catherine of Aragon, who was buried in Peterborough Cathedral, the greatest building in my home town; Ann Boleyn, mother of Queen Elizabeth I (unlike her daughter, the mother was executed [they used the sword, not the garrote]); Jane Seymour, Henry's favorite, since she provided him with a male heir (later to become King Edward VI and die young); Ann of Cleves, whom Henry did not like, and whom he divorced after a month; Katherine Howard, who seems to have committed adultery and was thrown from the throne to the axman's block; and Katherine Parr, who outlived the eminent king.

I found these Portales Archives led the way into students beginning to understand what Real Research rather than just Report Writing was actually like, and to start practicing it. Of course, I used examples of my own published and unpublished--sometimes ongoing— research (and not just into Literature or Linguistics), to give them useful models for such research (The Need to Avoid Hypocrisy).

There are of course, even where there are unsatisfactory working conditions, some relatively minor things that can be done to somewhat alleviate the situation. Thus, for example, apart from finding enhanced pay rates for people whose lot is mainly to teach four or five sections of Freshman Composition a term, they would work better perhaps if once in a while, but regularly, they could teach a sophomore literature course to give them some kind of relief. Further, as happened to some of my colleagues forced into this kind of program at Stevens Point and, to a lesser extent, at Kansas, allowing such freshman-composition teachers to choose as they taught a basic subject focus in literature or some other useful field of choice they were interested in would also seem to raise their spirits somewhat while introducing students to badly lacking extra control over general knowledge. I for one taught, with enhanced satisfaction all round, at both Stevens Point and Kansas Freshman Composition, classes whose base subjects were either The Bible as Literature or Twentieth-Century World Literature in Its Full Context of Situation. Instructors' morale of the teachers is, of course, a very important consideration.

They will probably teach better if their morale is high, and college supervisory staff and the instructors' departmental colleagues should do their very best to find ways to improve the morale of composition-teachers, which is for the most part very low these days and certainly not improved by the prevalent rise of the bullying fear culture. Further, as suggested earlier, current situations prevailing in many universities lead such instructors to be under the direction of composition directors who are in many cases forced by superiors to behave in dictatorial fashion, considering instructors' problems when they feel so inclined and ignoring them at will. Of course, there are many very good composition directors, especially ones who have been especially trained in the field, but, all too often, the authorities in any case force them to prove they have actually done something, and so, often against the directors' will, they feel forced to disturb the routines of the instructors drastically and introduce new method and materials, even though what has been done has in many cases been done both industriously and well.

This is bad for instructor morale and of course consequently for student progress, especially, as is so often the case, because of pressures above and below, composition directors stay one after another for only one or two years and these disruptive mini revolutions keep on happing to impede general progress. This is one of the many reasons why I think the position of composition director should be abolished, and composition-committees comprising the whole composition-teaching personnel should be substituted. Where such committees do in fact function, they have in my experience elevated the mission of the group. Another aid to the improvement of the situation, though one which I know is fraught with problems concerns continuity.

One of the problems compared with the British situation is that in North American higher education, students are faced with lack of continuity, and in the composition sequences they are frequently discouraged from having the same instructor for sections one and two of the sequence. Too bad, it takes time to get really acquainted, student or teacher, and in many cases if the same teacher can deal with the students in both classes, the over-all result will be better.

To sum up, we can't abolish college/university Freshman English Composition programs yet, much as we might like to. They are with us for the foreseeable future, so we might unite to do the best we can with them. Dictatorial methods must, of course be eschewed; we must remember that we are attempting to be formative towards our students (and towards our colleagues), in no way focused on punitive measures, no matter how frustrated we are with the status quo. We are in what I have always expected and hope to be the university scene, which focuses on civilized behavior to all, and in a thoroughly democratic fashion.

It would, I think, be best generally to abolish posts of composition director; instead, as I found the situation to work so well at the University of North Dakota, we should have situations with regard to Freshman Composition that involve maximal faculty governance, one in which all the personnel teaching these essential courses, no matter what their faculty levels might be, tenured full professors through part-time temporary graduate teaching assistants or adjuncts, has a respected voice free from any kind of punitive danger in voicing views about current composition practices and a vote on all decisions affecting the composition program—no exceptions.

After all, all personnel involved in this difficult venture are doing essentially the same thing, aiming at uniform goals, even if, as they perhaps should be, the methods employed in reaching these goals should be as individual as possible. In general, it seems to me, the Re:Learning approach, similar to the aims of many original universities.

Summary and Conclusion

From what I have written above, I hope it can be seen that I believe that composition classes can, with some changes of attitude and practice make a considerable positive difference to entering university and college students, though much more needs to be done in the pre-college English programs developed in K-12 classrooms. No panaceas should be expected, but attempts to work hard at progressively enhancing student literacy from the very earliest years at grade schools should be seen as an urgent priority. It is clearly totally inappropriate that this most important of subjects should be left in the hands of harassed teachers with enormous class loads.

I have made it abundantly clear that I think not enough care is taken generally in allotting the appropriate faculty to take care of Freshman composition courses.

Alas, the same problem also occurs from my observation in the high schools and probably in the earlier stages of students' education. One example I observed myself serves as a cogent example. I visited one school in my area, in part to observe a student teacher, in part, at her and the school's invitation to give a poetry reading in the school in question. The teacher in charge of English was a coach. He had been pushed into the role against his wishes and was quite clearly himself almost totally illiterate. Nevertheless, he was polite and decent, but seems to have been appointed to his position on the assumption that because someone can speak English, he or she must be able to teach it. I have heard of many cases of this kind of thing, both at the high school, and, alas, even at college level. The students have the idea all too often that English is an easy subject, and that they can pass Freshman Composition just about any time, and they'll leave it till later, knowing they'll pass it easily.

And, alas, again, all too often, considering a great inconsistency in teacher abilities and attitudes, many in fact run through system, unscathed by failures.

Since, the way beginning students are, there needs to be a great deal of care taken with a subject that is absolutely essential for all subjects—people cannot really do well in any profession without competence in English. Consequently, no matter how and when this is done, and especially in these times of new and rapidly changing technology, special courses may be necessary for instructors in English at all levels, and it would be a good idea for people teaching Freshman Composition to receive remuneration at a level or preferably somewhat above that of high-school teachers, instead of, as is all too often the case now, at a much lower level, hardly in fact a living wage.

Evidently, current climates emphasizing a generally bullying college culture and one where focus is increasingly on punitive rather than formative approaches all round needs to be abandoned and all elements in the higher-education matrices need to remember the kinder gentler atmosphere where student success, not failure, needs to be constantly in focus and increased faculty governance and democracy free from any kind of culture of fear should accompany that. Students need to be encouraged to believe that enhanced literacy is something to be proud of and will at the same time help them to secure better career chances, job satisfaction, and fiscal sufficiency. This can be done principally through encouraging students to respect and maintain a strong work ethic, one that recognizes that a great deal of willing effort will be required if they are to reach the necessary standards. For them to do this, they will have to be made to believe that their grades are awarded at all times objectively, and not through any kind of favoritism, but through receiving truly objective analyses verified by disinterested referees.

Students will do very well, it is maintained, if their efforts are geared so far as is possible to projects they have had a truly enthusiastic hand in initiating, and if their teachers and class colleagues have been able to help them focus and revise in all respects as they seek so far as is possible, to create published examples of written and researched excellence.

In bringing all this about, teachers must at all times make sure that they have started with each of their charges with a clear idea where he or she is in terms of literacy potential and striven with a positive and very genuine enthusiasm to help them develop as master with apprentices free of frivolous charges of encouraging academic dishonesty and plagiarism.

At no time must any professor or his or her professional supervisors at any level, simply sit back and give grades based on the supposition that high-school diplomas having suggested student literacy the best thing they can do is wait for the students to make mistakes, and then punish them.

The object must be always formative-first, explaining what has gone wrong and then assisting the students concerned to gain control of their errors. Of course, more money will have to be poured into the mix. It is hopeless to expect people bullied at their job though making less than is necessary to make a living at what they do to teach in lockstep fashion unhappy students in great numbers. The working conditions for all instructors at whatever level must be the very opposite at all times of those which characterize a hostile workplace.

Can Freshman Comp Classes Really Help Develop the Skills and Talents and Writing Abilities of Freshman, and If So, How Can This Be Done?

In the final analysis, the problems associated with College Writing programs are stymied because of money, just as were the decisions of the postwar British Labor government as they set about trying to implement the 1944 coalition governments relatively unbiased Education Act. In the end, instead of being able to very carefully and sophisticatedly being able to indicate accurate profiles of the needs and aspirations and probable capabilities of students through sophisticated diagnostic testing, then being able to place students for the best advantage in specialized schools, they had to wing it, finished up doing a little bit for the technologically inclined and suited, then set up examinations to identify the brainy from all classes, in a set of quite ancient kinds of intellectually based exams, which eventually let to a climate of passing or failing the eleven-plus, and letting those who passed have very traditional but very good elitist schooling, while the vast rest were dumped into holding cells, as it were, until they were fifteen, at which point, there being a vast treasury of unskilled labor opportunities that have now pretty well disappeared, they were released into the plebian work force hoards, perhaps in the main contented, who knows.

In the current fiscal climate of the United State, many really unemployable so-called plebians, unable to find easy mindless jobs in assembly lines, and unwilling or unable to find careers in the armed forces, gravitate into higher education where their needs are expected to be fulfilled. Without adequate communication skills, of course, which haven't for all sorts of reasons been provided for them by the K-12 schools, they need a quick fix, first of all into competence in the standard language of the country.

There are very few specialty-trained English professors who really know what would be best to do for Freshman Composition, so relatively unskilled personnel are pressed into the mire represented by the masses of the illiterate, and forced to do their best in an ill-paid set of situations. And the people concerned and their equally unprepared supervisors tend to wing it and hope that their students get something out of the process, hopefully something or other that aids their communicational competence a tad in some way or other.

It would, of course, be much better, (earlier training being unavailable), to have developed before they enter the process, sophisticated diagnostic activities that, just like medical doctors dealing with other kinds of health profiles, are able to tell just which kinds of problem profile each student possesses with regard to literacy and then, like the prescription of treatment and medicine and even perhaps in some cases surgery, apply necessary remedies and courses of maintenance and improvement to the patients—ones that really fit their needs. Of course, as with medical specialist, the people working with Freshman Composition students would have to be trained to deal with the special problems once they were discovered, and it would certainly be necessary for the students concerned as their lacks were dealt with, though have prescribed for them definite specialized sub courses that could perhaps be well provided in writing laboratories, if these could be transformed into something more that rooms with banks of computers doing very little more than serve as babysitting machines.

Needless to say, our present hoards of incoming Freshmen with more or less unknown profiles of flawed literacy are in practice bunged willy-nilly into classrooms, where they are constrained to learn together materials which may or may not be useful to them with their predicament, and all too often they come out of the morass no more (and in some cases perhaps less) literate than they were when they entered. It looks very democratic, all being treated equally, but their needs profiles are all quite different, and they need careful and extremely sophisticated accurate presorting so that their individual needs can be catered to effectively. The solutions concerned can with increasing sophisticated technology and properly trained or retrained personnel make a good go of radically improving incoming student literacy in a relatively short period of time, though frankly in most cases this would take rather more time and effort than is involved in the present all together two-term-class environment. But, there isn't the necessary money, nor is there in existence yet a pool of aptly trained remedial personnel. Students possessing a wide range of IQs and interests from very different language backgrounds and social and ethnic classes are all dumped together. They are taught inevitably with the basic crude idea of no child left behind according to rough rubrics that need considerable expert care in reworking if they are to be any good for any student at all, and then, things being what they are and all depending on flawed humans with a meager budget of financial support, there comes the obvious sequel that eventually students in college will be taught to a minimal set of examination questions graded according to blind rubrics and instead of no child left behind, it will be increasingly the case that no child will be advanced.

Nevertheless the people who work to try to keep colleges and universities going no matter what, will feel that the good scores coming out of the poor assessment tools will grant all those failing to advance degrees and honors and feel satisfied that the problems of mass literacy will have been solved. So, let us start trying to change things for the better as a result of reading and listening to jeremiads like mine. With money and trained personnel and sophisticated diagnostics and labs, it will be possible to let all children advance in their own ways. In the meantime, until such halcyon days arrive, each teacher must try his or her best in small ways only perhaps to have each student put into his or her change make some discernible improvement in actual literacy along with a radically improved awareness of what each of their literacy needs are, so that they can, if they wish, work on them themselves.

REFERENCES

Dickens, C. (1854) Hard Times--For These Times. London: Bradbury and Evans

Dickens, C. (1839) The Life and Adventures of Nicholas Nickleby. London: Chapman and Hall

Ehrlich, E. (2000) English Grammar. Third Edition. Schaum Outline Series. New York: McGraw Hill

Ehrlich, E. (1992) Punctuation, Capitalization and Spelling. Second Edition. Schaum Outline Series. New York: McGraw Hill

Firth, J. R. (1957) Papers in Linguistics 1934-1951. London, Oxford University Press.

Graves, R, and Hodge, A. (1994) The Reader over Your Shoulder: A Handbook for Writers of English Prose. London: Jonathan Cape.

Mitford, J. (1963) The American Way of Death. New York: Buccaneer Books.

Oldknow, A. (2009) Precision Writing. 2nd Ed. Portales, New Mexico: Scopcræft

Sizer, T. R. (1973) Places for Learning. Places for Joy. Cambridge, MA: Harvard University Press

Waugh, E. (1928) Decline and Fall. London: Chapman and Hall.

Waugh, E. (1948) The Loved One. London: Chapman and Hall .

INDEX

D

E

N

O

P